IRISH WOMEN AND THE VOTE

IRISH WOMEN AND THE VOTE
Becoming Citizens

Editors
LOUISE RYAN
MARGARET WARD

Foreword by
ROSEMARY CULLEN OWENS

IRISH ACADEMIC PRESS
DUBLIN • PORTLAND, OR

First published in 2007 by
IRISH ACADEMIC PRESS
44, Northumberland Road, Dublin 4, Ireland

and in the United States of America by
IRISH ACADEMIC PRESS
c/o ISBS, Suite 300, 920 NE 58th Avenue
Portland, Oregon 97213-3786

This Edition © 2007 Irish Academic Press
Chapters © Individual Authors

www.iap.ie

British Library Cataloguing in Publication Data
An entry can be found on request

ISBN 978 0 7165 3392 4 (cloth)
ISBN 978 0 7165 3393 1 (paper)

Library of Congress Cataloging-in-Publication Data
An entry can be found on request

Typeset by Carrigboy Typesetting Services
Printed by Creative Print and Design, Gwent, Wales

Contents

List of illustrations

With thanks to Rosemary Cullen Owens for her kind permission to reproduce images 1, 2, 3, 6, 8 and 9.

A Chronology of the Irish Suffrage Movement

1869	National Society for Women's Suffrage established in Dublin
1871	Northern Ireland Women's Suffrage Society formed; later known as Irish Women's Suffrage Society
1874	Three issues of *Women's Advocate* published by Thomas Haslam
1876	Dublin Women's Suffrage Association (DWSA) formed
1896	Irish women granted right to become poor law guardians
1898	DWSA becomes Dublin Women's Suffrage and Poor Law Guardians Association
1898	The Local Government Act gives Irish women the right to vote and to be elected to District Councils
1901	Dublin Women's Suffrage and Poor Law Guardians Association changes name to Irish Women's Suffrage and Local Government Association
1908	Irish Women's Franchise League (IWFL) formed
1910	Six IWFL members imprisoned in England as a result of suffrage militancy
1911	Irish Women's Reform League formed
1911	Irish Women's Suffrage Federation formed
1911	Irish women win right to be elected to County Councils
1912	Irish Party votes defeat Conciliation Bill in Westminster
1912	*Irish Citizen* paper first published
1912	Irish women's united appeal for inclusion in Home Rule ignored
1912	IWFL declares war on Irish Party
1912	First militancy in Ireland – 8 IWFL members jailed

1912 Women's Social and Political Union (WSPU) members attack Primer Minister Asquith in Dublin

1913 Home Rule Bill passed. Irish women excluded

1913 Prisoners (Temporary Discharge for Ill-Health) Act – 'Cat and Mouse Act' passed in Westminster

1913 IWFL prisoners released under Cat and Mouse Act

1913 Ulster Unionists promise women the vote in separate Ulster parliament

1913 WSPU establishes 'Ulster Centre' in Belfast and Dublin branch

1913 The Irish Women's Suffrage Federation organises 'Dublin Suffrage Week'

1914 Ulster Unionists withdraw promise of the vote for women

1914 WSPU arson campaign begins in the north

1914 WSPU activists imprisoned

1914 United deputation of Irish suffragists lobby House of Commons

1914 First World War begins

1914 WSPU suspends militancy and pulls out of Ireland

1914 Irish suffragists establish 'Watching the Court Committee'

1915 Attempt to establish Belfast branch of IWFL fails

1915 Women's International Peace Congress at The Hague

1916 Easter Rising – murder of Frank Sheehy Skeffington

1918 End of First World War

1918 The Representation of the People Act gives women over 30 in Ireland and Britain the right to vote and to stand for parliament

1918 Constance Markievicz becomes first female MP elected to British House of Commons, taking her seat in Dáil Éireann

1922 Women in the Irish Free State gain equal suffrage rights with men and can vote at 21 years of age

Foreword

ROSEMARY CULLEN OWENS

In 1870, in the course of a paper on 'The Emancipation of Women' read to the Cork Literary and Scientific Society, John Walter Bourke noted that 'an impending change is manifest in the present social and political position of women'. Forty-eight years later, in December 1918, Anna Haslam, Hanna Sheehy Skeffington and Louie Bennett – aged seventy-five, forty- two and forty-eight years respectively – voted in a general election for the first time. They were among those benefiting from the Representation of the People Act, passed earlier that year, which granted the parliamentary vote to women aged thirty and to men aged twenty-one. The story of what happened in the intervening forty eight years and beyond is contained within the covers of this excellent book on the women's suffrage movement in Ireland.

From the turn of the century, a number of significant developments occurred within the women's movement in Ireland. Key among these was the emergence of a younger, confident, articulate generation of women, most of whom had benefited from the work of their predecessors in accessing higher education. Many of these younger women had not been born, or had only been infants, when the earlier campaigns had commenced. They were, however, very much women of the new twentieth century, aware of contemporary women's campaigns worldwide, and prepared to use the media, humour and theatrics to advertise their campaign. Many of them were also prepared to use militancy, ultimately being imprisoned for their actions. All was grist to the publicity mill and to the attainment of their goal. Allied to the long established Irish Women's Suffrage and Local Government Association, the formation of the militant Irish Women's Franchise League in 1908, followed in 1911 by the non-militant Irish Women's Suffrage

Federation, demonstrated the commitment of women to play a public role in the life of their country. During the tumultuous years from 1912–18, these groups were influenced and sometimes divided by major political developments in Ireland. Amongst these were the campaign for Home Rule, the Labour and Sinn Féin movements and the outbreak of war in 1914. After the Easter Rising of 1916 and the executions and imprisonments that followed, women's groups co-operated on a number of related issues, particularly against the proposed extension of conscription to Ireland in 1918.

In 1977, Dr Margaret MacCurtain wrote of the Irish woman as 'one of the enigmas of twentieth century Ireland. Her public face is that of wife and mother, enshrined in the 1937 Constitution . . . Her private face is that of one who has been awarded no place at the conference tables and who, increasingly, knows she has been hidden from history'. From the 1970s, due to the support and commitment of historians such as Dr MacCurtain and Mary Cullen, the task of rediscovery of women's history commenced. As one of those who embarked on that journey during those years, I was not atypical. Despite having attained a degree in history, I knew only the 'token women' that were included in history text books – usually as an adjunct to a male political figure or movement. I knew nothing of the real history of women, nothing of the campaigns outlined above, or of the role played by women in the development of the Irish state. Those of us who have attempted to correct the 'hidden from history' phenomenon have sought to ensure that our rediscovered female heritage is included in all aspects of history teaching and publication so that succeeding generations can have the opportunity to learn of women's contribution. Crucial, also, is the encouragement of new interpretations and the protection of new sources in all areas of women's history and experience. This book will most certainly add to the store of knowledge about the early feminist movement in Ireland, in particular bringing together as it does a rounded picture of the suffrage movement in a way not presented before. It is a fitting tribute to those pioneering feminists who sought to ensure that Irish women would obtain political equality with Irish men, and I congratulate its editors and contributors for their vision and initiative.

Introduction

MARIA LUDDY

The year 2008 marks the centenary of the establishment of the Irish Women's Franchise League, the first new suffrage society to be organised in Ireland since the 1870s. Dora Mellone saw the Irish Women's Franchise League as a pioneer in rousing public interest in the suffrage question in Ireland.[1] Its foundation marked the beginning of a new period of suffrage activity in an Ireland that was experiencing considerable cultural, social and political possibilities. Other suffrage societies followed. In 1911 the Irish Women's Reform League was established and was the first suffrage organisation that united women's suffrage and trade unionism. Later in 1911 Irish Women's Suffrage Federation was established as an umbrella organisation for the varied suffrage societies that then existed. In 1912 the *Irish Citizen* declared there were about 3,000 active suffragists in Ireland. The organisation of the Irish Women's Franchise League brought new life to the suffrage cause and a new generation of men and women to political activism. It reasserted women's rights as citizens, and extended the range of protest to include militant activity, the possibility of imprisonment and hunger strike to advance their cause. It brought a new force to suffrage activism, the physical body of women, to fight the cause.

Any examination of suffrage ideas, activities or even militancy has to begin in the nineteenth century when issues of equality, citizenship and the relationship of women to the state were actively and publicly discussed. In Ireland, women's campaign for the parliamentary franchise has tended to overshadow women's considerable contributions to philanthropy, social reform and municipal politics. It was, however, in those arenas of activity that the rhetoric and practice of citizenship and ideas of political equality were shaped and formed. From the early nineteenth century, Irish women, through their philanthropic activity, began to argue for their essential presence in the realm of the public. Philanthropic work was seen as a natural extension of a woman's designated role in society, and that role was defined by her relationship to her family. Women's primary concerns were expected to be the physical and moral welfare of the family. Woman's natural role was in the home: woman was considered moral, spiritual, benevolent, modest, submissive, and compassionate. However, the rhetoric of woman's uniqueness, her maternal qualities, and her self sacrifice encouraged the idea that middle-class women had special responsibility for caring for the less fortunate in society. Women argued that they had a special duty towards the poor, and over the nineteenth century large numbers of Irish women, from all religious denominations, engaged in philanthropic work. Through their philanthropic work a number of women came to the realisation that it was only with the acquisition of the parliamentary franchise that substantial social change could be brought about.[2]

It was in their participation in reform societies from the 1860s, societies such as the Ladies' National Association for the Repeal of the Contagious Diseases Acts (1871), the National Society for the Prevention of Cruelty to Children (1889), the Philanthropic Reform Association (1896), and the Irish Workhouse Association (1896), that women gained practical experience of political activism and developed and enhanced the rhetoric of equality which became central to their suffrage work. The societies listed above were the most progressive of the reform societies that existed in Ireland in the late nineteenth century. Each of these societies, with the exception of the LNA, having mixed executive committees, actively sought changes in the law with regard to the safety of children and the protection of the destitute and of women. The women on these committees, through their involvement in these philanthropic societies, developed a new awareness of women's disabilities that encouraged them to attack discriminatory social practices. These reformist women associated the acquisition of the vote with social change.

One of the major advances made by women as philanthropists and reformers was to become poor law guardians. Women had begun to seek admittance to the workhouse as visitors soon after the establishment of the poor law system in 1838. It is difficult to gauge the extent of philanthropic women's involvement in these institutions. It was not until 1880, for example, that the North Dublin Union Board of Guardians allowed Catholic and Protestant women 'to visit the sick of their own persuasion'.[3] For many philanthropists, workhouses were dens of iniquity where young girls would grow up to be idle and immoral. The vulnerability of children within the workhouse system infused many philanthropists with a reforming zeal and a campaign of practical action that eventually saw women becoming eligible to be elected to boards of guardians. In 1896 a bill was passed which allowed women, with certain property qualifications, to serve as poor law guardians. Many of those elected were supporters and activists in the suffrage campaign.[4]

It appears that the majority of women who were involved in the suffrage campaign in the late nineteenth century were Protestant. The founding figures of the suffrage campaign, Isabella Tod and Anna Haslam, a Presbyterian and Quaker respectively, were brought to an awareness of women's political disabilities and civic weakness through their philanthropic work. Many of the women who joined them had a tradition of philanthropic involvement and social activism. Lay Catholic women did not have a tradition of social activism and were much slower to organise for social reform. Catholic women who became politically active tended to join nationalist organisations that sought freedom from England rather than social reform as a first step. It was nuns who became the primary providers of welfare within the Catholic Church in the nineteenth century. They were socially conservative, their own social structures reflecting the social divisions that were deemed natural to society. They did not inspire social revolution nor encourage the political or independent aspirations of women.

Roughly one quarter of the women on the Dublin Women's Suffrage Association had a background in philanthropic work. Besides Haslam and Tod, other women, such as the Congregationalist, Rosa M. Barrett, were active philanthropists and suffrage activists. Barrett, for example, opened a crèche in Dun Laoghaire in 1879, later converting it into an orphanage called the Cottage Home for Little Children. Concerned with the plight of orphaned and destitute children she was also a founding member of the National Association for the Prevention of Cruelty to Children and a supporter of the Philanthropic Reform Association. In the early years of the twentieth century she helped to establish the Women's National Health Association of Ireland that aimed to heighten public awareness about the prevention of disease, especially tuberculosis.[5] Anna Haslam, née Fisher, had established a lace making industry in her home town of Youghal as a means of providing employment to the local girls. She was an active member of the Ladies' National Association and became a member of the English executive of that society in 1888. She was also a committee member of the Philanthropic Reform Association and the Irish Workhouse Association. She campaigned vigorously to bring about improvements in girls' education in the late nineteenth century and also campaigned for the admission of women as poor law guardians.

Isabella Tod, like Haslam, was a campaigner on a range of issues of concern to women from the mid-nineteenth century. Her initial attempts to promote the interests of women arose from her campaigns to improve the educational opportunities of middle-class girls. She was the first woman in Ireland to demand that women be admitted to universities. She organised the first suffrage group in Ireland, from Belfast, in 1871 and was an active member of the Ladies' National Association. She was also an active temperance advocate and a prominent member of the Belfast Women's Temperance Association. Tod established the Northern Ireland Society for Women's Suffrage (NISWS) in 1871 and joined it to the London Women's Suffrage Society. She remained secretary of the NISWS until the 1890s. Tod travelled the country tirelessly, speaking at public meetings to persuade both men and women of the need for the vote. In 1873, for example, between 6 and 14 February she spoke at meetings in Belfast, Carrickfergus, Coleraine, Armagh and Dungannon. In one week in May 1874 she had spoken from platforms in Cork, Limerick, Bandon, Clonmel and Waterford. She also appeared regularly at suffrage meetings in London. During this time she still campaigned for educational rights for women, was organising petitions to support the reform of property laws and was also organising a campaign against the Contagious Diseases Acts.[6]

As far as we are currently aware, Isabella Tod has perhaps left the best record of suffrage beliefs in nineteenth-century Ireland, though whether she was a 'typical' suffragist remains to be seen. Tod, like many nineteenth century suffragists, always admitted a practical purpose when seeking any improvement for women and argued for the vote on the basis of need and justice and on women's rights to citizenship. She sought a relatively restricted franchise and often, in her earlier speeches, based her claim on what she termed were inconsistencies in the laws between Ireland and England. In 1875 she claimed that some Irishwomen could vote for Poor Law Guardians, for Harbour and Water Board Commissioners; in towns which were not incorporated they could vote for Town Commissioners but could not vote for Town Councils. These she noted were 'capricious' arrangements. She referred to the importance of aiding middle-class women's constructive work of philanthropy in 'elevating the classes who naturally come under their care'.[7] It was also important to grant women the vote in view of their maternal responsibilities. 'Not only in the details of management of a workhouse (which needs an experience in housekeeping), but in the care of the sick, of the old, of the children, and the training of girls to earn their bread, no less than in the discrimination between honest poverty and imposture, there is work which must be shared by women to be done efficiently.'.[8] The majority of early suffragists did not desire the vote for all but demanded that women property owners should have as much right to the vote as male property owners. This demand for suffrage did not then extend in practical terms to all women but all women would benefit from even a limited suffrage. The benefits to be conferred on all women were not just legislative but also would improve the quality of relationships between men and women. Poorer men, who Tod considered had little regard for women, would, with the granting of the franchise recognise immediately the importance of all women, even their own wives, daughters and sisters. 'Women who suffer', she stated, 'need the franchise for protection and women who work for others need the franchise for efficiency.'[9] She wanted not only political power for women but also, much more importantly, their admission as citizens. In the nineteenth century she noted that 'neither the humanity of women nor their citizenship is acknowledged by a large proportion of uneducated men'. Granting the vote can teach men that 'women are citizens of the state'.[10] Even more importantly, the acquisition of the vote would allow women to exercise 'moral responsibility and freedom of action'. Suffragists, like Tod, expected to gain concrete powers with the acquisition of the vote. By strategic and moral use of their vote, women would be able to transform society into their own vision of moral and spiritual rightness. Not only would the vote allow for concrete changes in society but of much more fundamental importance for Tod was the belief that enfranchisement would transform women's consciousness, it would strengthen her self image in the individuality and self determination that she saw in citizenship. She demanded that women be allowed to participate directly in the political decisions that affected their lives. The demand for the vote revealed her protest against all the abuses to which women were prone in a single demand for a right to shape the social order through action in the public sphere.

Though nineteenth-century suffrage activists clearly failed to win the parliamentary franchise, they achieved a great deal, not least in the changes that were effected with regard to the education of girls and young women, the legislative changes that marked increased rights, particularly for married women, and through their work on the Contagious Diseases Acts where issues of sexuality, and the 'double-standard' were publicly debated. The suffrage campaign that emerged in the twentieth century differed in significant ways from that of the nineteenth century, even if their goals were the same. The most striking feature of twentieth-century suffrage activism in Ireland is the range of strategies that Irish women were able to engage to develop their arguments and bring those arguments to the public. More than ever, Irish women now appeared on public platforms to argue their case. From 1912 the *Irish Citizen* became a central forum for the articulation of ideas about suffrage, citizenship, duties and rights, gender and sexuality in Irish society. For the first time, fictional representations of Irish suffrage activists were published. Suffrage conferences were organised and by 1913 activists were able to organise a 'suffrage week', a project, according to one source, 'which was crowned with success'.[11]

In this collection, contributors throw new light on the suffrage campaign in nineteenth and twentieth-century Ireland. Mary Cullen provides the necessary intellectual backdrop for women's activism by discussing and tracing the development of republican ideas in women's political activism from 1798. As she clearly shows, even with the development of socialism, liberalism and nationalism, elements of republican values, 'the concept of citizens committed to individual freedom and the common good', remained central to the thinking of suffragists and feminist activists in their agreements and disagreements. Both Carmel Quinlan and Myrtle Hill provide comprehensive surveys on the suffrage campaigns in the south and north of Ireland from the 1860s to 1918. Quinlan's recovery of Anne Robertson is an important contribution to the genealogy of suffrage thought and activism in nineteenth-century Ireland. Quinlan also provides a clear account of why it was so difficult for suffrage concerns to be addressed in parliament. The dichotomy that existed between the nineteenth-century suffrage campaign and the apparent radicalism of the Ladies' Land League is notable. Hill focuses attention on the suffrage issue in Ulster and specifically on the contribution that unionist women made to the campaign. It is evident that unionist women were substantially involved in suffrage activism, but the encroaching sectarianism of political life made it difficult, and sometimes impossible, for unionist, nationalist and non-aligned women to work together. Hill acknowledges the different motivations of women working for suffrage in the North, and the significance of the Women's Social and Political Union (WSPU) in shaping that campaign. Mary Clancy's article provides a detailed case study of suffrage activism in the west of Ireland. The activism of women in the west offers a story of collaboration between women of different backgrounds, ages and even political views. Her emphasis on the ways in which women of the west created a space in which they could argue and debate suffrage and citizenship issues marks a major advance for the twentieth-century campaign. The creation of the *Irish Citizen* newspaper was one such space, the suffrage week organised in 1913, as discussed in Paige Reynolds's article, was another, the consistent publication of articles and viewpoints on Irish suffrage activism in English and international periodicals and magazines was yet another. The evolving sophistication of the campaign's creation of public and intellectual space marks one of the major differences between the campaign of the nineteenth and twentieth centuries.

In the nineteenth century, issues of sexuality and particularly the double standard of morality had been raised by Irish suffragists who were involved in the campaign to repeal the Contagious Diseases Acts. Issues of sexuality were to enter suffrage debate in the twentieth century. As Louise Ryan notes, suffragists reconstructed the problems of sexual crime and abuse as ones that crossed the public/private divide. Just as the courtroom became a key space, indeed a theatre, in which suffragettes made their cause public, so courts were, for many suffragists, the arena where crimes against the bodies of women and children remained unpunished, where men escaped justice. Reynolds argues that suffragists regularly 'invoked sexual morality in their political discourse both to generate interest in their cause and to support their claims that female virtue could cure the corruptions of modern life'. Women's oppression and sexual corruption apparently went hand in hand. Margaret Cousins had advanced views on vegetarianism and sexuality, though as Catherine Candy points out, it is important to view and explore Cousins' ideas as being mediated by the history of imperial orientalism. There is no doubt that research on the views of Irish suffragists towards empire would repay investigation.

Cliona Murphy reveals how humour operated within the suffrage campaign and how suffragists used it as a weapon against their detractors. Suffrage campaigning was often a case of managing ridicule. The literary work of Susanne Day and her novel 'The Amazing Philanthropists' is highlighted for its particularly satirically humorous views on the poor law, and on public reaction to women's suffrage. The value of fictional accounts for an understanding of suffrage in twentieth-century Ireland is explored by Murphy and to a greater extent by Leeann Lane in her article on the writer and activist, Rosamond Jacob. Like Hanna Sheehy Skeffington, Jacob has left an invaluable archive recounting her social and political world. Her first novel, 'Callaghan', is the only Irish novel currently known to deal specifically with the suffrage issue and written by an activist of the period. For contemporary reviewers, 'Callaghan' was a 'most readable story'[12] but the novel tells us much about Jacob's views on suffrage, nationalism, the role of the British in Ireland and the place of militancy in the fight for freedom.

Denise Kleinrichert's chapter focuses attention on the much neglected subject of suffrage and socialism in Belfast. Suffragists found it difficult to engage working women in their cause; there seemed to be little benefit for these women from a campaign that sought to advance middle-class, rather than working-class women. There were a number of suffragists, Margaret Connery and Winifred Carney among them, who were aware of the disabilities under which working women laboured. The difficulties faced in organising working women, as workers, never mind suffragists, may very well have slowed their recognition of an identity based on their collective interests. The trade union activist Cissy Cahalan noted in 1914 that: 'A woman has no tradition behind her, she enters the labour market with the quiet hope of leaving it on marriage. When she did wish to become unionised most of the men's unions refused to admit her.'[13] While the expansion of women's trade unionism was believed to be 'the best possible contribution to the whole cause of feminism',[14] working women appeared to have little to gain from the suffrage campaign. What trade unionist women, such as Winifred Carney, attempted to do was create another public space for women, where they were recognised as workers with rights and as women who were citizens.

While discussions of sexuality in the suffrage press reveal an inherent fear of the abuse of women's bodies, suffragettes used their bodies through their willingness to be imprisoned and to hunger strike in ways that made women's bodies bodies of protest. William Murphy's article reveals how suffragettes brought new tactics to Irish political life. While the period of suffragette militancy ended in August 1914, suffragette prison militancy was adopted as a template by other Irish protest groups. In refusing to pay fines, by undergoing imprisonment, the Irish suffragettes used the courtroom as a place of protest and their bodies as a fundamental form of resistance to their lack of political recognition.

Margaret Ward's article explores the reaction of Irish suffragists to the outbreak of war in 1914. She evaluates the conflicting views of suffragists towards the war; a number of Irish suffragists were pacifist, some argued that the suffrage campaign must be set aside until the war was won, some argued for continuing the campaign for the vote. The suffrage campaign in Ireland was able to accommodate women of diverse political and social views, just as it could accommodate women who held profoundly divergent views on the war. Caitriona Beaumont's article explores what happened to Irish women's political activism once the vote had been won and Irish independence achieved. Irish women had played an active role in the fight for Irish independence through their involvement in the Easter Rising of 1916, the War of Independence 1919–21 and the Civil War 1922–23. Equal citizenship had been guaranteed to Irish men and women under the Proclamation of 1916. Irish women over the age of 30 who filled particular property requirements won the right, with their British counterparts, to the parliamentary franchise in 1918. Active lobbying, particularly by women, saw all Irish citizens over the age of 21 enfranchised under the Irish Free State Constitution enacted in June 1922. It would appear that Irish women were well placed to benefit from the roles they had played in the fight for Irish independence. However, women did not retain a high profile in the political affairs of the country and from the foundation of the Free State, women's political, economic and social rights were gradually eroded.[15] It was perhaps the struggle itself, the ways in which it formed women's political activism, the ideas and modes of action it generated, rather than the acquisition of the vote that was the most important aspect of the suffrage campaign. The lessons learned in that campaign were to stand women well in the continuing struggles for political equality throughout the twentieth century.

NOTES

1. Dora Mellone, 'Woman suffrage in Ireland', *The Englishwoman*, 20, 58 (October 1913), p. 3.
2. For further information on women and philanthropic work, see Maria Luddy, *Women and Philanthropy in Nineteenth-Century Ireland* (Cambridge: Cambridge University Press, 1995), Margaret H. Preston, *Charitable Words: Women, Philanthropy, and the Language of Charity in Nineteenth-Century Dublin* (Westport, CT: Praeger, 2004), Jacinta Prunty, *Dublin Slums, 1800–1925* (Dublin: Irish Academic Press, 1997), Alison Jordan, *Who Cared? Charity in Victorian and Edwardian Belfast* (Belfast: 1993).
3. *English Woman's Review*, 15 April 1880, pp. 172–3.
4. See Anna Clark, 'Wild workhouse girls and the liberal imperial state in mid-nineteenth century Ireland', *Journal of Social History*, (Winter, 2005), pp. 389–409.
5. See Luddy, *Philanthropy*, pp. 92–3.
6. For Tod's activism, see Maria Luddy, 'Isabella M.S. Tod, (1836–1896)', in Mary Cullen and Maria Luddy (eds), *Women, Power and Consciousness in Nineteenth-Century Ireland* (Dublin: Attic Press, 1995), pp. 197–230; Noel Armour, 'Isabella Tod and Liberal Unionism in Ulster', in Alan Hayes and Diane Urquhart (eds), *Irish Women's History* (Dublin: Irish Academic Press, 2004), pp. 72–87.
7. *Women's Suffrage Journal*, 1 March 1875, p. 29.
8. *Women's Suffrage Journal*, 1 March 1886, p. 38.
9. *Women's Suffrage Journal*, 1 March 1875, p. 30.

10. *Ibid.*
11. Report of the Executive Committee of the Irish Women's Franchise League, 1913, p. 9.
12. *Irish Times*, 14 January 1921, in Jacob manuscripts, 33, 115, National Library of Ireland, Dublin.
13. The Drapers' Assistant, January 1914.
14. *Irish Citizen*, October 1917.
15. For recent work on the role of women in politics and social life in these years, see Maryann Gialanella Valiulis, 'Defining Their Role in the New State: Irishwomen's Protest Against the Juries' Act of 1927', *Canadian Journal of Irish Studies* 17, 1 (July 1992), pp 43–60; *idem.*, 'Power, Gender and Identity in the Irish Free State', *Journal of Women's History* 6/4/7/1/ (Winter/Spring 1995): pp. 117–36; *idem.*, '"Neither Feminist Nor Flapper": the Ecclesiastical Construction of the Ideal Irish Woman', in Mary O'Dowd and Sabine Wichert (eds), *Chattel, Servant or Citizen: Women's Status in Church, State and Society* (Belfast: Institute of Irish Studies, 1995), pp. 168–78; Mary E. Daly, 'Women in the Irish Free State, 1922–1939: the Interaction Between Economics and Ideology', *Journal of Women's History* 6/4/7/1/ (Winter/Spring 1995), pp. 99–116; *idem.*, '"Oh, Kathleen Ni Houlihan, Your Way's a Thorny Way!": the Condition of Women in Twentieth-Century Ireland', in Anthony Bradley and Maryann Gialanella Valiulis (eds), *Gender and Sexuality in Modern Ireland*, (Amherst: University of Massachusetts Press, 1997), pp. 102–26; Mary Clancy, 'Aspects of Women's Contribution to the Oireachtas Debate in the Irish Free State', in Maria Luddy and Cliona Murphy (eds), *Women Surviving: Studies in Irish Women's History in the 19th and 20th Centuries* (Dublin: Poolbeg Press, 1990), pp. 206–32; Caitriona Beaumont, 'Women, Citizenship and Catholicism in the Irish Free State, 1922–1948', *Women's History Review* 6, 4 (1997), pp. 563–85.

CHAPTER ONE

Feminism, Citizenship and Suffrage: A Long Dialogue

MARY CULLEN

INTRODUCTION

Organised action by Irish feminists to gain the parliamentary franchise developed from the 1860s and achieved final success when the 1922 Constitution of the Irish Free State gave full political rights to both sexes. During the nineteenth century the franchise came to be seen as the hallmark of citizenship and essential for participation in political decision-making. Yet throughout, suffragists saw the vote as one part of a far-reaching concept of citizenship. More specifically, it appears to me that Irish suffragists' understanding of citizenship consistently incorporated basic components of civic republicanism. This essay aims to discuss this.

NORMATIVE 'LANGUAGES'

In every generation and place individuals grow up absorbing an inherited body of ideas, values, and traditions, or political 'languages'. Depending on the issues seen as most pressing, participants draw on various components, emphasise some, ignore or challenge others, alter original meanings, add new ideas and values as the process of develop-ment in the whole continues. Modern feminism emerged in the interaction between economic, social and political developments and the political languages current in the eighteenth century.

The republican tradition was one of these languages. More than just a form of government, it combined political and social ideals and values. The American historian Gordon Wood sees republican values 'spread everywhere in the culture of the Western world' in the eighteenth century, and essentially 'the ideology of the Enlightenment'.[1] Republican origins go back to ancient Greece and Rome, to the idea of the *res publica*, the 'public thing' belonging to and created by the individually free citizens of an independent city state. For classical theorists the organisation of the city state or *polis* aimed at 'the common good of its members and enabled them to cooperate in the pursuit of ideals that were fundamental to humanity'.[2] Freedom and interdependence went hand in hand. Citizens remained free as individuals and as a group only if they put the common good before private interests when necessary. Citizenship demanded civic virtue, including public spirit, justice, courage, prudence and moderation, to protect the state from outside aggression and internal corruption. In turn, participation contributed to the development of citizens as human persons.[3]

Republicanism ceased to be a central focus in political debate for centuries after the fall of the Roman Republic until the emergence of the city states of Renaissance Italy. Its reworking then and during the revolutionary period in seventeenth-century England produced what is called 'classical republicanism'. The growth of large territorially-defined states with large populations made representative systems appear more feasible than direct citizen participation in government, while the interests of the growing commercial classes prioritised the protection of individual property rights in emerging theories of natural rights. In her study of civic republicanism, Iseult Honohan identifies two diverging strands of thought on republican freedom in the eighteenth century. One saw it as 'security of life, liberty and property, protected by a form of representative government in which interests and power were separated and balanced'. For the other, citizens' freedom depended on 'their being active, united and virtuous participants in their own self-government'.[4] An interacting set of values came from Enlightenment, or Age of Reason, emphasis on the equality of all human persons on the basis of shared rational nature and its critical analysis of accepted ideas and institutions. These broadened ideas of eligibility for citizenship, and added an optimism that reason and education could improve human nature and, emulating advances in scientific knowledge of the natural world, discover the laws governing human societies.

Yet another long-standing normative language, seldom seriously addressed by historians and political scientists, pervaded all the others. This was the language of masculine superiority. It saw women as dependants, subject to male authority, inferior to men in various ways, including capacity for rational judgement, and ineligible for citizenship. It co-existed with, and justified the exclusion of women from, many civil and political rights. Republican citizenship, from its origins, had been confined to a minority of men and excluded all women. Now, in the late eighteenth century, pioneering women used the democratic implications of Enlightenment thinking to claim recognition as full human beings and citizens possessing the right and duty to direct their own lives, make rational moral decisions, share responsibility for the organisation of society, and develop as human persons, all basic republican values.

THE FEMINIST CHALLENGE: MARY WOLLSTONECRAFT

One of the most influential pioneers was the radical English writer Mary Wollstonecraft (1759–97). *A Vindication of the Rights of Woman* (1792) was an assertion of the full humanity of women. It challenged restrictions on women's freedom, stereotypes of women's 'nature' as irrational and emotional, and books by men 'of genius' that treated women as 'a kind of subordinate beings, and not as part of the human species . . .'. Women were rational human beings as men were, and the same standards of freedom, virtue and responsibility applied. Rousseau had argued, in *Émile* (1762) that, because their duty was to serve men's needs, women should be educated to submission and away from independent judgement. Wollstonecraft responded that it was a farce 'to call any being virtuous whose virtues do not result from the exercise of its own reason. This was Rousseau's opinion respecting men; I extend it to women . . .'[5]

She did not defend women's actual behaviour. Restrictions on autonomy and conformity to stereotypes corrupted women and damaged the common good. Women who used feminine deceits instead of reasoned argument exercised a harmful influence on family, household and society. Yet, the main culprit was the 'tyranny of men', compounded by the 'plausible epithets men use to soften their insults . . . . [such] as fair defects, amiable weaknesses, etc'. It was 'time to restore to [women] their lost dignity – and make them, as a part of the human species, labour by reforming themselves to reform the world'.[6]

Reciprocal relationships between freedom, citizenship, the common good, civic virtue and personal development permeate the book. It recognised no boundary between public and private life. Women and men might have different duties, but they were all 'human duties' pertaining to citizenship. '[M]ake women rational creatures, and free citizens, and they will quickly become good wives, and mothers; that is – if men do not neglect the duties of husbands and fathers'. But it was not as mothers but as human beings that women claimed civil and political rights. Women's 'first duty is to themselves as rational creatures, and the next, in point of importance as citizens, is that, which includes so many, of a mother'. Economic independence was vital, since women could not be virtuous until 'in some degree, independent of men'. She opened the question of political participation, arguing that women should have their own representatives and not be 'arbitrarily governed without having any direct share allowed them in the deliberations of government'.[7]

UNITED IRISH WOMEN: MARTHA McTIER AND MARY ANN McCRACKEN

In eighteenth-century Ireland, as elsewhere, republicanism was one of the main political languages in use.[8] So far there has been little research on the political thought of Irish women. However, the letters of two contemporaries of Wollstonecraft, Martha McTier (1742–1837) and Mary Ann McCracken (1777–1866), both members of middle-class Presbyterian and United Irish circles in Belfast, are permeated by the language and values of republican citizenship.

For over forty years, Martha McTier and her brother, William Drennan, a founding member of the United Irishmen, maintained a correspondence where political information, ideas and advice inter-mingled with family matters, gossip, career, courtship and marriage.[9] Martha read the political writers of the day, sometimes before William did, and offered her opinions. Throughout, both maintained a commit-ment to liberty, the common good, justice and courage. Despite the personal danger to William, developing a medical practice in Dublin while engaged in anti-establishment politics, Martha gave support, encouragement, advice and sometimes exhortation. Prudence should temper action, but to a limited extent. Justice and principle could not be subordinated to personal concerns, whether William's trial for sedition, the alienation of his patients, or Martha's own safety as an open supporter of the United Irishmen. She used republican language: 'I can never believe that good policy in a state and justice and common honesty must be set at variance . . . they are really one. . . .' Reminding William of the reasons he entered politics, she exhorted him: '. . . so virtue and honour regulate the conduct of those I love, with the prudence *they* allow of, I feel equal to every other trial . . .'. In December 1797 she lamented that 'if there is any public virtue here she dwells with the young . . . She must first be got acquainted with in Greece and Rome, yet later writers have given I believe a more enlarged view of her'. She had read Wollstonecraft and spoke of her a number of times, without declaring her own position on feminist claims. That she agreed with them is suggested by her insightful yet sympathetic comment on the discrepancy between Wollstonecraft's love affairs and her advocacy of reason-controlled emotions. '[N]obly did she assert her sex's independence – yet what a miserable slave *she* was. Virtue and prudence must ever be absolutely necessary to independence'.[10]

Mary Ann McCracken was close to her older brother, Henry, who led the United Irishmen at the Battle of Antrim in May 1798. While he was in hiding after defeat, she helped him, organised an escape plan that nearly succeeded, and finally attended his trial and walked hand-in-hand with him to the place of execution. While the affection in her letters is obvious, Nancy Curtin[11] notes that she appears better read than he in the classic republican and radical texts and to have been comfortable lecturing him on politics, while John Gray remarks on her 'apparent leadership' in their relationship.[12] She had read Wollstonecraft and put the case for women's emancipation in Enlightenment and republican language in a letter to Henry in Kilmainham Jail in Dublin in 1797. Speaking of the United Irish auxiliary women's societies in Belfast, she criticised the men for having separate female societies 'as there can be no other reason for having them separate but keeping the women in the dark' and making 'tools of them . . .'. Women should have 'rational ideas of liberty and equality for themselves' and reject their 'present abject and dependent situation, degraded by custom and education . . .'. It was time to 'throw off the fetters with which they have been so long mentally bound . . .'. They needed a 'genuine love of Liberty and just sense of her value . . . as without Liberty we can neither possess virtue or happiness . . .'. '[T]here can be no argument produced in favour of the slavery of women that has not been used in favour of general slavery and which have been successfully combatted by many able writers'.[13]

EARLY SOCIALISM AND FEMINISM: ANNA WHEELER[14] AND WILLIAM THOMPSON

Just over a quarter of a century later, the joint work of an Irish man and an Irish woman 'offered perhaps the most comprehensive treatise on sexual equality and social and economic reform provided in the nineteenth century . . .'.[15] From the eighteenth-century ferment of ideas the political languages of liberalism and socialism were emerging. Both developed the republican values of individual liberty and the common good plus the democratic thrust of Enlightenment thinking, in the context of the economic and social upheaval created by the industrial revolution. Liberalism, which was adopted as its ideology by capitalist interests, defined individual liberty and equality as essentially freedom from all imposed restrictions including government interference. Socialism saw unfettered capitalist pursuit of individual profit as inimical to equality and the common good, and argued that the economy must be consciously managed in the interests of the whole community. Many early socialists aimed to achieve this by harmonious co-operation between social classes and the initiatives of middle and upper-class philanthropists.

Anna Wheeler (1785–c1850), born Anna Doyle, the daughter of a Church of Ireland clergyman, left an abusive marriage and became active in early socialist circles, both those of Henri Saint-Simon and Charles Fourier in France and of Robert Owen in England, where she met William Thompson. Thompson, a Protestant landowner from Cork, was one of the most radical and egalitarian thinkers of the Owenite co-operative movement, and he and Wheeler collaborated in the *Appeal of One Half of the Human Race, Women, Against the Pretensions of the other Half, Men, to Retain them in Political, and Thence in Civil and Domestic, Slavery*.[16] Its immediate genesis was the assertion by the Utilitarian philosopher James Mill that women could be excluded from political rights because the interests of 'almost all' women were included in those of their fathers or husbands. Like Mill, Thompson and Wheeler based their argument on Jeremy Bentham's thesis that laws and government policies should promote the greatest happiness of the greatest number of individuals. The *Appeal* developed a detailed analysis of the logical flaws in Mill's claim that women's happiness was safe in male hands while at the same he asserted that men needed political rights to protect their civil rights 'of property and person' against their propensity to exploit each other. It pointed to the evidence of men's actual behaviour towards women, giving particular emphasis to the marriage laws. It argued that in reality the happiness of the greatest number of both women and men would be increased if both sexes had equal rights in civil and criminal law. A further increment would result from equal political rights as their exercise would develop women's intellectual powers and expand their sympathies beyond the immediate family, thereby increasing their own capacity for pleasure and their contribution to the general happiness. Women were exhorted that, to be free they had 'only to desire it, to perceive their real interest, always harmonising with the interest of the whole race, and fearlessly to advocate it'. Finally, the *Appeal* asserted that only a socialist organisation of society could deliver the fullest possible happiness of the greatest number. All previous systems, from slavery to republicanism, had subjected women to men. Only under a new system of 'Association, or of Labour by Mutual Co-operation' could 'perfect equality and entire reciprocity of happiness between women and men' be achieved, by '[l]arge numbers of men and women co-operating together for mutual happiness, all their possessions and means of enjoyment being the equal property of all – individual property and competition for ever excluded . . .'[17]

TOWARDS FEMINIST ORGANISATION: THE ROLE OF PHILANTHROPY

By the 1860s, organised action for women's emancipation was emerging in Ireland. The new middle classes were growing in wealth, numbers and influence with the expansion of commerce, manufacture, banking, and the professions, all increasingly male-dominated, while the separation of workplace and home grew, and with it the ideology of public–private division and 'separate spheres'. The Westminster parliament was recognised as the location of political decision-making in the United Kingdom of Great Britain and Ireland. The middle classes were wresting political power from the aristocracy. Middle-class men won the parliamentary vote in 1832 and male heads of households in 1867. The parliamentary franchise was increasingly seen as the hallmark of citizenship and the gateway to political participation.

Republicanism was no longer as prominent among political languages, though, as already noted, both liberalism and socialism continued some of its values, while developing nationalism emphasised the idea of the republic as a self-determining nation where the people replaced the monarch as ruler.[18] The language of masculine superiority still flourished, described by one prominent feminist as a 'tone of depreciation of women . . . [in the 1860s] frightfully common, both in society and the press – whether it was an attitude of groundless or misplaced compliment, or of patronage, or of mockery or contempt'.[19] In Ireland, no large-scale organised socialist movement had emerged and the ideas of Wheeler and Thompson do not appear to have had a conscious formative influence on the early women's emancipation campaigns.

Liberalism was the generally dominant language; while the logic of its rejection of restrictions on individual freedom of choice implied support for civil and political rights for women, in practice liberal men as a group failed to actively advocate these.

The immediate route to feminist organisation for most of the pioneering Irish activists was through the interaction between republican values, Enlightenment emphasis on the individual plus its optimism that action and education could improve human nature and society, and the challenge the Christian churches faced in responding to changing social and economic conditions. From this emerged evangelical religion, or revivalism, and it influenced all denominations. It preached a dynamic Christianity, based on the individual life of self-denial, humility, submission and obedience, virtues particularly associated with women, leading to action to regenerate a sinful world. Seeing women as naturally closer to its ideals, it authorised them to uphold moral standards inside and outside the home, and associate together in charitable organisations.[20] In the process it provided a new normative language of a limited female superiority in the area of morals.

Starting in the late eighteenth century and continuing throughout the nineteenth, Western societies saw a huge expansion of middle- and upper-class female voluntary charitable work. Irish women philanthropists developed a wide range of services aimed at improving the moral and physical condition of the poor, particularly women and children.[21] They moved outside the home into more meaningful, challenging and personally-fulfilling work than was previously open to women, work for the most part initiated and organised by themselves. This gave them experience of management, finance, dealing with the male-run 'public' world and, not least, the opportunity to judge that women could manage many things as well or better. It could develop awareness of gender inequality and the limits this imposed on their work. For the few who joined anti-slavery associations, attention was directly focused on discrimination in civil and political rights, while these and temperance organisations gave experience of campaigning with male colleagues to change the laws. A minority of philanthropists moved further to openly challenge restrictions on women's autonomy and freedom of action, while a larger number were ready to move into new areas of activity opened by the feminists. Shared commitment to the common good, to being 'useful' to society, maintained on-going interaction between philanthropy and feminism.

Overall, women's response to evangelicalism indicates how widespread dissatisfaction was with the limited scope for action and development of potential sanctioned by conventions and normative languages. Its scale suggests that more than purely religious motivation was involved, powerful as this undoubtedly was. Motivations are often complex and, like all human thinking, can accommodate apparently contradictory elements. Historically, challenges to the status quo have often been represented as returns to an earlier situation or as mandated by accepted normative languages. Historians of religious congregations regularly have to decode the language of self-effacement in which women religious attributed their own initiatives to male ecclesiastics. A religious mandate was less challenging to many women – not to mention their families and communities – than open defiance of the accepted norms of female behaviour.

THE NINETEENTH-CENTURY CAMPAIGNS FOR CIVIL AND POLITICAL RIGHTS

The first generation of pioneering feminists in Ireland came from Protestant denominations, with Quakers especially prominent. While Catholic women were equally involved in philanthropy, at an early stage Catholic lay pioneers translated their societies into religious congregations in a move seen as a trade-off with the hierarchy whereby they gained long-term security and support for their work at the cost of some autonomy – and perhaps the incidental side-tracking of potential feminists.[22]

Discrimination against women in civil and political rights made the contrast between their position and that of men, particularly of the developing middle classes, wider than ever. Under the common law, married women 'had no civil existence: they owned no personal property, they could neither sue nor be sued, they could not divorce their husbands, or claim any rights over their children'.[23] Women could not vote in parliamentary elections or hold public political office. They were excluded from the universities, entry to the higher professions, while the education of girls at second level aimed more at accomplishments and preparation for marriage than intellectual formation and employment. In theory, middle and upper-class women were supported by their menfolk. Failing this, the only 'respectable' employments were poorly paid governessing, teaching or needlework. The law made women the punishable party in sex-related offences such as prostitution, illegitimate births and adultery.

Campaigns developed around all these areas in Ireland from the 1860s.[24] Taken together, their combined objectives could be seen as a programme for republican citizenship. Married women's control of their own inherited or earned property was a prerequisite for their own personal autonomy, and the issue affected all women, single or married, and all social classes. Raising standards of female education so that it aimed at intellectual development was central to development of human potential and ability to reform society, as well for employment, economic independence and autonomy. Opposition to government regulation of prostitution in the Contagious Diseases Acts upheld the common good in the moral improvement of society, and challenged double sexual standards that punished prostitutes while leaving male clients untouched. The parliamentary vote was linked to recognition as full human persons, to freedom and self-determination, and was increasingly seen as essential to empower women to influence legislation that would benefit society as a whole. Campaigners used two different but complementary lines of argument; firstly, the Enlightenment case that women and men were equally human persons with the same rights and responsibilities to themselves and to society; and secondly, that each sex had a different contribution to make, both important and both needed for the proper management of society. The latter drew on the language of women's moral superiority, seen as needed to control male lust, protect the family and raise moral standards generally.

These ideas were constantly articulated by the leaders. Anne Jellicoe (1823–80), a Quaker and a major figure in the reform of women's education, wrote in 1873:

> By education is not merely meant instruction, but the cultivation of all those faculties – intelligence, affection, will, conscience – such training, in short, as will enable each individual to guide herself right through the circumstances of life – to know her duty, and to do it – an education which, if so considered, is as important to women as to men, to poor as to rich.[25]

Anna Haslam (1829–1922), a Quaker in Dublin, and Isabella Tod (1836–96), a Presbyterian in Belfast, were to the forefront in all the campaigns. Thomas Haslam, Anna's husband and co-feminist, published three issues of the *Woman's Advocate* in 1874. It argued the case for women's suffrage as 'the moral right of properly qualified women to some share in the enactment of the laws which they are required to obey'. Women demanded political and educational rights and to be 'treated as reasonable beings, who are personally responsible for the

talents which have been confided to their care'. In 1875, Isabella Tod
wrote that women were:

> . . . citizens of the state, inheritors with men of all the history
> which ennobles a nation, guardians with men of all the best life of
> the nation; bound as much as men are bound to consider the good
> of the whole; and justified as much as men are justified in sharing
> the good of the whole.

Experience showed that women 'felt a deeper responsibility resting upon
them, and . . . attempted to carry their religious principles into the
common things of life to a greater extent than men did'. Men were often
drawn to politics from selfish motives while women did not campaign
'only for themselves. They fight for others; and it is because we have so
much work to do that we fight as hard as we do . . . '.[26] For Tod, suffrage
was 'not merely a claim of abstract right, but of necessary means for
performing duties'.[27] It was 'the only practical means of redressing
wrongs'.[28]

When women gained eligibility for election as Poor Law Guardians
in 1896, Anna Haslam rejoiced that women voters crossed sectarian
lines to vote for a candidate whom they knew could be 'absolutely
trusted to do her duty by [the poor]'. Conscious of the links between
philanthropy and feminism, she explained that many women had not
become active suffragists because success seemed so impossible that they
threw their energy into 'charitable work . . . the results of which would
be visible within their own life-time'.[29] In 1906, Thomas asserted that
women 'have been brought into the world, like men, to cultivate their
whole nature, physical, intellectual, moral, spiritual, political and so on,
in the way most conducive to their happiness, and the well-being of the
world at large'.[30] There is a fuller discussion of the Haslams in Carmel
Quinlan's chapter in this book.

THE *IRISH CITIZEN* NEWSPAPER 1912–20

By the early twentieth century, educational standards at second level had
been substantially raised and entry to the universities achieved, though
not yet to all the higher professions. Married women had gained
considerable, though not complete, control of their property. The
Contagious Diseases Acts had been repealed. The vote and eligibility for

election had been won in local government. The major campaigning issue was now the parliamentary vote. The numbers of active suffragists expanded rapidly around the western world. In Ireland, women from Catholic and nationalist backgrounds were joining in significant numbers, though Protestants and unionists still formed the majority.

Nationalist–unionist differences reached a climax during the lifetime of the *Irish Citizen*. Some form of Home Rule became inevitable after 1911 when the House of Lords lost its indefinite veto on legislation. An armed force, the Ulster Volunteers, was organised in 1913 to resist the imposition of home rule on Ulster, followed in the south by a corresponding force, the Irish Volunteers. World War I, the 1916 rising, the establishment of Dáil Éireann and the War of Independence followed. Irish feminists took varying attitudes to these developments. However, for this discussion I want to consider their thinking on citizenship as it emerges in the pages of the *Irish Citizen*, the newspaper published in association with the Irish Women's Franchise League, the most prominent of the new suffrage societies, between 1912 and 1920. It is a unique source that provided a forum for a wide range of opinion and argument.[31]

The political languages drawn on included socialism (now more developed in Ireland and interacting with the labour movement), nationalism and pacifism, as well as women's moral superiority and mission to regenerate society. Themes prominent in the earlier emancipation campaigns were discussed and new issues raised. The motto on the paper's masthead made an immediate statement: 'For men and women equally the rights of citizenship: From men and women equally the duties of citizenship.' The first editorial stated that the paper stood for the 'fullest development of a complete humanity . . .' and against limits on 'human freedom and human character'.[32] Another spoke of 'adjustment between the needs of the individual and the needs of the community'.[33] An unsigned contribution argued for co-operation between men and women in a 'voluntary bond' to create a 'social organisation . . . capable of giving the maximum opportunity of personal freedom to the maximum number of persons'.[34] E.A. Browning, press secretary of the Irish Women's Reform League, wrote that 'we have become sensitive to the common needs and satisfactions . . . the joy of one is a gain to all, and the suffering of one an injury to all'. Women might be denied the hallmark of citizenship, but 'should this not make us anxious to prove ourselves citizens in all but name?'[35]

There was considerable agreement that women were morally superior to men in some ways, and had a different set of values; they were sexually more chaste, more concerned with the common good, with 'true life-values' – both the preservation and quality of life – and were more opposed to war and militarism. Whether these qualities were seen as biologically determined, or arising from women's experience in maternal and domestic roles, it was imperative to bring them into political decision-making. This could be done by direct participation in political decision-making or by citizen-mothers educating future citizens. For either role, education was crucial. Among others, Mary Hayden, Professor of Modern Irish History at University College Dublin, argued that girls' education must go beyond the selfish interests of the individual family, specifically include politics, economics, the place of the family in society, and prepare her 'to do her duty efficiently', whether in the 'corporate life of the city or country' or as a mother.[36]

Some contributions acknowledged that women were not morally superior to men in all ways, and were held back from developing their full potential by the narrow range of opportunities open to them. Margaret Connery of the Irish Women's Franchise League saw suffrage as part of a bigger movement aiming at the 'unity of humanity . . . a universal brotherhood of man'. This was not possible while half of humanity, women, were 'sunk in servitude and degradation'. Women's roles and work had become seriously impoverished and 'new forms of labour and the right to labour' were essential. If woman 'may not grow and develop, and exercise all her powers of body and mind, she, and the race through her, are threatened with ultimate extinction'.[37] Marion Duggan, a law graduate of Trinity College Dublin, argued that, while women were 'in some ways superior to men', they had 'failed to cultivate certain qualities which men have learned by experience', and wider opportunities, including the practice of law, 'may materially assist [their] moral development'.[38]

Socialist contributors, themselves mostly middle-class women, agreed that suffrage and feminism were integrally linked to the common good. In Belfast, Margaret McCoubrey, describing herself as a socialist, claimed that when women gained equality 'existing systems for maintenance of law and order, our gigantic farce called Courts of Justice' will go and there will be 'no need for charitable organisations, for prisons, or for rescue-homes'. Only with the help of women 'dare you dream of true Internationalism'.[39] However, socialists also challenged the leadership role of middle-class feminists, arguing that working-class women must achieve their own emancipation. Middle-class leadership was defended by Margaret Connery on the grounds that the poorest, most oppressed and overworked women could hardly lead the movement.[40] Marion Duggan, a regular contributor over the years (and discussed in more detail in Louise Ryan's chapter in this volume), asked could 'wealthy or educated women . . . be trusted to make laws for poor working women?' Should the latter be 'free and independent, or humbly receiving the legislative bounty of their better-off sisters?' [41] When demands for suffrage had first emerged only middle-class men had the vote and the demand for suffrage on the same terms as men appeared relatively unproblematic to middle-class women who saw it as their duty to improve both the physical and moral conditions of their poorer sisters. As more categories of men gained the vote, and as socialism and trade unionism developed in Ireland, such assumptions came under attack.

One editorial reported the English Fabian Society's finding that the majority of working women contributed to the support of dependents. This discredited calculations of women's wages on the needs of an individual, and only the votes of working women would change this.[42] However, most socialist contributors argued that economic reform came before the vote as a priority for working women. Economic justice was the first essential and the only basis on which international harmony and equality between men and women could be built. Working women needed to organise to improve pay and gain admission to a wider range of work. This would educate them to use and appreciate the franchise. Then they 'themselves must decide how best to get the vote, by full, frank, free discussion'.[43] Louie Bennett, later to become general secretary of the Irish Women Workers' Union, also pressed the prior need for trade unions. When women had cured sweated labour conditions they would turn to civic reforms 'which only the workers themselves will ever achieve'. She urged the *Irish Citizen* to look at 'broader aspects of feminism than purely suffrage'. Feminism and Co-operative Internationalism were 'dependent upon economic justice'. Economic justice, for workers and in international relations, was the only way to a world 'safe for democracy'.[44]

Trade unionists also recognised that the exploitation of working women in conditions, unequal pay and limited employment opportunities had to be addressed in the context of the labour movement as a whole and the co-existing exploitation of working men. Bennett went so far as to argue that the demand for equal pay and equal work for women was problematic in the present industrial system and organisation of society where 'the financial burden of keeping the home lies upon the male wage-earner, working under a system so heedless of human needs'. 'When co-operation has succeeded capitalism' the distribution of work can be 'completely readjusted'. Women workers needed to raise their whole status, pay and working conditions to have 'that self-respect as a worker which gives a note of happiness to any toil . . . '[45]

On the related question of women's trade unions versus mixed unions, Bennett supported separate unions on the grounds that they gave women's voices and needs a better hearing. She was challenged by Cissie Cahalan, of the Linen Drapers' Assistants' Association and a member of the Irish Women's Franchise League, who argued that only by the sexes closing ranks, and women and men working 'shoulder to shoulder' in mixed unions could they reach the 'goal of Irish Labour – the Workers' Republic'.[46] Throughout all the debates, agreements and disagreements, the concept of free, self-determining citizens working together for the common good continued as a unifying principle and objective.

CONCLUSION: FEMINIST AND REPUBLICAN VALUES TODAY

Some significant points emerge from this brief overview. Firstly, the pioneering feminists identified their problem as the non-recognition of women as full human persons, in Wollstonecraft's words 'not part of the human species'. Secondly, their chosen model incorporated the values of that strand of republican citizenship emphasising individual autonomy, active co-operation with others to create the common good, and self-development through participation. Thirdly, these values continued to inform Irish feminism throughout the late nineteenth and early twentieth centuries, when civic republicanism was no longer a political language in widespread use and to most people in Ireland republicanism meant complete independence from Britain.[47]

The demand was never simply for equality of rights with men within existing structures and value systems. Nor did feminists promote men's patterns of behaviour as the human norm to which they should aspire. Their aim was more ambitious, a transformation of society through the promotion of 'female' values. The nineteenth-century activists antici-pated that women's admission to citizenship would bring new standards of morality, compassion, equality and justice into public decision-making. In the early twentieth century feminist socialists and trade unionists agreed with this but insisted that economic justice was a prerequisite for working-class women's autonomy and the common good of society.

Events since then have shown that these expectations were not fulfilled. Women's full citizenship has not transformed society in the ways envisaged by feminists. Women as a group have not supported the same political policies, but, like men, have been distributed across a wide range of often conflicting philosophies and ideologies. Universal suffrage has not delivered effective participation in political decision-making to all citizens. Nor has any consensus been reached as to whether observed differences in behaviour between women and men are the result of nature or nurture. It is more useful to look to feminist analysis of women's experience as a force for change in human society. This is not to suggest that feminist thinking has never been mistaken. Feminists have been legitimately criticised for being unduly optimistic at times, élitist, over-maternalistic or blind to class issues, and so on. Similar criticisms can and have been made of most radical ideas and, if all political thinkers or schools of thought were dismissed for these criticisms, there would be few left. Weak links in a chain of argument do not necessarily negate the values being promoted.

Today there appears be a real need for these feminist values. For most of the nineteenth and twentieth centuries, liberalism and socialism have been the dominant political languages in the West. For some people the claims of socialism were undermined by the subordination of individual freedom to a controlling elite's definition of the common good in the USSR experiment. More recently, neo-liberalism has pushed the emphasis on individual freedom to an extreme in the deregulated pursuit of corporate profit and the ideology of politics as a struggle between competing interests. Disillusionment is mounting at its failure to deliver the common good it promised. Over recent decades, political theorists have been turning again to the tradition of civic republicanism in the hope that its concept of the interdependence of individual liberty and the common good, plus the need for active, participatory citizenship to ensure both, may help to solve some of today's problems. There are many problems and no obvious solutions; not least among them how to achieve meaningful participation, and how to reach agreement on what comprises the common good.

The feminist contribution to these debates can come, not by providing a blueprint for the ideal polity, but by its long commitment to a world-view that combined political and social values and saw the personal development of the individual as part of the political process, and its insistence that women be recognised as citizens and values associated with women recognised as human values essential for achieving and maintaining the common good. For this contribution to be made, the feminist tradition must be remembered, revisited, and reworked for today's world. The current pervasiveness of neo-liberalism endorses a definition of feminism as aiming solely at equal participation by women and men in existing socio-political systems. Such a definition loses the potential of the historical feminist rejection of an ideology that sees some human values as appropriate in private life while a contradictory set are acceptable in public political life. This rejection opens the way to envisioning new models of human nature and behaviour and new models for the organisation of society, something a narrow definition of equal rights does not.

History has a central role here. Societies rely largely on historians for their group memory and understanding of how contemporary institutions and values have evolved. Knowing how we got to where we are is essential for potentially better and more realisable decisions as to where we go next. Most history is still written within a paradigm that sees males as the active agents in the patterns of continuity and change in human history. In the case of Irish history, most general surveys and specialist monographs devote no analysis or questioning to the political, social and economic consequences of being born a male or a female in a specific place at a specific period in history. They take for granted the centuries-long historical reality of laws, regulations and custom that combined to channel control of resources, wealth, property, access to education and political power to males and away from females. If feminism is mentioned at all, it is seen essentially as women trying to reach a stage of development already achieved by men. The result is that successive generations grow up absorbing this world-view and unaware of an important part of their historical heritage.

Gender relationships have always been a fundamental factor in human history. Until they are incorporated into 'mainstream' histories of Irish and other societies, history and group memory will continue to disseminate a distorted view of that history. Succeeding generations will have no understanding of where contemporary gender relationships came from, and no basis from which to assess their value, defects and possibilities. It is as important for boys as for girls, for men as for women, to realise that the male role in society is not *a priori* the human norm, but, like the female role, a social construct open to change over time, and equally problematic.

As the body of research in women's history grows, we move closer to the point where the paradigm of male agency, and the male role as the human norm, will no longer be sustainable and will be replaced by a more inclusive model. Incorporating the suffrage and emancipation campaigns into a general history of modern Ireland could be a good start towards a more accurate representation of the past. These campaigns show women as autonomous political actors who succeeded in changing the law to win civil and political rights for over half the total adult population and who in the process made a significant contribution to political theory. We already have a considerable body of knowledge, at present largely confined to the specialist field of women's history. Beginning to make this breakthrough may be the next stage in the development of women's history.

NOTES

1. Wood, G.S. *The Creation of the American Republic 1776–1787* (Chapel Hill: University of North Carolina Press, 1998), pp. vii–viii.
2. Morrow, J. *History of Political Thought; a Thematic Introduction* (Basingstoke and London: Palgrave, 1998), p. 19.
3. See Honohan, I. 'Freedom as citizenship; the republican tradition in political theory', *The Republic* 2 Spring/Summer 2001, pp. 7–24.
4. Honohan, I. *Civic Republicanism* (London and New York: Taylor & Francis, 2002), p. 110.
5. Wollstonecraft, M. *A Vindication of the Rights of Woman* (Oxford: Oxford University Press, 1993), pp. 7, 86–7.
6. Ibid., pp. 100, 113.
7. Ibid., pp. 119, 221, 227, 228, 265.
8. Connolly, S.J. 'Introduction; varieties of Irish political thought', in S.J. Connolly (ed.), *Political Ideas in Eighteenth-Century Ireland* (Dublin: Four Courts Press, 2000), p. 18; Ian McBride, 'The harp without the crown; nationalism and republicanism in the 1790s', ibid., p. 159; Stephen Small, *Political Thought in Ireland 1776–1798; Republicanism, Patriotism and Radicalism* (Oxford: Oxford Univeristy Press, 2002), passim.
9. Jean Agnew (ed.), *The Drennan–McTier Letters* (Dublin: Women's History Project in association with the Irish Manuscripts Commission, 1999). As the general editor, Maria Luddy, points out, they are a marvellous source for social and political history. For present purposes, the letters of the 1790s provide an example of republican citizenship in action.
10. Ibid., vol. i. 14, vol. ii. 255, 255, 387. William Godwin's *Memoir* of Wollstonecraft and her *Posthumous Works*, published early in 1798, discussed her love affairs and printed some of her love letters. The resulting scandal provided many with an excuse to ridicule her arguments. See Claire Tomalin, *The Life and Death of Mary Wollstonecraft* (London: Penguin Books, 1974), p. 233.
11. Curtin, N.J. 'Women and eighteenth-century Irish republicanism', in Margaret MacCurtain and Mary O'Dowd (eds), *Women in Early Modern Ireland* (Edinburgh: University of Edinburgh Press, 1991), p. 140.
12. Gray, J. 'Mary Ann McCracken' in Daire Keogh and Nicholas Furlong (eds), *The Women of 1798* (Dublin: Four Courts Press, 1998), p. 55.
13. McNeill, M. *The Life and Times of Mary Ann McCracken 1770–1866: A Belfast Panorama* (Belfast: The Blackstaff Press, 1988), pp. 125–6.
14. For Wheeler, see Dooley, D. 'Anna Doyle Wheeler', in Mary Cullen and Maria Luddy (eds), *Women, Power and Consciousness in 19th Century Ireland: Eight*

Biographical Studies (Dublin: Attic Press, 1995), pp. 19–53, and *Equality in Community: Sexual Equality in the Writings of William Thompson and Anna Doyle Wheeler* (Cork: Cork University Press, 1996).

15. Dooley, 'Anna Doyle Wheeler', p. 31.
16. The *Appeal* was first published in London in 1825 under Thompson's name. In the 'Introductory Letter to Mrs Wheeler', Thompson explicitly stated that his purpose was to put Wheeler's ideas on paper, as her 'interpreter and the scribe of your sentiments', and reqretted that only a few of the pages were actually 'written with your own hand'. Thompson, W. *Appeal of One Half of the Human Race, Women, Against the Pretensions of the other Half, Men, to Retain them in Political, and Thence in Civil and Dometic, Slavery.* (London: Virago, 1983), p. 27
17. Thompson, *Appeal*, pp. 121, 122–3, 195, 199.
18. Honohan, *Civic Republicanism*, pp. 113–19.
19. Isabella Tod, cited in Helen Blackburn's obituary of Tod, *Englishwoman's Review*, 15 October 1898, p. 59. The similarity to Wollstonecraft's description seventy years earlier is striking.
20. Rendall, J. *The Origins of Modern Feminism; Women in Britain, France and the United States, 1780–1860* (Basingstoke: Macmillan, 1985), pp. 73–6.
21. See Luddy, M. *Women and Philanthropy in Nineteenth-Century Ireland* (Cambridge: Cambridge University Press, 1995); Raughter, R. 'A natural tenderness: the ideal and reality of eighteenth-century female philanthropy', in Maryann Valiulis and Mary O'Dowd (eds), *Women and Irish History* (Dublin: Wolfhound Press, 1997), pp. 71–88.
22. For these developments and discussion of the issues, see Fahey, T. 'Nuns in the Catholic Church in Ireland in the nineteenth century', in Mary Cullen (ed.), *Girls Don't Do Honours: Irish Women in Education in the 19th and 20th Centuries* (Dublin: Arlen House, 1987), pp. 7–30; Clear, C. *Nuns in Nineteenth-Century Ireland* (Dublin: Gill and Macmillan, 1987), and 'The limits of female autonomy; nuns in nineteenth-century Ireland' in Maria Luddy and Cliona Murphy (eds), *Women Surviving: Studies in Irish Women's History in the 19th and 20th Centuries* (Dublin: Poolbeg Press, 1990), pp. 15–50; Luddy, M. *Women and Philanthropy in Nineteenth-Century Ireland;* Raughter, R. 'A natural tenderness', and (ed.), *Religious Women and Their History: Breaking the Silence* (Dublin: Irish Academic Press, 2005).
23. Rendall, *Origins of Modern Feminism*, p. 4. The United Kingdom divorce law of 1857 gave women the right to sue for divorce, though on more stringent conditions than applied to men, and it was not extended to Ireland.
24. Since changes in the law for all parts of the United Kingdom were made at Westminster, there was considerable co-operation between the British and Irish campaigners and, in the cases of married women's property and the Contagious Diseases Acts, Irish activism was part of an England-based campaign.
25. Cited in Anne V. O'Connor, 'Anne Jellicoe' in Cullen and Luddy, *Women, Power and Consciousness*, p. 152.
26. Cited in Maria Luddy, 'Isabella M. Tod', ibid., pp. 217–18
27. Cited in Helen Blackburn's obituary of Tod, *Englishwoman's Review* 15 January 1897, p. 60.
28. Cited by the Mayoress of Belfast at the unveiling of a memorial to Tod, *Englishwoman's Review* 15 January 1898, p. 53.
29. *Englishwoman's Review*, 15 October 1898, pp. 222, 224. For more on the close relationship between philanthropy and feminism see Carmel Quinlan's chapter on the Haslams in this book.

30. Haslam, T. *Women's Suffrage from a Masculine Viewpoint* (Dublin: 1906), p. 15.
31. For this section I have found both Hearne, D. 'The Development of Irish Feminist Thought: A Critical Historical Analysis of The Irish Citizen 1912–1920', (PhD thesis, Ontario, 1992) and Ryan, L. *Irish Feminism and the Vote; an Anthology of the Irish Citizen newspaper 1912–1920* (Dublin: Folens, 1996) very useful.
32. *Irish Citizen*, 25 May 1912.
33. Ibid., 17 May 1913.
34. Ibid., 13 July 1912.
35. Ibid., 2 Aug 1913.
36. Ibid., 6 and 13 July 1912.
37. Ibid., 29 Dec 1912, 4 Jan 1913.
38. Ibid., 24 April 1915.
39. Ibid., 27 Feb 1915.
40. Ibid., 3 Jan 1913.
41. Ibid., 8 Aug 1914.
42. Ibid., 19 July 1913.
43. Marion Duggan, ibid., 20 Feb 1915.
44. Ibid., Jan 1918.
45. Ibid., Nov 1919.
46. Ibid., Dec 1919.
47. Irish feminism continued to incorporate the same values up to and including the second wave of feminism of the 1970s and 1980s.

CHAPTER TWO

'Onward hand in hand'[1]: The nineteenth century Irish campaign for votes for women

CARMEL QUINLAN

INTRODUCTION

The prime movers in the campaign for votes for women between 1860 and the end of the nineteenth century were Anna and Thomas Haslam, a married couple who were both Quakers.[2] The Haslams are noteworthy in that they were multi-cause campaigners; interested and active in many movements for social reform. Thomas had written a treatise on birth control in 1868 in which he recommended family limitation by use of the 'safe period'. Their perception of the inequity of the prevailing double standard of sexuality moved them to campaign for the repeal of the Contagious Diseases Acts.[3] Thomas was an avid student of social theories; his reading on heredity and evolution coloured his writings on marriage and the rearing of children.[4] Anna worked for increased educational opportunities for women for many years.[5] She also had worked for the anti-slavery movement in the mid-nineteenth century; the involvement of Quaker women in the cause of anti-slavery has been credited 'as giving impetus to the evolution of the women's suffrage movement'.[6] Above all, they both believed in the equality of the sexes, a cause to which they devoted their long lives.[7]

There had been some faint stirrings of feminist activism in Ireland some decades before the start of an organised campaign for women's suffrage. A meeting in the Library of Friends' Meeting House, in Eustace St. Dublin in 1861 was attended by Bessie Raynor Parkes,[8] Mrs Lloyd,[9] Mrs Jellicoe[10] and Miss Corlett.[11] The meeting 'urged the need for providing employment for educated women'. From this and other meetings came the Queen's Institute, and subsequently Alexandra

School,[12] established in 1861 with the purpose of training girls for employment opportunities as machinists, law writers, telegraph clerks, office clerks, ornamental writing, engravers and lithographic workers.[13] This meeting is evidence of the existence of a network of mainly Quaker women involved in reform and innovation in the cause of increased opportunities for women as early as 1861.

PETITIONING PARLIAMENT

The petition for votes for women presented to parliament by the recently elected member of parliament, John Stuart Mill, in 1866 was signed by 1,499 women, of whom seventeen had Irish addresses.[14] The majority of signatories were Dublin based with three from Belfast, three from Waterford, and one from Cork. In April 1866, Mill promised that he would present a petition to parliament seeking votes for women if a hundred signatures could be obtained. From the available evidence it appears that the obtaining of signatures and the presentation of the petition was a rushed affair. Logistical difficulties in the collection of signatures in a very short space of time probably account for the very small number of Irish signatures, a mere one per cent of the total. From their surnames, it seems likely that all Irish signatories of the petition were Quakers or had Quaker connections.

The petition claimed: 'That the participation of women in the Government is consistent with the principles of the British Constitution inasmuch as women in these islands have always been held capable of sovereignty, and women are eligible for various public offices.' The petition further sought 'the representation of all householders, without distinction of sex, who possess such property or such rental qualification as your honourable House may determine'.[15] Mill's success in bringing about the first debate on women's suffrage was, in his opinion, the most important public service he performed in the House of Commons. In May 1867, during the debate on the Reform Bill, he moved that the word 'man' be replaced by the word 'person', thus ensuring 'that the question of a woman's right to vote was heard for the first time in modern history in the legislative assembly of a civilized country'. After a short debate a division was taken and Mill's amendment received 73 votes or almost a 'third of the thin attendance'.[16] He was pleased that the introduction of the topic had given an 'immense impulse to the question'.[17]

The perceived success of the first petition was the catalyst for the formation of a 'provisional' London committee to suffrage. In January

1867, a committee was formed in Manchester for the 'promotion of the enfranchisement of women'.[18] In the autumn of 1867, the 'provisional' London committee became the London National Society for Women's Suffrage.[19] Correspondence between Mill and Thomas Haslam in August 1867 and again in 1868 discussed the possibility of spreading the movement to Ireland.[20] There is little evidence of organised suffrage activity in Dublin before 1870 although there were petitions for suffrage presented to parliament from Ireland in 1869. Signatures came mainly from Dublin and environs although there were some also from Cork, Waterford, Queen's County and twenty-one signatures from Bruree, Co. Limerick.[21] By 1869 the National Society for Women's Suffrage was listed as established in London, Edinburgh and Dublin.

THE BEGINNING OF SUFFRAGE ACTIVITY IN IRELAND

Anna Haslam, with her husband Thomas as helper and propagandist, is usually credited with being the instigator of suffrage activity in Ireland. Evidence would suggest, however, that Annie Robertson was the initial organiser in Dublin. Miss Robertson, from 2 St James's Place, Blackrock, Co. Dublin, was named as Honorary Secretary of the Dublin branch of the National Society for Women's Suffrage (London, Edinburgh, Dublin) in a circular of 1869.

The first public manifestation of interest in, and potential support for, an Irish campaign for women's suffrage came in 1870. In April of that year, Annie Isabella Robertson organised a successful public meeting in the Molesworth Hall, Dublin on the theme of 'electoral disabilities of women'. The meeting was addressed by Millicent Fawcett[22] and received extensive coverage in the *Freeman's Journal* where it was reported that the body of the hall was crowded and the reserved seats and the platform were also 'completely occupied'. Fawcett's speech, reported in full, appears forceful and compelling and was essentially a demolition of the contemporary arguments put forward against votes for women. The attendance included such luminaries as Sir William and Lady Wilde, Sir Robert Kane, Reverend Lloyd, Provost of Trinity College, Reverend Mahaffy, also of Trinity College and Sir John Gray MP.[23] In her scrapbook of cuttings, Anna Haslam, who had been present with her husband Thomas, added the names of Isabella Tod,[24] Barbara Corlett, Miss Gough and Mr and Mrs Eason as being present at the meeting.[25] Anna, recalling the meeting over forty years later, described it as 'the best meeting that was held in Dublin –

no such names have been got together for any meeting since'. Millicent Fawcett's cogent and well-argued speech was reprinted in full in the *Freeman's Journal*.

In the *Irish Citizen* article of 1914, Anna recalled the 1870 meeting: 'It was got up by Miss Robertson who worked alone in the suffrage cause for some years. Petitions were her chief form of activity'.[26] This supports the view that Haslam was not actively involved in the early organisation of public meetings but rather that Robertson was her precursor in activism.

Isabella Tod established the Northern Ireland Society for Women's Suffrage in 1871 and 'travelled the country tirelessly speaking at public meetings on the suffrage issue. As well as speaking in towns all over Ulster, she spoke in Cork, Limerick, Bandon, Clonmel and Waterford'.[27] These meetings were reported in the English published *Women's Suffrage Journal*. Meetings were sometimes marred by disturbance, a fact rarely acknowledged in the official accounts. A vivid, and perhaps approving, description of the heckling endured by the female speakers at suffrage meetings survives in the private journal of Charles Ryan:

> A Woman's Rights meeting was held in Cork but it was very disorderly. When Miss Beed[y] MA came forward a ruffian called out: "Hurrah for the Venerable Bede." Miss Downing was requested to "Speak up darling" . . . "What are women's rights without women's charms" said another when a particularly ill-favoured lady, Miss Todd (sic) came forward. Singing and disturbance made the meeting very lively.[28]

Isabella Tod did not complain about difficulties experienced at meetings; on the contrary, she wrote to London that 'everywhere they received good local support and met with much cordial sympathy, and nowhere opposition'.[29]

THE *WOMEN'S ADVOCATE*

A short-lived, but interesting, periodical appeared in 1874, in which Thomas Haslam penned his ideas on the rights of women to a 'more positive legal status'. There were only three issues of this journal, which might be more correctly called a series of pamphlets, which they resembled in layout and content. The first issue of *The Women's Advocate* published in April 1874 was implicitly addressed to Irishmen. In it

Haslam challenged the perception that women 'degrade themselves by stepping out of their natural sphere of unobtrusive modesty' by seeking political equality. He trenchantly countered criticism of women's public agitation for the vote: 'If you are grieved to see so many of our best and noblest women "unsex themselves" – as you affect to call it – what have you done to prevent the necessity for their so demeaning themselves?'[30] Ray Strachey has synopsised contemporary [1873] arguments against granting of votes to women, using uncited quotes: 'It would "unsex" women, "contaminate" them, "drag them down to our own coarse and rough level", and "defile their modesty and purity".[31] *The Women's Advocate* carried under its title the words of Herbert Spencer: 'Equity knows no difference of sex. The law of equal freedom applies to the whole race – female as well as male,' a quotation that had been used by Millicent Fawcett in her 1870 speech in Dublin. Haslam attributed his allegiance to the cause of women's suffrage to his having read this quotation in 1851.[32]

Haslam's analysis of the rightful place of women is complex. While he is adamant about the rights of women to equality, there is in his early writings on suffrage evidence of an ambiguity in regard to the vexed question of campaigning women leaving themselves open to charges of 'demeaning themselves' by being forced into the 'field of controversy' by entering the public sphere. There seems to be in his writing at least a tacit acceptance of this viewpoint, or perhaps more correctly, an ability to argue from an angle of acceptance. It must be remembered that his arguments were addressed to men in an effort to persuade them to become advocates of women in their search for the vote. There is, I think, a degree of sophistry in his arguments. In addressing his entreaties to men, he exploited the common perception of the indelicacy of women being forced to enter the public sphere. He used this ploy in order to persuade men that they should campaign on behalf of women, thus removing the necessity of such women behaving in what might be deemed an 'indelicate' manner. In practice, Haslam enthusiastically supported his wife's entry into the public sphere, and regularly and enthusiastically attended public meetings addressed by women. He was above all a pragmatist, who acknowledged the possible prejudice of his audience and sought to persuade within its constraints, rather than risk alienating it by attacking dearly held opinions. His later writings reveal his unambivalent disapproval of an attitude that claimed women needed to be 'protected' from participation in public life.

The second (May 1874) edition of *The Women's Advocate* contained practical advice on successful campaigning methods. His practical advice reveals him not only as a theorist but as someone with experience of organising protest, albeit of the most law-abiding and constitutional nature. Anna revealed, in an interview in *The Irish Citizen*, that his advice was considered so useful that 5,000 copies of this leaflet were ordered by Lydia Becker,[33] the English suffragist pioneer, for distribution to English activists.[34] *The Women's Advocate* was not produced in June 1874 and in July the third and final number contained a brief rebuttal of the *Spectator's* hostile attitude to suffrage entitled 'Woman Suffrage versus *The Spectator*'.[35] Interestingly, a further year and a half was to elapse before the Haslams' suffrage association came into being.

THE DUBLIN WOMEN'S SUFFRAGE ASSOCIATION (DWSA)

A suffrage meeting held in Dublin on 26 January 1876 in Exhibition Palace Hall, Earlsfort Terrace (now the National Concert Hall) seems to have been the catalyst for the formation of the DWSA.[36] Among the speakers were Lydia Becker, Lilias Ashworth,[37] Eliza Sturges of Birmingham and Isabella Tod. They were supported by Mr W.H. Allen and Sergeant Sherlock MP, both of whom were subsequently DWSA members. The meeting was constantly interrupted by disturbance 'from the lower part of the room' and 'hisses' during the speeches. When the motion 'that the exclusion of women otherwise legally qualified from voting in the election of members of Parliament is injurious to those excluded' was put to the house, there were 'cries of aye and some confusion at the end of the hall'. The chairman, Maurice Brookes MP asked that 'any person of opinion it should not pass . . . say no'. There was no response . . . 'and the resolution was carried unanimously'.[38] It should be noted that this account, admitting that all was not harmonious at the meeting, came not from a suffrage publication but from the *Freeman's Journal*.

The minute book of the Dublin Women's Suffrage Society shows the first recorded meeting to have taken place on 21 February 1876 in the Leinster Hall, Molesworth Street. Charles Eason chaired the meeting.[39] The account of this meeting does not include a list of attendance but a partial list can be reconstructed from resolutions passed. Abraham Shackleton (treasurer), Miss Corlett, Miss McDowell and Mrs Haslam were present. A resolution passed confirms that a committee had been in place before this meeting: 'That Mrs Haslam and Miss McDowell be requested to act as secretaries for a short time longer'.[40] The report of the second meeting of 6 March includes a list of the attendance: Henry Allen (chairman), Mrs McCarthy [probably the wife of Justin McCarthy MP), Lady Murray, Miss E. Webb, Miss Geoghegan, Miss Russell, Miss Corlett, Miss Laffan, Mrs Butler, Miss Helen Webb, Miss McDowell, Mr And Mrs Haslam. An executive committee was formed which included Mr Eason, Mrs Haslam, Miss Corlett, Miss McDowell, Miss Emily Webb and Miss Helen Webb.[41] Again Quakers predominate: Corlett and the Webbs were also associated with the Society of Friends.

The formation of the DWSA executive committee at the February meeting marked the start of a formal movement dedicated to the campaign for equality for women. Mrs Haslam proposed that an annual subscription of one shilling per annum 'shall constitute membership in the association'. Mrs Haslam and Miss Rose McDowell were appointed secretaries. Initially the meetings were irregular, usually about four per annum, and mainly concerned with the presentation of petitions to parliament. A notable characteristic from the beginning was the involvement of influential men in the suffrage society. Members of Parliament regularly attended meetings, including T.W. Russell,[42] Maurice Brookes,[43] Colonel Taylor[44] and William Johnston.[45] The Sergeant-at-Arms, David Sherlock, was a frequent participant.[46] The DWSA was proud of the male input to the society: 'Co-operation with men has been a distinguishing feature of the policy of the Association from the first'.[47]

The essentially middle class nature of the association, a fact invariably remarked upon by historians, is not surprising. The feminist socialist Helena Moloney remarked that the Irish women's movement 'which aroused such a deep feeling of social consciousness and revolt among Irish women of a more favoured class, passed over the head of the Irish working woman and left her untouched'.[48] Education was a vital element in the development of feminist consciousness, and while there is evidence of working class involvement in England, particularly among the textile unions, there was no similar involvement in Ireland, a fact regretted by Anna Haslam.[49]

Accounts of DWSA meetings contained in the minute book of the society are perfunctory but reveal that much effort was invested in the obtaining of signatures to petitions that were subsequently forwarded to Westminster. In 1877, there were '13 petitions containing 2,912 signatures . . . forwarded to the House . . . presented by Sir A. Guinness and Colonel Taylor'.[50] One year later we learn that '15 petitions were forwarded during the 1878 session' which contained 3,191 signatures.[51]

There was a veritable deluge of petitions presented to parliament in this period, particularly whenever a private member's suffrage bill was being introduced. In the decade of the 1870s there was a Bill introduced every year except 1875.

Other than collecting signatures for petitions, the main work of the DWSA in its early stages consisted of striving to overcome the 'prevailing ignorance' of Dubliners regarding the cause of votes for women. The committee placed emphasis on the educational role of the society. It strove to spread the message by holding meetings and circulating periodicals that advocated suffrage for women. At a meeting in September 1876, the secretaries were requested 'to obtain leave from the various reading rooms in the city to permit copies of *The Women's Suffrage Journal* to be laid on their tables'.[52] In January 1877, it was reported that the DWSA had arranged that the reading rooms of Trinity College, the Chamber of Commerce, The Royal Dublin Society, Mechanics' Institute, Coffee Palace and The Friends' Institute 'now receive *The Women's Suffrage Journal*'.[53] By 1879 the following establishments were included in the list of venues to which 'suffrage journals were sent': the Free Libraries in Thomas St., Capel St. and Kingstown, the Workman's Club, Charlemont Place, Law, Historical and Philosophical Societies of Trinity College, and the Constitutional Club.[54] A great number of the above reading rooms were male only preserves, revealing the commitment of the society to raising male awareness to the cause of women's franchise.

Drawing room meetings in private houses were a favoured method of getting the message across to small numbers of invited guests. The minute book frequently mentions that such meetings had taken place, e.g. 'Successful drawing-room held at Mr Eason's'[55] and 'Two drawing rooms were held . . . excellent addresses'.[56] The committee did not neglect self-education. It was regularly addressed by visiting activists from London. The committee instructed Mrs Haslam to 'purchase *The Women's Question in Europe*' for eleven shillings to lend to members. The DWSA were aware of contemporary social and intellectual movements and on at least two occasions held meetings in conjunction with congresses in Dublin.

Accounts of the nineteenth century Irish suffrage movement describe the DWSA as 'preaching to the converted'[57] at 'small meetings, usually in the drawing rooms of members' houses'.[58] In reality, in the first years, the major resources of the committee were expended on large public meetings to which prominent speakers were invited. The first arranged by the fledging association was in the Antient Concert Rooms on

6 April 1877. This was judged not 'so successful as we had wished . . . especially owing to the determined hostility of a small knot of disturbers',[59] obviously not a case of merely preaching to the converted. Eliza Wigham, visiting from Edinburgh, gave 'a few words of encouragement in the full conviction that though the work is uphill and the opposition at present envenomed, eventual victory is *certain*'.[60] Another public meeting was held in Leinster Hall on 19 August 1878. It was reported that 'much good has been done by this meeting' with which Lord Talbot De Malahide was associated.[61] The Lord Mayor presided at the DWSA public meeting at Leinster Hall in 1879.[62] A 'large and most influential' meeting was held in Leinster Hall in October 1881 which was 'crowded . . . many people had to be turned back as there was not even standing room to be had'.[63] The publicity for this meeting, held in conjunction with the Social Science Congress, was impressive: '750 cards and 1,000 fly leaves' were printed and distributed, the 'usual' advertisements were placed in the newspapers and placards placed in the tram cars.[64]

The embryonic Dublin suffrage movement had been affiliated to the English movement from the beginning. Mrs Haslam attended the 'Great Manchester Demonstration' in February 1880 for which she claimed expenses of £2.10.0. When asked to give an account of the meeting she demurred that she was no speaker; rather than speak from memory she had taken the precaution of preparing notes. Her account highlights the excitement of the occasion and conveys the impression that women present had a sense of being mould breakers in the tradition of great reform movements of the past:

> The famous Free Trade Hall where in bye-gone (sic) times the voices of John Bright and Richard Cobden so often rang out during the Corn Law agitation was crowded by thousands of women who thronged the steps of the platform, passages and every available spot so that an overflow meeting had to be improvised in the Memorial Hall adjoining . . . the meetings were managed from first to last by women – gentlemen, except the reporters were not to be seen in the body of the hall – they were relegated to the gallery on payment of 2/6 each (the entire hall being free to women).[65]

Although Anna Haslam's efforts for equal opportunity for women never included comments, nor suggested actions, which might be termed anti-male, there is in this account a rarely exhibited sense of glee in her comments of how, for once, when women were in control they neatly turned the tables on the male audience. Gentlemen who complained of the arrangements in the Free Trade Hall were reminded that: 'in the most august assembly in the land, ladies were not only condemned to sit in a gallery perched up in the clouds, but were carefully caged in where they could not be seen and could very badly see and hear', whereas gentlemen at the Manchester meeting were offered 'their choice of seats in a fine spacious gallery where they could see and hear the ladies'.[66] These comments express familiarity with the *purdah*-like conditions to which women were condemned when they visited the Houses of Parliament. Female suffrage campaigners attended the debates of the many defeated bills, confined to quarters that effectively reinforced 'their unfranchised state in emphatic physical terms'.[67] Anna does not mention that she had addressed the Manchester demonstration, a fact documented by Blackburn.[68]

When the first suffrage bill passed its second reading in 1870 by a majority of 33, the pioneer suffragists were 'full of happy anticipation of easy achievement' which proved 'delusive'.[69] Forty-eight years were to pass before women were granted the vote. Why? One practical reason was the difficulty of introducing a private members' bill, a procedure subject to numerous hazards. Such bills could easily be stymied and needed the government's tacit support or, at the very least, the absence of government hostility. Private bills had time allocated to them by ballot at the beginning of each parliamentary session. In the event of success in the ballot, it was still possible, and indeed all too easy, for the previous business on the agenda to be prolonged so that no time remained for the private bill. If the bill were reached on the order of business, the debate could be prolonged until the limited private members' time expired and the bill was 'talked out'. In 1905, for example, 'a second reading victory was . . . averted by Mr. Labouchere, who in order to ward off a possible suffrage success, distinguished himself by speaking for some hours about the lighting of vehicles'.[70] Even if the bill successfully passed the first stage, it was notoriously difficult to find time for the later stages, as it had to join the queue of other private members' bills. However, despite the frequent frustration of unsuccessful private members' bills, the suffragist leaders encouraged and supported them, for they considered that they were the only course open to them, and that they always engendered publicity for the cause.[71] Constitutional suffragists' campaigns were also frustrated by the vicissitudes of party politics. A fundamental difficulty was that the major parties neither officially supported nor opposed women's suffrage but allowed members a 'free vote'. By the end of the nineteenth century the futility of the strategy of introducing private members' bills was causing frustration within the more radical sections of the suffrage movement which resulted eventually in the militant suffrage campaign.

Between the foundation of the DWSA in 1876 and the granting to Irishwomen the right to become poor law guardians in 1896, there was a steady stream of unsuccessful suffrage bills presented to parliament. The DWSA lobbied assiduously for each bill. The *modus operandi* was simple but effective and the campaign was not confined to Dublin. As well as initiating petitions, letters were sent to women all over Ireland by Anna Haslam as Honorary Secretary of the DWSA, asking them to organise local suffrage committees and to write to Irish members of parliament urging their support. Such letters, she argued, 'would have great weight with our Members; and the total expense need not exceed a pound at the farthest'.[72] Occasionally, an example of a suitable letter to members of parliament was included; recipients were asked to 'send a similar letter in your own language to all members in your town and county and any others over whom you can exert influence'.[73] In March 1884, when the campaign to include franchise for women householders in the forthcoming Reform Bill was at its height, a circular letter requested that the recipient 'not only write personally' to both 'Borough and County members' but that she 'induce the largest number of . . . friends and acquaintances, men and women to do the same'. The circular continued forcefully: 'Write to members; to Mr Gladstone; to other Cabinet members; to Mr Trevelyan; insisting and entreating that they will not deny to Women householders a measure of long withheld justice . . . But our action should be prompt and universal; we should not lose a day in pressing our claim.'[74] In April 1884, Anna mounted a newspaper campaign. She wrote to the *Daily Express* regarding the 'Household Franchise Bill'. She wished to 'solicit the kind support of the newspaper'. She argued that 'we have justice on our side as well as constitutional principle; our claim is a . . . reasonable one'. Her letter reveals her methods and also the other reforms to which she was committed:

> The only debatable argument is whether we shall be included in the present Franchise Bill or be compelled to go on agitating, petition-ing, addressing public meetings, interviewing members of Parliament memorializing Cabinet Ministers . . . for another ten or fifteen years, to the exceeding waste of time of these energies which we might be devoting to the improvement of our educational, sanitary, licensing, poor law and other systems which greatly need reform.

She claimed supporters 'among all shades of opinion – Conservative, Liberal and Home Ruler'.[75] This letter was one of fifty-four sent to newspapers in Leinster, Munster and Connaught, thirty of which were published. A circular containing the history of Irish MPs' voting record on women's suffrage was 'largely distributed among friends of the movement requesting them to write to their members' and provoked a 'good response'.[76] Sixteen petitions were forwarded to the House of Commons, twelve to the House of Lords and 'numerous letters sent to members'.[77] Anna's obituary in *The Woman's Leader* praised her prodigious workload: 'No work appeared to her too great; no detail too small or tedious. To circularize every Irish Member, or to write thirty or forty letters to prominent public men with her own hand was mere child's play'.[78]

In the event, the Reform Bill did not include a clause enfranchising women householders. The defeat of the clause for the enfranchisement of women was a bitter disappointment. The sums had been done and victory seemed assured. The provisions of the Act, when passed, meant that 'the male population was now very fully enfranchised, and the impetus for pushing democracy farther appeared to be spent'.[79] Simultaneously, the provisions of the Corrupt Practices Act (1883) resulted in the recruitment of women as unpaid party workers, as it was no longer legal to pay professional canvassers. Strachey has stated that activities of women in party politics did a great deal for the suffrage cause, as it could be no longer argued that women were unfit for the 'rough and tumble' of politics: 'They proved their utility; and by so doing they broke down the ancient belief that politics was exclusively a man's job'.[80] An acrimonious split occurred in the English suffrage movement between those who wished to include party political associations as affiliates and those who wished to keep the suffrage movement free from the 'intrusion of party spirit into the neutrality hitherto so carefully preserved'.[81] The DWSA were firmly behind Mrs Fawcett who wished to remain independent of any party political affiliation. She subsequently formed the National Society for Women's Suffrage (NSWS) established on the old non-party lines, and Mrs Haslam was appointed to the London Executive.[82] The Dublin committee remained independent and non-party.

There is no documentary evidence extant of the attitude of the DWSA towards the Ladies' Land League that operated in Ireland from January 1881 to August 1882. One might have expected an organisation that demonstrated that women were capable of organising and operating a countrywide campaign under the most difficult of circumstances to have elicited comment from the executive committee of the DWSA. The women of the Ladies' Land League displayed the same organisational efficiency as the DWSA. It famously compiled 'The Book of Kells', a detailed register of all land rentals in the country, and also efficiently administered the Land League's considerable funds. The feminist press in England was opposed to these ladies' 'illegal' activities, however, and greeted news of the arrest of members with satisfaction. The alleged leniency of the constabulary towards the ladies prior to the arrests was deplored as the principle of men and women being equal before the law was one of the basic tenets of the feminist movement. There is no evidence of the attitude of the Haslams to the Ladies' Land League. They would, however, have been bitterly opposed to what they would have perceived as the illegal nature of the Ladies' Land League operations, although they might well have been sympathetic to its work to alleviate distress caused by evictions. Dublin was a small city. Anna Parnell walked home to Hatch Street every evening from the League's offices in Sackville St. It is extremely likely that members of the DWSA were acquainted with Ladies' Land League executive members – they may even have been friends. The actions of the Ladies' Land League were given much press coverage. However, the minutes of the DWSA never mentioned them, but they rarely dealt with anything other than suffrage matters. I think it fair to say that women of the calibre of the Parnell sisters and their co-members would have believed in female suffrage, despite the evidence of the embryonic Ladies' Land League in America being careful to point out that it had no connection with the suffrage movement.[83]

POOR LAW GUARDIANS

Despite the continued failure of the successive bills in the 1880s and 1890s, the Irish movement had cause for rejoicing when in 1896: 'That indefatigable friend of women's interests W. Johnston M.P. undertook to introduce a Women's Poor Law Guardian (Ireland) Bill and successfully carried through all its stages in the House of Commons in a few days thereby ensuring its subsequent enactment'.[84] This legislation, which meant that qualified women could now stand for election as Poor Law Guardians, was the catalyst for a resurgence of the association. At once the committee focused upon the election of women as poor law guardians. A letter was sent in March 1896 to eighty 'leading ladies . . . urging them to look out for suitable women who would be prepared to offer themselves as candidates at future elections'.[85] The election of Miss Martin as first female Poor Law Guardian was 'felt to be the cause for much congratulation'.[86]

Although Anna Haslam did not herself stand for election as a Poor Law Guardian, preferring to spearhead a campaign to persuade other women to go forward, she involved herself with standards in workhouses, a key issue for guardians. She visited Holyhead, Bangor and Caernarfon Workhouses, 'some of the arrangements in which are decidedly superior to those adopted in our Dublin environs'.[87] When attending the Conference of the Women's Suffrage Association in Birmingham, and a conference of women workers in Manchester, she availed of the opportunity to visit workhouses and children's homes in the Birmingham, Manchester and Kettering areas.[88] She saw the advantages gained there by the presence of women as guardians, a role which exemplified the links between philanthropy and activism. Her remarks reveal her as having a strongly compassionate nature; her perception of the workhouse was as a place that should be made as comfortable as possible for the poor, whom she clearly saw as deserving the best treatment it was possible to provide within the constraints of the system. She was struck by the facilities provided by Welsh and English institutions, including swings and playrooms for children and superior sanitary facilities. These facilities she attributed to the 'womanly element in the management of the institutions'.[89] Haslam addressed many election meetings where she exhorted her audience to vote for women as poor law guardians.

The 1897 DWSA[90] report rejoiced in the election of twelve women poor law guardians 'fulfilling their most sanguine expectations'. It was noted that the women's election had been to the 'entire satisfaction of the great body of ratepayers but also to the acknowledged advantage of their respective boards'.[91] The importance of Irishwomen standing for election of as poor law guardians was recognised as a powerful stimulus 'to the willingness of our more capable fellow country women to take their legitimate share in the public work which our social needs require'.[92] Local committees were formed in Strokestown, Skibbereen, Tralee and Miltown Malbay with the intention of 'moulding public opinion . . . bringing electoral influence to bear upon such of our Representatives as are either hostile or indifferent to women's claims'. Women poor law guardians were subsequently elected in these four towns demonstrating the effectiveness of the DWSA strategy.

THE LOCAL GOVERNMENT ACT

The second reading of the Parliamentary Suffrage Bill in February 1897, which was carried by 230 to 159 votes, was 'exceedingly encouraging' and Irish members' voting had been 'satisfactory'. Michael Davitt was one of the Irish members who voted for the bill.[93] Despite continued disappointment in the search for the parliamentary franchise, 1898 was a 'red letter year for Irishwomen', as the government 'honourably redeemed their pledges, in the passing of the Local Government Act'. The practical result of this, announced the committee, was that qualified women in Ireland:

> ... now enjoy all the franchises possessed by their English sisters together with the lodger franchise not yet conferred upon the latter. They now also enjoy all the franchises possessed by their fellow countrymen except the parliamentary; and if they have not yet obtained seats upon the County and Borough Councils, there is every probability that these will be thrown open to them at no very distant date.[94]

Once again Anna had worked closely with sympathetic MPs, most notably William Johnston of Belfast, to secure amendments to the bill that would enhance the position of women. Qualified Irishwomen were entitled to vote under the act, and to stand for office as district councillors and as poor law guardians. She 'had reason to sound a triumphant note since she had played a leading role' in ensuring that successful outcome.[95] Her political acumen was displayed in the campaign for the local government franchise for women. She was convinced that 'because of political causes' in Ireland, in single seat electoral divisions women would have very little chance of heading the poll. The intervention of the committee, who addressed 'appeals and remonstrances to numerous Members of both Houses of Parliament', ensured the dual membership proviso, permitting the election of not fewer than two members in each electoral division in the case of District Councils and Board of Guardians [which] was not in the original draft of the Bill.[96] A letter from Anna to Mr Balfour in which she points out the 'the single member principle ... will throw a serious obstacle in the way of Poor Law lady guardians especially in rural districts' elicited the reply that Mr Balfour 'thinks it not improbable' that the vote in the House of Lords 'will be in the direction you require'.[97] Because of similar representations, including a letter sent to the chief secretary of Ireland,

a further amendment ensured that persons who were not local government electors were eligible to stand as candidates if they fulfilled the
residence qualification. This provision was particularly important as it
enabled many married women to stand as district councillors.[98]

By the end of 1898 there were eighty-five women elected as poor law
guardians, thirty-one of whom were also rural district councillors. These
results furnished:

> . . . a conclusive answer to those who affirm that Irish women are
> too exclusively wrapped up in their family concerns to take their
> rightful share in the duties of Local Government and it also
> conclusively proves that they will be well qualified to perform their
> duties as intelligent electors when the Parliamentary vote has been
> conferred upon them.[99]

Despite this upbeat account of victory the committee deplored that,
'strange to say', Cork was still without a woman guardian, nor was there
a single woman elected in Galway, Waterford, or Limerick.[100] The lack
of an active feminist movement in Cork was a recurring cause for
concern. This lack of an 'influential Committee' in the 'southern
metropolis' meant that there was little progress in Munster. It was
surprising that the existence of Queen's College did not bring
'enlightenment'.[101]

The DWSA committee regularly published lists of elected women
poor law guardians and Mrs Haslam never lost an opportunity to
publicise the advantages of women's contribution when elected. She saw
them not merely as administrators, but as compassionate philanthropists
who brought a practical humanity to their role as poor law guardians.
Above all, she saw them as reformers who 'added to the inmates'
comfort' by improving the 'dietary', the kitchens and the clothing of the
inmates.[102] Twenty-first century feminists might well deplore her
perception of women poor law guardians' strengths as essentially the
application of their domestic skills to the workhouse. Anna Haslam,
however, saw such skills as uniquely equipping the women for the task
of bringing much needed reform to the institutions that they
administered. She felt that, prior to the election of women, the voting of
poor law guardians 'was carried out upon exclusively party lines and
with . . . little regard for the well-being of our destitute poor'. Now when
women voted for 'the lady candidate' they 'rose above all sectarian
prejudices and gave her their vote . . . simply because she was well known
for her deeds of mercy to the poor and can be absolutely trusted to do

her duty by them'.[103] Thus women, as electors and elected, were presented as superior beings whose concerns were service to those who were the denizens of the workhouse. Anna was ever conscious of the need to convert those prejudiced against the election of women to public office and saw the perceived excellence of the service provided by these women as an important step in the inevitable, if lengthy, progress towards the granting of the franchise. She continually reiterated this point and although the parliamentary franchise obviously continued to be the main aim of the DWSA, its energies, and especially those of Anna herself, were from henceforth also channelled into more immediately attainable goals.

In 1898, the DWSA, now calling itself the Dublin Women's Suffrage (and Poor Law Guardians') Association published a pamphlet entitled *Suggestions for Intending Lady Guardians* which offered practical advice to suitably qualified women on gaining support for their candidacy. It advised the formation of a committee 'of influential men and women of all shades of political opinion and of all religious denominations – to promote the election of two or more capable and judicious women ... in all the more important Unions in Ireland'.[104] Anna revealed herself as possessing considerable public relations skills in advocating the desirability of electing women as poor law guardians. In November 1900 she wrote a letter to *The King's County Chronicle* in which she commented on a recent meeting of the Roscrea Board of Guardians at which 'a laundry case' was discussed. She declined to comment on the particular case as she did not know the circumstances but she asked to be allowed make 'one obvious suggestion' that would provide 'true remedies for such disorders not only in your Union, but in all our Unions'. Her solution, of course, was the election of women as poor law guardians 'who would have the same power as the other Guardians and will meet them on equal terms on the Board'. From 'intimate personal knowledge' she could assure readers that elected women 'in their brief term of office, have already done invaluable service by their unfailing tact, good sense, discretion and undying vigilance as their brother guardians freely and generously acknowledge'. She enclosed reports of the conference of women guardians of April 1900 that revealed the 'sterling good sense' of the participants.[105] The DWSA produced a pamphlet with advice for 'philanthropic Irishwomen' who wished to avail of the opportunities afforded by the legislation of 1896 and 1898. Readers were given all relevant information on the categories of person eligible to vote in local government elections and detailed instructions on the mechanics of registration. There were also clear instructions on the procedures for candidates to go forward for election as poor law guardians and as rural and urban district councillors. Although it was pointed out that 'as yet women are not eligible for membership of Borough and County Councils' there were 'several important offices' for which they could apply. These included 'Sanitary Inspectors, School Attendance Officers, Inspectors of Workhouses . . . members of the Governing Committees upon the District Hospitals'.[106] It is likely that Anna Haslam was the author of this work and of 'Suggestions for Intending Lady Guardians' which advised the formation of committees 'of influential men and women of all shades of political opinion and of all religious denominations to promote the election of . . . capable and judicious women . . . in all the more the important Unions in Ireland'.[107] *The Englishwoman's Review* printed 'Irishwomen and the Local Government Act' by Anna Maria Haslam, containing much the same information as that contained in the two pamphlets and written in a similar style. These works have been described as 'carefully drafted, clear explanations of new rights and of steps which should be taken to implement them'.[108]

Above all, Anna saw the local government successes as a stage in the battle for the vote rather than an end in itself. She wrote: 'For my-self personally the Local Government Act is interesting, far more as a political educator than from the specific benefits that may in other directions spring from it.' Heretofore, she argued, 'many women saw no practical good in agitating for reform which never seemed likely to be realised'; instead they involved themselves in charitable works 'the result of which would be visible in their lifetime'. Now, however, 'sitting side by side with men upon their respective councils will revolutionise their ideas and make them not only desire the Parliamentary vote but willing to take some little trouble to obtain it'.[109] Susanne R. Day, suffragist and poor law guardian, recognised that the election of women to local government bodies was a vital factor in their politicisation, and made the case for parliamentary suffrage compelling:

> On County Councils, Boards of Guardians and Committees they have vindicated their public-spiritedness. But her position on administrative boards has only increased women's demands for the vote. In administering the law she has learnt how to criticize it, and its weak spots stare up at her in helpless and hopeless and often tragic confusion.[110]

The election of women as public officials empowered them to administer laws that they had no part in formulating, nor had they a vote in the election of those who did. Women's participation in local government must have created confidence in their competence. Anna Haslam's constant reiteration of the improvements achieved by women poor law guardians bears witness to this. Their public profile, their canvassing for election, the fact that women could vote in those elections surely lessened fears about women's inability to participate in public life.

CONCLUSION

As is evident from its labours to involve women all over Ireland in the campaign for the vote, in its efforts to promote the election of women in local government and to encourage the employment of women as public officials, the Dublin Women's Suffrage Association endeavoured to become a countrywide pressure group. Anna had written in 1898 that: 'The immediate duty of women's suffrage in Ireland is the establishment of active working Committees' in centres of population 'and to this indispensable work our Dublin Committee are now more especially addressing themselves'.[111] The DWSA did not confine itself to Ireland but also participated in the international women's movement that emerged in the 1880s.

By the end of the nineteenth century, the Haslams had been engaged in the cause of suffrage for over thirty years. The suffrage organisation they had founded was in its twenty-fifth year. Much had been achieved in legislation, the extension of the provisions of the Married Women's Property Act, the Repeal of the Contagious Diseases Acts, the participation of women in local government, the increased availability of education to women, the increase of employment opportunities. The criticism levelled against the nineteenth-century suffrage movement, with the Haslams at its head, was that they were conformist, ineffective and middle class. But by their patient and decorous methods they had achieved reforms central to the basic cause of equality. Ray Strachey thought it 'obvious to all the suffragists, that the education movement and the political movement . . . were all part of the same thing'. Millicent Fawcett, too, understood the importance of the gradual reforms:

> Women's suffrage will not come, when it does come as an isolated phenomenon, it will come as a necessary corollary of the other changes which have been gradually and steadily modifying during this century the social history of our country. It will be . . . based upon social, educational and economic changes which have already taken place . . . The revolution has been quietly taking place.[112]

The Haslams worked within the existing power structures but in reality they were challenging the very fundamental tenet that political life was the prerogative of a male government. From her surviving speeches it is clear that Anna Haslam was not a passionate or inspiring speaker. She appealed to the reason of her listeners. She was a respected figure who, in her person, made nonsense of the gibes of 'howling viragos' or 'shrieking sisterhood' which were levelled at the women who wanted the vote. While she rationally argued women's right to the vote, helped by the writings of her feminist theorist husband, she was also determined to demonstrate that, by their responsible actions and devotion to duty, they deserved it.

The DWSA evolved into IWSLGA (Irishwomen's Suffrage and Local Government Association) and continued to agitate for the vote, although overshadowed by the militant suffragette movement of the twentieth century. When the vote was finally granted in 1918, Anna Haslam (now 89) triumphantly processed to the polls, surrounded by flowers, and supported by women of all political hues.

NOTES

1. Thomas Haslam, *The rightful claims of women*, (Dublin: Ormond, 1906) pp. 21–2.
2. The Haslams had been disowned by the Society of Friends around the time of their marriage but always referred to their Quaker background and enjoyed an extensive network of like-minded Quaker activists.
3. The Contagious Diseases Acts were enacted in the 1860s and allowed for the examination and detention of women deemed to be prostitutes to ascertain whether they suffered from venereal disease. The Acts were discriminatory as the women's clients were not examined. They epitomised the double standard of sexuality deplored by the Haslams.
4. Thomas Haslam's works included *The Marriage Problem*, (Dublin: Webb, 1868); *A few words on prostitution and the Contagious Diseases Acts* (Dublin: Webb, 1870); *The Duties of Parents* (London: Burns, 1872) as well as booklets on suffrage.
5. See my *Genteel Revolutionaries: Anna and Thomas Haslam and the Irish Women's Movement* (Cork: Cork University Press, 2002) for an in-depth study of the Haslams.
6. See Helen Blackburn, *Women's Suffrage: A Record of the Women's Suffrage Movement in the British Isles* (London: Williams & Norgate, 1902) p. 15. Quinlan, *Genteel Revolutionaries*, pp. 139–140.
7. See Mary Cullen's 'Suffrage, feminism and citizenship' in this volume for a discussion of the evolution of the ideology that drove the campaign for votes for women.
8. Bessie Rayner Parkes was the organiser of petitions in 1856 'representing the injustice of the law respecting the property and earnings of married women'. She was the co-founder with Barbara Leigh Smith of the feminist periodical *The Englishwomen's Journal*. See Helen Blackburn, *Women's Suffrage: A Record of the*

Women's Suffrage Movement in the British Isles (London: Williams & Norgate, 1902). p. 47.

9. Perhaps the wife of Provost Lloyd of Trinity, an early supporter of suffrage.
10. Ann Jellicoe (1823–80) was the wife of John Jellicoe, a miller from Mountmellick. She was responsible for the setting up of a lace school in Mountmellick. She moved to Dublin and was involved in the setting up of Alexandra College. She was a member of the Society of Friends.
11. Barbara Corlett was a signatory of the John Stuart Mill petition in 1866. She was involved with all early suffrage meetings in Dublin. She was a member of the Society of Friends.
12. 'Mrs. Anna M. Haslam: The 'At Home' to Celebrate her Eightieth Birthday', 5 April 1909. Unidentified newspaper cutting from newspaper in Dublin Friends' Historical Library scrapbook, p. 21.
13. Helen Blackburn, p. 128; Anne V. O'Connor and Susan M. Parkes, *Gladly learn and gladly teach* (Dublin: Blackwater Press, n.d.) p. 7.
14. Although there were seventeen names with Irish addresses attached to the petition, I suspect there were only fifteen signatories, two of whom added the name of another female family member.
15. Petition *To the Honourable the Commons of the United Kingdom of Great Britain and Ireland in parliament assembled*, presented by John Stuart Mill on 7 June 1866.
16. Michael St. John Packe, *The Life of John Stuart Mill* (London: Secker & Warburg, 1954), p. 492.
17. Mill to the editor of *The Anti-Slavery Standard* 4 July 1867. Cited in Packe, *Life of John Stuart Mill*, p. 492.
18. Helen Blackburn, *Women's Suffrage: A Record of the Women's Suffrage Movement in the British Isles with Biographical Sketches of Miss Becker* (London: Williams & Norgate, 1902), pp. 58–9. Helen Blackburn (1842–1903) was a native of Valentia Island, Co. Kerry, secretary to the Central Committee of the National Society for Women's Suffrage from 1880 to 1895 and editor of *The Englishwoman's Review* from 1881 to 1889. Her *Women's Suffrage* is a valuable source for the history of the first wave of suffrage activism. Perhaps because of her Kerry origins, the work includes much information on Ireland and on the Haslams.
19. *Ibid.* p. 63.
20. *The Later Letters of John Stuart Mill* (Toronto: University of Toronto Press, 1972), p. 1,315.
21. *Englishwoman's Review,* vol. 1 (new series), p. 13.
22. Millicent Fawcett, leader of the emerging English movement, was wife of a member of parliament. She was the acknowledged leader of the suffragist movement.
23. *Freeman's Journal,* 10 April 1870.
24. Isabella Tod, from Belfast, was a committed suffragist. A talented public speaker, she also worked for education for women and campaigned against the CDAs.
25. Scrapbook held in Dublin Friends' Historical Library, Dublin.
26. *Irish Citizen,* 21 March 1914, p. 347.
27. Maria Luddy, 'Isabella M.S. Tod', in Mary Cullen and Maria Luddy (eds), *Women, Power and Consciousness in 19th Century Ireland* (Dublin: Attic Press, 1995) pp. 215–16.
28. *The Journal of Charles Ryan,* (Wed. 13 May 1874), TCD Ms. 10,349. f 39.
29. Blackburn, *Women's Suffrage: a record,* p. 128.
30. *The Women's Advocate,* no. 1, Apr. 1874.
31. Strachey, *Cause,* p. 266.

32. Thomas Haslam, *Women's Suffrage from a Masculine Standpoint* (Dublin: IWSLGA, 1906), p. 4.
33. Lydia Becker (1827–90) was a worker for the cause of suffrage from 1866. She was secretary to the Manchester Suffrage Society from 1867. She was 'a woman of unusual political insight' who was intellectually convinced of the rightness of the suffrage cause. See Strachey, *Cause,* p. 106, and Blackburn, *Women's Suffrage: A Record,* pp. 23–43.
34. *Irish Citizen,* 21 March 1914, p. 347.
35. *The Women's Advocate,* no. 3, July 1874.
36. Máire O'Neill, 'The Dublin Women's Suffrage Association and its successors', *Dublin Historical Record, v.* 38, no. 4, September 1985, p. 127.
37. The 'lovely' Miss Ashworth was reputedly popular as a speaker in that, according to Strachey, she successfully belied the stereotype of the 'rather hirsute female with spectacles and large feet who figured so freely in the comic Press'. Strachey, *Cause,* p. 120.
38. *Freeman's Journal,* 21 January 1876. p. 6.
39. Charles Eason (1823–99) was the founder of the bookselling and stationery firm Eason & Son.
40. DWSA *Minute book,* 21 February 1876.
41. *Ibid.* 6 March 1876.
42. Thomas Wallace Russell, Liberal MP for North Tyrone from 1886 to 1910 and for South Tyrone from Oct. 1911 to 1918. He was created a Baronet in 1917.
43. Maurice Brookes, Liberal MP, pro-Home Rule, was member for Dublin between 1874 and 1885.
44. Colonel Thomas Edward Taylor was a Conservative MP. He was Chancellor of the Duchy of Lancaster in the period during which he was involved with the DWSA. Colonel Taylor initially voted against Mill's amendment to the Representation of the People Bill on 20 May 1867, but he afterwards voted in favour of women's suffrage. (See Blackburn, W*omen's Suffrage: A Record,* p. 255.) He died on 3 February 1883.
45. William Johnston was a Conservative MP for Belfast from 1868 until 1902. He was educated at TCD.
46. David Sherlock QC was a member for Queen's County, 1868–80. He was at various times Chairman of the Board of Excise and Sergeant at Arms. He was a Liberal, pro-Home Ruler who died in 1884. He was a Roman Catholic.
47. *Reports of the Irish Women's Suffrage and Local Government Association from 1896 to 1918* (Dublin: Ormond, 1918), pp. 7–8.
48. Helena Moloney, 'James Connolly and Women' *Dublin Labour Year Book,* 1930 cited in Cliona Murphy, *The Women's Suffrage Movement and Irish Society in the Early Twentieth Century* (New York: Harvester Wheatsheaf, 1989), p. 21.
49. IWSLGA *Annual Report,* 1903, p. 10. Delegates to a convention in Holborn reported the 'newly awakened zeal throughout England' including considerable working class support. Such support 'unimaginable in Ireland, except, perhaps, in Belfast'.
50. DWSA *Minute Book,* 11 July 1877.
51. *Ibid.* 10 July 1878.
52. *Ibid.* 20 September. 1876.
53. *Ibid.* 22 January. 1877.
54. *Ibid.* List entitled 'Suffrage journals sent to the following:' DWSA *Minute Book.* Although undated, it would appear, from its position in the volume, to refer to 1879.

55. *Ibid.* 13 February 1878.
56. *Ibid.* 29 April 1879.
57. Rosemary Cullen Owens, *Smashing Times: A History of the Irish Women's Suffrage Movement 1889–1922* (Dublin: Attic Press, 1984), pp. 23, 27.
58. Louise Ryan, *Irish Feminism and the Vote* (Dublin: Folens, 1996), p. 7.
59. DWSA *Minute book,* 11 July 1877.
60. *Ibid.*
61 *Ibid.* 15 January 1879.
62. *Ibid.* 29 April 1879.
63. *Ibid.* 1 February 1882.
64. *Ibid.* 4 August 1881.
65. *Ibid.* 18 February 1880.
66. *Ibid.*
67. Niamh O'Sullivan, 'The Iron Cage of Femininity: Visual Representation of Women in the 1880s Land Agitation', in Tadgh Foley and Seán Ryder (eds), *Ideology and Ireland in the Nineteenth Century* (Dublin: Four Courts Press, 1998) p. 181.
68. Blackburn, *Women's Suffrage: A Record,* p. 154.
69. Blackburn, *Women's Suffrage: A Record,* p. 67.
70. Strachey, *The Cause,* p. 291.
71. Rover, *Women's Suffrage and Party Politics,* p. 190.
72. Circular with letterhead of DWSA in scrapbook in IHA archive.
73. *Ibid.*
74. *Ibid.*
75. Letter from Anna Haslam in *Daily Express,* 17 March 1884 (from scrapbook).
76. DWSA, *Minute Book* of 26 June 1884.
77. DWSA, *Minute Book* of 27 October 1884.
78. *The Woman's Leader,* 8 December 1922, p. 358.
79. Strachey, *Cause,* p. 278.
80. *Ibid.* p. 280.
81. Blackburn, *Women's Suffrage: A Record,* p.175.
82. DWSA, *Minute Book* 28 December 1888.
83. Accounts of the Ladies' Land League include: Anna Parnell, *The Tale of a Great Sham* (Dublin: Arlen House, 1986); Margaret Ward, '*Unmanageable revolutionaries* (London: Pluto Press, 1983); 'Gendering the Union: imperial feminism and the Ladies Land League', Women's History Review, vol. 10, no 1, 2001. See also Michael Davitt, *The fall of feudalism in Ireland* (London: Harper, 1904), T.W. Moody, 'Anna Parnell and the Land League', *Herm Athena,* Summer 1974.
84. DWSA, *Annual Report* 1896, p. 3.
85. DWSA, *Minute Book* 5 March 1896.
86. DWSA, *Minute Book* 15 September 1896.
87. *Ibid.*
88. *Ibid.* 11 Nov. 1896.
89. Address by Anna Haslam at an election meeting in Dublin in support of Mrs Lawrenson's candidacy as PLG, 10 Feb. 1897. Scrapbook, in IHA archive.
90. The DWSA briefly became the Dublin Women's Suffrage (and Poor Law Guardian) Association. Next known as the Dublin Women's Suffrage and Local Government Association, its name was changed in 1901 to Irish Women's Suffrage and Local Government Association (IWSLGA), which name lasted until 1918. To avoid confusion I have used only two versions, viz. DWSA and IWSLGA.
91. DWSA, *Annual Report 1897,* p. 4.

92. *Ibid.* p. 5.
93. *Ibid.* p. 7.
94. DWSA, *Annual Report 1898*, p. 3.
95. Virginia Crossman, *Local Government in Nineteenth-century Ireland* (Belfast: The Institute of Irish Studies, The Queen's University of Belfast, 1994), p. 94.
96. DWSA, *Annual Report 1898* pp. 3–4.
97. Anna Haslam to Arthur Balfour, 20 July 1898 and reply of 22 July 1898, IHA archive.
98. Crossman, *Local Government.* pp. 94–5.
99. DWSA, *Annual Report 1899*, p. 3.
100. *Ibid.* p. 7.
101. *Ibid.*
102. 'Women and Local Government in Ireland: A Chat with Mrs Haslam'. *Sunday Times,* 8 July 1900.
103. 'Irishwomen and the Local Government Act' reprinted from *Englishwoman's Review* (Oct. 1898). Copy in Haslam Scrapbook, IHA archive.
104. DWSA, *Suggestions for Intending Lady Guardians* (Leaflet). Scrapbook, IHA archive.
105. Anna Haslam to the editor of *The King's County Chronicle,* 9 Nov. 1900.
106. DWSA, *Suggestions for Intending Women Workers under the Local Government Acts* Rev. ed. (Dublin: DWSA, n.d), pp. 1–8.
107. DWSA, *Suggestions for Intending Lady Guardians* (Dublin: DWSA, n.d.).
108. O'Neill, *DWSA and its Successors.* p. 150.
109. Anna Haslam, *Irishwomen and Local Government Act.* Reprinted from *The Englishwoman's Review,* 15 Oct. 1898.
110. Susanne R. Day, *Women in a New Ireland* (Cork: MWFL, 1912), p. 3.
111. Anna Haslam, *Irishwomen and the Local Government Act.*
112. Millicent Fawcett, *Nineteenth Century,* May 1886. Cited in Rover, *Women's Suffrage,* p. 2.

CHAPTER THREE

Women of the West: campaigning for the vote in early twentieth century Galway, c1911–c1915

MARY CLANCY

INTRODUCTION

This chapter explores how women in the west of Ireland defined and created a political space to discuss the question of votes for women. Irrespective of their geographical location, suffragists argued, essentially, about equality – that the vote be granted to women on the same terms as it was, or might be, held by men; its long, uneven, history reflecting the ebb and flow of parliamentary interest.[1] What happened in rural regions of 'the Celtic fringe'[2] is, however, somewhat neglected, though its history has enormous potential in showing how women collaborated at a point of change in Ireland. In addition, the experience in Galway also shows how women in relatively isolated contexts worked for an international cause. This chapter, then, will take as its focus one aspect of suffrage organising in the west of Ireland, selecting, in particular, the cluster of events, meetings and writings that most noticeably marked out the years in question.[3] There was interest in women's suffrage in Galway during the nineteenth century – mostly within the confines of university circles[4] – and more curiously through the agency of Lilias Ashworth Hallett,[5] the leading west of England suffragist. There is not space in this chapter to consider the peculiarities and the personalities of the earlier period, however, except to note that there was a context of organising and influence that pre-dated the more public form of the twentieth century campaign.

There are no suffrage minute books or private papers, letters, diaries or photographs to guide the investigation.[6] Local newspapers, however, provide a more vicarious route to the words, if not the thoughts, of the activists and will form an important source in the recovery of their history. Census returns offer up important additional biographical details.[7] To establish personal narratives, with much certainty, from such public sources would only have partial success. As the memoir of Frances Moffett, *I also am of Ireland*, all too briefly reveals,[8] this world was far more real and troubled than newspaper print admits.

THE NEW CENTURY

Access to university education for women was the important influence in the new century.[9] From about 1904, for instance, students debated the women's suffrage question in the Literary and Debating Society, had rows about discrimination in student societies and were elected to college committees,[10] and thus developed skills, confidence, contacts and awareness. It is important to acknowledge the role of schools attended by these students – the High School and the Dominican convent[11] – in inculcating the sense of achievement that marked out this generation. Some took part in suffrage events later in Galway; others, however, left to pursue academic and professional careers elsewhere.[12] Student interest, however, did not result in any formal suffrage organisation in Galway.

Nonetheless, outside of explicit suffrage organising, there was public activism and achievement in Galway. Town and county women worked in various types of philanthropy, religious women ran convents, schools, industrial schools, worked in workhouses as nurses and teachers, managed and expanded the town's Magdalen asylum, women contested local government elections and took up positions as public officials.[13] District nurses, likewise, were part of the expansion in public, professional roles that marked out the decades after the 1890s. The public nature of their work, especially when working for state institutions, meant that the local press frequently published reports of meetings and speeches. In this way, some women became well-known to the general public. For example, Nurse Hedderman, the enterprising district nurse in the Aran Islands, left an excellent archive through the press, in addition to her valuable autobiography, *Glimpses of my life in Aran*.[14] The range of women involved in such effort was wide, certainly, though changing; the old world of landed women, in particular, was giving way to the democratic, reformist organising of the middle classes or the 'modern new women' nurses, college lecturers, teachers and instructresses.

While the context locally includes some organisational experience and visibility, the visit of the Irish Women's Franchise League to Galway in October, 1911 appears almost to have been imposed by outsiders. Mrs Earl, the chief organiser, was a stranger to Galway[15] and Margaret Cousins, though a visitor to Connemara, was also unknown publicly.[16] 1911 was, however, yet another crucial moment in engendering public and political support as the all-party Conciliation Bill, another moderate enfranchisement measure, once more gave rise to expectations.[17] In Galway, Mrs Earl briskly organised a special meeting of the Urban District Council and easily persuaded the councillors to pass a resolution in support of the bill. This was an important achievement, as such resolutions were valued for propagandist purposes, and so, despite some reluctance and much uncertainty about its meaning,[18] the Urban District Council voted in favour of the Conciliation Bill and thus Galway's local representatives played a role in the broader campaign to enfranchise women.[19]

The IWFL also organised a public meeting in the Town Hall where Christabel Pankhurst promised to deliver 'a spirited address'. Cousins, having worked briefly with the Pankhurst organisation in London, describes bringing Christabel to Ireland as their 'biggest venture in organisation'.[20] Whether or not Christabel conquered in Galway, as Cousins felt she did in Dublin, the event was an important one in the political history of the town.[21] Pankhurst's status as a political figure ensured that the meeting would be 'well attended', yet, it is noteworthy that a woman in her mid-twenties could attract such a formal audience on a cause that was not about nationality or empire.[22] Meetings of this scope usually involved male platform speakers only, with women as participants in the audience or as social organisers; to have mostly women, and no clergymen, as platform speakers further marks out the significance of the meeting as a political event.

Christabel Pankhurst's approach was to situate the talk in an Irish context, arguing on such qualities as rural equality and women's emigration, an approach that was, initially, effusive in its emphasis on Ireland, the Irish and Irishwomen, and ill-suited to its middle class audience. During question time, she joked about prison, likening her experiences of being in the House of Commons to Holloway;[23] there was no discussion of hunger-striking and forcible feeding. She also indicated to the audience that she was not interested in parliament. Like Mrs Earl, with her flattery of the urban councillors,[24] it was the 'charming' Pankhurst of Margaret Cousins' memory that Galway saw.

Mostly, however, Christabel Pankhurst explained why the parliamentary vote should be extended to women, raising the arguments so important to north of England suffragists about women's labour and

working conditions[25] before turning attention to the Home Rule legislation. In 1911, suffragists were still hopeful that the bill would make
provision for women.[26] The politically mixed audience that came along
to hear Christabel was to listen, then, to discussions on Home Rule as a
possible route to enfranchisement, recognised by Pankhurst the tactician
as important. The speakers' insistence that the IWFL was distinctively
Irish may have further discomfited unionist women in the audience and
– perhaps – might explain why the IWFL did not establish a successful
branch in Galway. Neither did the assertions of the IWFL, or Christabel
Pankhurst's claim to be a woman from 'another country', fully satisfy
nationalist critics,[27] and criticism of women of English descent bringing
an English woman over to Ireland led to an interesting old-style
confrontation in the local press.[28]

1913

The branch that was reportedly established in the aftermath of the
Pankhurst visit did not survive,[29] though Edith Young, the woman who
helped to organise it, remained active in suffrage. She exemplified the
new type who was displacing the more usual landed aristocratic woman
activist. Edith, though participating also in Catholic charity, was more
prominent in public health campaigning through the Women's National
Health Association.[30] Also, with other young women and men of the
town, Edith Young was involved in drama, performing the lead role in
the Dramatic Society's production of the popular West End play, *Peter's
Mother*.[31] Later, in 1920, she was to become the first woman elected as
poor law guardian in the town (though not the county) of Galway,
unusually enough for a suffragist.[32] These occasions also gave a public
face to Edith Young through the relatively new medium of newspaper
photography. Though Edith Young provided important continuity with
the earlier events, it was another woman, Mary Fleetwood Berry, who
instigated the next phase. In January 1913, she was instrumental in establishing a branch of the constitutional Irishwomen's Suffrage Federation,
an organisation then linking twenty-six societies nationally.[33] Galway
called itself the Connacht Women's Franchise League.

The role of Mrs Fleetwood Berry, whose political contacts were
conservative and religious, represents yet another shift in influence.
A temperance advocate, and former president of the Irish Women's
Temperance Union, Mary Berry had worked with other advocates
including those who were central to IWSF organising.[34] Berry, through

her marriage to the Rector of St Nicholas Church, had a strongly Protestant evangelical identity.[35] To organise on women's suffrage, and to engage in work that was non-sectarian, as well as non-party, is an interesting step for Mary Fleetwood Berry to take in the context of her personal and religious history. In working with Edith Young, for instance, she was working in a formal capacity with a Catholic woman for what appears to be the first time. Electing Edith Young as its president, rather than Berry – although there may have been practical reasons, too – attests to the political importance of having a Catholic rather than a Protestant at the head of this organisation. Mrs Berry, who stayed with the group until its demise, remained, too, the contact with the Federation in Dublin.

The work of the Connacht Women's Franchise League took the form of holding public lectures and publishing suffrage papers. Its activity was confined mostly to Galway town. Margaret Cousins mentioned interest in the west of the county,[36] and while Connemara had a strong tradition of general activism in agrarian politics, and had returned women poor law guardians and officials, no further evidence of formal suffrage organising has been found. There are also reports of suffrage activity in the better-off and English-speaking parts of the county, including by a Home Rule district nurse.[37] The town of Tuam experienced some of the exciting scenes that were increasingly associated with the suffrage question when two visitors, Miss Chenevix, of the Federation, and Miss Helen Fraser,[38] held an open-air meeting and distributed literature. To look for suffrage societies in country areas, outside the small towns in particular, is, however, to apply an urban framework to a rural setting.[39]

Stephen Gwynn, a local MP, and one marked out as sympathetic by suffragists until he disappointed on Home Rule, was an obvious route to parliamentary influence. Mostly, Galway's parliamentarians lived outside of their constituencies, including David Sheehy, of the prominent suffrage family,[40] and so scope for direct contact was limited. The only meeting of note, for instance, occurred in June 1914, when a delegation of the suffrage league called upon Stephen Gwynn, at the Railway hotel, in connection with Birrell's Intermediate Education Bill. The deputation, composed of Mary Donovan,[41] Edith Young and Florence Moon, presented a lengthy, well-considered statement laying out their thinking on the subject of women's equality as workers, protesting against the 'gross injustice' of paying women teachers less than men, the damage that low pay caused to women's health, arguing that working women had to support as many dependents as men.[42] This was the first, and only, time that the suffragists engaged in a type of work that was so typical of the constitutional movement but more easily available in larger urban centres, the absence of resident parliamentarians affecting such possibility within local contexts. It was also an interesting political moment, just after the election of 1914, when the imminent prospect of Home Rule, as much as the election of Gwynn, was celebrated with banners and bands, illuminated windows and bonfires in the town.[43]

SUFFRAGE ACTIVITIES IN GALWAY

The group mostly organised within its means, holding monthly committee meetings in the homes of various members, its chief role to undertake educative work on the suffrage question. As one of its most influential members, Hannah Anderson, stated, the group was 'not rich enough'.[44] Research was important, however, and a Dublin friend helped to provide a suffrage library. Influenced by their reading of suffrage texts, the Galway suffragists wrote about core arguments like taxation without representation, being subject to laws that they had no say in making, discrimination in pay and prejudice in employment, sweated labour, housing and the protection of children. Whatever the stance of the individual suffragist, there was a singular focus on the concept of citizenship and a sense of injustice that women were denied a political voice in formulating the laws to which they were subject. The candidate at election time could afford to ignore the demands of the voteless woman citizen and so, in the able words of Florence Moon 'we want power'.[45]

Perhaps the most astute method at communication used by the group was to send the papers that they prepared for their monthly meetings to the local press for publication. The topic was 'Why I am a supporter of women's suffrage' and, between May and November 1913, a total of five papers appeared in two local newspapers, the *Galway Express* and the *Connacht Tribune*. Mary Donovan, Miss Mary O'Neill and Miss Perry, BA were the voices of working women making their way in a professional world where they faced discrimination and prejudice. Donovan's piece suggests some personal knowledge of discrimination in her delineation of women who were better qualified than men receiving half the salary for 'the crime of being a woman'.[46] The more detached and authoritative prose of Miss Perry's paper,[47] also on the subject of injustice to women workers, advances the strategic possibility of political expediency, arguing that in co-operating with industrial workers who were economically and politically discontented 'a remedy might be found for their social and political grievances'.[48] Miss O'Neill, with particular emphasis on women who were self-supporting (a key theme of this era) and in arguing for legislative and social change, proclaimed that 'the woman's vote is especially needed to safeguard the interests of the working woman'.[49] Other authors, Florence Moon and Mrs Tennant, reflected the interest of the older suffragist in the value of the local vote and the importance of England as a reference point. Tennant, also a prominent temperance suffragist, hoped that the vote would enable women to 'make colossal raids . . . against the drink traffic'.[50] Florence Moon offered a link to the early days of suffrage organising by revealing that she was born into a suffragist home in Birmingham, where her mother attended suffrage meetings. Though allowed 'much freedom of thought', the influence of her mother was such that it led her to take up the cause of 'woman's rights'.[51] Birmingham, along with other centres such as Manchester and Bristol, had been organising around the suffrage question since the late 1860s. Moon, with Mary Fleetwood Berry, was the most public name within the Galway group, given her connection to the large, well-patronised, drapery establishment of the same name.

For Moon and Tennant, and other influential Presbyterian women within the group, their family links with England or Scotland seems to have encouraged arguments that were suited to industrial and urban environments rather than a small town in the west of Ireland. The arguments of the younger women, to an extent, were more relevant to a new, and increasingly populous, generation of professional women. The publishing of these papers brought the question into the public domain and left a public archive whose value is to be noted, especially given the absence of private papers. The Fisher household, with Edith Fisher hosting committee meetings and Mr Fisher, as editor of the *Express*, publishing the material, was also important to the success of the League.[52]

The local press also continued to publicise the broader suffrage campaign. Anna Haslam remained prominent,[53] for instance, and the influential Millicent Fawcett wrote articles to publicise the opposition to forcible feeding of hunger-striking suffragettes in England.[54] Increasingly, however, once the suffragettes had re-started their militant campaign after the collapse of the Conciliation Bill in late 1911, the press was unsympathetic, printing lurid denunciations throughout 1912 and 1913.[55] There is mention of a Galway woman, Kathleen Kean, being arrested for her involvement in 'suffragist riots' in London in 1911[56] – she is probably one of the Misses Kean who attended the Pankhurst meeting in the Town Hall – but the reference was brief and unadorned.

PUBLIC MEETINGS

The Galway suffragists also organised a number of public meetings, in January and October, 1913. The well-attended meetings are good evidence of how the question, as much as the personality, was of interest. In addition, some travelled from outlying areas to hear the speakers. The inaugural public meeting, held on 17 January 1913, reportedly enjoyed a 'packed' large room, with 'hundreds' turned away. Miss Moser, the delegate of the Irishwomen's Suffrage Federation, defined its object as 'non-militant, non-political and non-sectarian'.[57] This object apparently offered sufficient scope to the diverse group of women who decided to join together in the local branch. Miss Day, who travelled to Galway to hear Christabel Pankhurst in 1911, argued that of the two standpoints, she concluded that it was the non-militant, constitutional approach that would persuade the thousands of men currently indifferent on the subject. In a difficult context – male students had attended intent upon disrupting the meeting – the audience heard Day speak, as a Protestant, of her regret about the treatment of Catholics in penal times, which was unusual[58] though also useful in that she could extend the analogy to the situation of the disfranchised woman. It is also an insight into how the suffrage speakers were adapting and devising some kind of balance or neutrality before the new audience provided for by the objects of the organisation. In identifying the home as the ideal starting place for women to discuss the question, Day was claiming significant public status for the concept of the suffrage mother, the propagandist in the home converting husband, son and daughter. Such argument also suggests that many of those in Day's audience were older and married.

The second public event of 1913 was held in October, when the League hosted the visiting suffragist, Miss Abadam. There was a 'large and enthusiastic' turnout while Edith Young, who chaired the meeting, spoke of the 'sympathy and support' encountered since setting up the League.[59] The interest in challenging indifference – as well as in arguing for equality – is also once again evident in Young's introductory comments. Typically, at meetings, suffragists posed the question 'What good is the vote to me?' before explaining its potential in affecting legislation on a host of issues affecting women, the home and children. The speaker, Alice Abadam, a Welsh woman, was, essentially, a travelling lecturer who, by the time she reached Galway, had already taken a number of positions within the suffrage movement. Starting out as a militant in the WSPU, in 1907 she was part of the group that broke away to form the Women's Freedom League and more recently had been associated with the Catholic Women's League.[60] Abadam offered yet a different perspective. In contrast to her former colleague, Christabel Pankhurst, an earlier visitor to the town, Abadam dispensed with any preamble of local or Irish relevance except to tell her audience that Galway was 'still non-emancipated'. An emphasis on emancipation, as opposed to enfranchisement, was a distinctive theme of the Women's Freedom League and one that, as her speech showed, still held significance for Abadam. The speaker's tendency to incorporate 'empire' in discussions of the universal nature of citizenship struck a discordant note, in contrast with local practice and other visiting speakers. Abadam presented a talk of some breadth, drawing on a broad range of historical and contemporary evidence, American, English and European, secular and religious, with especial attention to indecent assault, sweated labour and prostitution.[61]

WAR WORK

There is not space in this chapter to examine in detail how the Galway suffragists worked during the war years and negotiated the complex issues of pacifism and war work. However, there is one final event held in October, 1915, that is important to document. The guest speaker, Helena Swanwick, was in Galway to discuss 'Women and the War'.[62] The suffragists were interested in 'the part' that women could play and how the war had 'upset old theories' about women's work; there was still an attempt made to associate the new conditions and the role of women. Their war propagandist intent is clear, however, though somewhat self-effacing, stating Galway was 'somewhat out of touch with things' and that they had 'scarcely realised the work that women have been called upon to do since the ranks of the male workers have been thinned'.[63] It is somewhat improbable that women who were associated with men involved in, for instance, recruiting would be so out of touch, though why they selected Helena Swanwick raises a question about their understanding of the politics of wartime suffrage involvement. Swanwick, whose campaign against the war led to her resignation from the National Union of Women's Suffrage Societies (the Fawcett-led constitutional organisation to which the Galway suffragists owed its ideological references) was already established as a pacifist.[64] Galway suffragists would have known of her through the *Common Cause*, a journal that they drew upon.[65] How much they were aware of Swanwick the pacifist, rather than Swanwick the suffragist, is the intriguing question. Swanwick, in her autobiography, *I Have Been Young*, makes only passing reference to Galway, though explains that she has been invited to Ireland by suffragists and the Union of Democratic Control.[66] This time, it was Mary Berry who chaired the meeting, instead of Edith Young, who usually did so with visiting speakers.

In arguing about how the war was extending the scope for women's powers, and thus influencing public opinion to extend women's rights in post-war society, Berry reiterated a commonplace argument of wartime suffrage thinking. This suggests that the Galway women were keeping track of the new arguments. What did it mean to Mary Berry that her son was now at the front one year into a war that had resulted in the deaths of numerous local men? Her public words did not reveal such personal detail, though chairing Swanwick could suggest less than full support for the war.[67] Context, too, seemed to shape the Swanwick speech as she mostly fitted the question of women's equality in the context of the dangers that the war posed for women. She discussed the strain of war, its meaning for women who had men at war, criticised the doctrine that 'might is right', Home Office prejudice and obstinacy on women volunteers and questioned the nature of a flawed democracy where only men decided on 'issues of peace and war'.[68] The focus was firmly on women's rights, and she acknowledged the work done by women in relief work. However, as noted by Margaret Ward in her chapter in this book, women's war relief work was not without its critics within the pacifist movement. Swanwick had already experienced the difficulties of trying to attend an international peace meeting at The Hague earlier in the year and, later, with other campaigners, was subject to having pacifist meetings attacked and broken up.[69] The Galway meeting, despite the by now inevitable disruptions, was receptive, with, for instance, regular applauding throughout. In line with its thinking over the years, the situation of women, children and the home – this time as refugee, fatherless or ruined owing to war – seemed to resonate with the audience. 'If you are going to devastate the homes of the women, you ought to take them into your counsels' was one such applauded proclamation. It was a meeting of mostly older women, Swanwick then in her late forties and Berry about fifty. There was 'a good attendance' but unfortunately this vague observation is left without the detail of names in the local press. It would have been interesting to see the audience who came to hear Swanwick speak.

The immediate context, too, for the Galway talk was the imprisonment and execution of the English nurse, Edith Cavel,[70] an event that more fully politicised the role of the nurse in war work. In the rare testimony offered by her autobiography, the teenage Frances Moffett, who already had a horror of killing and war, feared further that Cavell's execution meant that anyone could be subject to death in war.[71] Nonetheless, less than three months after proposing thanks to Swanwick, local suffragists gave prominent support to a Ladies Recruiting Committee as the 'best means by which the women of Galway could help the men at the front'.[72] It is, however, beyond the scope of the chapter to explore the subsequent militaristic turn of the Galway suffragists (or some of them).

CONCLUSION

The effort of women in Galway, then, is chiefly that of creating a political space to debate and highlight a cause that did not fit conventional criteria. As the London demonstrations so visibly revealed, women of all sectors found the suffrage question relevant. What is known of the Galway group, however, is that women of different backgrounds – age, religion, politics, social class, education – were sufficiently taken with the question to work together in the non-party space that women's suffrage offered. Suffrage – internationally – involved a different set of political colours and while the Galway group did not appear to display ribbons or scarves, neither did they close meetings with the national anthem. How many nurses, teachers, clerical and shop workers were involved? How did family, friends and employer regard the suffragist? What did domestic servants in the larger households think about their suffragist employer? Who did not join the women's suffrage society and why? The questions, as always, continue to intrigue and point to the potential of investigating the personal and political histories of forgotten women.

NOTES

1. For an excellent overview, see, for instance, June Purvis and Sandra Stanley Holton, (eds), *Votes for Women* (London and New York: Routledge, 2000). On Ireland, see, in particular, Rosemary Cullen Owens, *Smashing Times: A History of the Irish Women's Suffrage Movement, 1889–1922* (Dublin: Attic Press, 1984); Cliona Murphy, *The Women's Suffrage Movement and Irish Society in the Early Twentieth Century* (Hertfordshire: Harvester, 1989); Margaret Ward, *Hanna Sheehy Skeffington: A Life* (Dublin: Attic, 1997); Diane Urquhart, *Women in Ulster Politics, 1890–1940* (Dublin and Portland, Or: Irish Academic Press, 2000); Carmel Quinlan, *Genteel Revolutionaries: Anna and Thomas Haslam and the Irish Women's Movement* (Cork: Cork University Press, 2002).

2. A term for women from Ireland, Scotland and Wales: see marches where women wore distinctive professional or national dress, e.g., *The Times*, 19 June 1911. For some rural studies, see M. Clancy, C. Clear et al., 'Oral History and Biography', *Women's Studies Review*, Volume 7 (Galway: Women's Studies Centre, 2000).

3. For further details, see M. Clancy, 'The "Western Outpost": Local Government and Women's Suffrage in County Galway 1898–1918', in Gerard Moran et al., *Galway: History & Society* (Dublin: Geography Publications, 1996) and M. Clancy, "' . . . it was our joy to keep the flag flying": A Study of the Women's Suffrage Campaign in County Galway', *Women's Studies Review*, Volume 3, pp. 91–104, (Galway, 1995). Unless otherwise stated, biographical information is derived from these studies and from on-going research.

4. Since c1870, women of academic families expressed interest in educational access; women's suffrage was a subject of debate in college societies.

5. Lilias Ashworth Hallett, a signatory in 1866, and, through her mother, connected to the Bright family, was a stalwart of the Victorian era who continued her interest into the new century. The family owned the Galway Fishery, in addition to their property in Bath. After marriage to T.G.P. Hallett, Lilias resided for periods in Galway. Though influential in establishing suffrage organising in Ireland in the 1870s, there is no evidence of success locally. A close associate of Millicent Fawcett, she shared, too, the latter's politics and was involved in anti-Home Rule activity in Galway.

6. The papers of Mary Donovan O'Sullivan, suffragist and later professor of history, held in the James Hardiman Library (Special Collections), NUI, Galway have no reference to her suffrage activity though a draft lecture prepared for the centenary of 1949 has invaluable, if brief, reference to contemporaries.

7. Information derived from census returns is documented more fully in my earlier publications on suffrage.

8. Frances Moffett, *I also am of Ireland* (London: BBC, Ariel Books, 1985).

9. For important background information on women's education, see, for instance, Mary Cullen, *Girls Don't Do Honours: Irish Women in Education in the 19th and 20th Centuries* (Dublin: Women's Education Bureau, 1987); Carol Dyhouse, *No distinction of sex? women in British universities 1870–1939* (London: UCL Press, 1995). For Galway, see also Tadhg Foley & Thomas Boylan, (eds), *From Queen's College to National University: Essays towards an academic history of QUC/UCG/NUI, Galway* (Dublin: Four Courts, 1999).

10. Based on examination of student publications from 1902, *Q.C.G.* and *UCG: A College Annual*

11. The High School, established in 1888, catered for Protestant girls. Later, the Dominican convent opened a school for Catholic middle-class girls, which some Protestant girls also attended.

12. The Perry sisters seem to have left c1908; Janet Perry taught Spanish in King's College, London, Agnes worked at North London Collegiate School, and Alice, the engineer, worked as an Inspector of Factories in London and Glasgow before moving to Boston in the early 1920s.

13. Among the prominent women throughout the county, there were: Aleen Cust, the first woman veterinary surgeon, Ada English, a medical doctor in Ballinasloe Asylum and later a deputy of the Second Dáil and Alice Perry, the first woman to qualify as an engineer in Ireland.

14. B.N. Hedderman, *Glimpses of My Life in Aran* (Bristol: John Wright, 1917).

15. Earl had experience of London demonstrations. See, for example, *Irish Citizen*, 25 May, 1912. On her November visit, she described herself as a 'mother of four sons',

Galway Express, 18 November, 1911. Earl had also accompanied Emmeline Pankhurst in Dublin: see *Irish Indpendent*, 6 April 1911.

16. James and Margaret Cousins, *We Two Together* (Madras: Ganesh & Co., 1950)
17. See, for example, Constance Rover, *Women's Suffrage & Party Politics in Britain, 1866–1914* (London: Routledge & Kegan Paul, 1967).
18. Emily Wilding Davison subsequently wrote to congratulate and to correct. *Galway Express*, 28 October 1911.
19. One month later, when Mrs Earl returned to seek the support of the county council, the Conciliation Bill was already dead.
20. Cousins, *We Two Together*, p. 171.
21. Margaret Cousins, who travelled with Christabel Pankhurst in Ireland (though there is no date given), describes Pankhurst as 'charming', a 'kind of Joan of Arc', and 'the brain of the campaign' (*We Two Together*, p. 172), interesting assessments to retain all those decades later.
22. *Galway Express*, 21 October 1911.
23. Interestingly, the governor of Galway jail was in the audience.
24. Mrs Earl praised Galway, its people and the Galway policeman who rescued her in London and re-assured the councillors that only one in seven women would be enfranchised. See, for example, *Galway Express*, 14 October 1911.
25. For required reading on the north of England radical suffragist, see, as always, Jill Liddington and Jill Norris, *One Hand Tied Behind Us: the Rise of the Women's Suffrage Movement* (London: Virago, 1978).
26. In November, 1912, Philip Snowden's amendment to Clause 9 of the Home Rule Bill (to substitute the local government register, which included women, for the parliamentary register) was lost by a resounding 173 votes. For details and explanations, see, for example, the *Freeman's Journal*, 6 November 1912.
27. Pankhurst's Home Rule background, through her father, Richard Pankhurst, may have influenced her thinking, too.
28. *Connacht Tribune*, 4, 11, 18 November 1911.
29. *Galway Express*, 21 October 1911. This branch does not appear to be documented in later *Irish Citizen* accounts.
30. Branches of the Women's National Health Association were established throughout the county in 1908. It remained an important organisation in these years. The Women's National Health Association annual reports, 1908–12 (N.L.I., IR 6140941 w 2) and local newspapers.
31. *Galway Express* 25 January, 1913. The play, by the prolific novelist and dramatist, Mrs Henry De la Pasteur, with Miss Marion Terry in the lead role, was a London success. See, for example, the *Times*, September, 1906–February, 1907.
32. She was also the only woman elected in 1920 who was not returned for Sinn Féin.
33. Irishwomen's Suffrage Federation annual reports, 1911–14 (N.L.I., IR 39963); *Galway Express*, 25 January 1913.
34. For important context, see, for example, Olive Banks, *Faces of Feminism: A study of feminism as a social movement* (Oxford: Martin Robertson, 1981) and further relevant discussion, for example, Megan Smitley 'Inebriates', 'Heathens', Templars and Suffragists: Scotland and imperial feminism, c1870–1914', *Women's History Review*, Vol 11, no. 3, 2002, pp. 455–80.
35. Mary (Chatterton) Berry from county Cork and James Fleetwood Berry, Tullamore were married since 1887. Their only son, Edward, was in the army. 1901 and 1911 Census of Ireland, county Galway (47/34); *Galway Express*, 17 August 1912.

36. *Freeman's Journal*, 6 November 1911.
37. *Connacht Tribune*, 15 March 1913.
38. For details on Helen Fraser, an experienced campaigner in Scotland and England, see Elizabeth Crawford, *The Women's Suffrage Movement: a reference guide 1866–1928* (London: UCL Press, 1999) and Oxford Dictionary of National Biography (2004).
39. Instead, the approach that I am using is to look for household-based suffragists.
40. David Sheehy was MP for South Galway, 1885–1900. Information on parliamentarians derived from Who's Who of British Members of Parliament; B. Walker, *Parliamentary election results in Ireland 1918–92* (Dublin and Belfast: Royal Irish Academy & Institute of Irish Studies, 1992); newpapers.
41. Mary Donovan (1887–1966), educated at the Dominican convent, won prizes and scholarships at school and university, undertaking further study in Germany. In 1914, she was appointed professor of history, in Galway. For further details of her career, see *Analecta Hibernia*, Number 26, (1970).
42. *Galway Express*, 20 June 1914.
43. *Connacht Tribune*, 6 June 1914.
44. *Galway Express*, 3 January 1914. Hannah (Perry) Anderson, like her husband, Professor R.J. Anderson, was from the North and later, after his death, she returned to university to study medicine.
45. *Connacht Tribune*, 17 May 1913.
46. *Galway Express*, 10 May 1913.
47. Perry's piece was possibly sent to the group from England.
48. *Galway Express*, 5 July 1913.
49. *Galway Express*, 14 June 1913. Miss O'Neill's identity is less easy to confirm, though she is likely the woman of the same name who also supported industrial enterprise locally.
50. *Galway Express*, 15 November 1913. The Tennants were a Scottish-born, Presbyterian family whose six daughters were prominent in local education, including the Dominican convent.
51. *Connacht Tribune*, 17 May 1913.
52. H.D. Fisher was a nephew of Anna Haslam.
53. See, for example, *Galway Express* 9 December 1911 and 3 May 1913.
54. *Galway Express*, 3 May 1913.
55. Captions like 'Female Hooligans' and 'Women Terrorists' were typical.
56. *Galway Express*, 2 December 1911.
57. *Galway Express*, 25 January 1913.
58. Susanne R. Day was a member of the Munster Women's Franchise League. There is no mention of Violet Martin (from Ross), also a member of the Munster grouping, and cited by Millicent Fawcett as a leading suffragist in her *What I Remember* (London: Fisher Unwin, 1924).
59. *Galway Express*, 11 October 1913.
60. Alice Abadam (1856–1940) was also known for her musical and artistic talents; Obituary, the *Times*, 3 April 1940.
61. Abadam's talk may have been connected with the national week of prayer organised by the United Religious Woman Suffrage Societies; see, for example, the *Times*, 1 October 1913.
62. *Galway Express*, 16 October 1915.
63. ibid.
64. For biographical details, see, for example, Elizabeth Crawford, *The women's suffrage movement*, pp. 666–8.

65. Extracts were printed in the local press.
66. Helena Swanwick, *I Have Been Young* (London: Victor Gollancz, 1935), p. 281.
67. Her son would die in the war, as would the sons of Edith Fisher and Anna Holmes, another suffragist.
68. *Galway Express*, 16 October 1915.
69. For important Irish context, see, for example, Rosemary Cullen Owens, 'Women and pacifism in Ireland, 1915–1932', in M. Gialanella Valiulis and M O'Dowd, (eds), *Women and Irish History* (Dublin: Wolfhound, 1997), pp. 220–330.
70. The *Times*, 16 October, 1915. Edith Cavell was executed on 13 October, charged with harbouring fugitives and Belgians of military age.
71. Frances Moffett, *I also am of Ireland* (1985). Moffett also reveals how local girls enforced their own code of persuasion by sending white feathers to young men regarded as recalcitrant.
72. *Galway Express*, 8 January 1916.

CHAPTER FOUR

Staging Suffrage: The Events of 1913 Dublin Suffrage Week

PAIGE REYNOLDS

INTRODUCTION

This chapter considers two events presented as part of Dublin
Suffrage Week. During this week, the Irish premiere of Ibsen's
social drama *Rosmersholm* invoked aesthetics to advance the cause of
emancipated personal relationships and a liberal public sphere, while the
political arguments of the 'Suffrage Conference' deployed critiques of
social and political realities to demonstrate how the world might change
if women were granted the vote. Like Louise Ryan's chapter in this
collection, this essay demonstrates how the suffragists engaged with
notions of publicity and sexual morality. In doing so, it also reveals how
they simultaneously employed art and political rhetoric, theatricality and
actuality to illustrate their hopes for the future and to persuade
audiences to support their agendas.

In the second week of December 1913, the Irish Women's Suffrage
Federation (IWSF) sponsored 'Suffrage Week in Dublin', a conference
that promised the public a dizzying array of activities including political
speeches, a debate between suffragists and anti-suffragists, programmes
of music and recitations, light luncheons and teas, and a great Christmas
fair offering for sale 'Suffragist Turkeys, Suffragist Sweets, Suffragist
Flowers, Suffragist Toys, Suffragist Dolls, and Suffragist Homes'.[1] The
IWSF, which was established in 1911 by Louie Bennett and Helen
Chenevix, imagined Dublin Suffrage Week as a means of drawing
together women and men from across Ireland to celebrate the diversity
of the Irish feminist public and its various religious, political, and
geographical affiliations. Representing itself as non-party, non-sectarian,
and non-militant, the IWSF sought to unite the many Irish suffragist
groups. Because it censured none of the divergent tactics deployed in the

campaign for the vote, this organisation seems to have successfully appealed to suffragists of all political stripes. For instance, the organisation's 1913 membership roster included the ascendancy authors Edith Somerville and Violet Martin, the arch republican Mary MacSwiney, and the author and nationalist social reformer George Russell, who served as the organisation's vice-president in 1915.[2]

Similarly, the IWSF's Dublin Suffrage Week claimed the support of a wide range of socio-political organisations from both England and Ireland, including the National Union of Women's Suffrage Societies, the Women's Freedom League, the Church League for Women's Suffrage, the Tax Resistance League, the Actresses Franchise League, the New Constitutional Society, and the Men's League. The effectiveness of this event in solidifying cooperation from the increasingly fragmented feminist and suffragist community in Ireland might well be attributed to its structure. The conference activities allowed participants to identify individually with the fight for suffrage in a multiplicity of ways – as consumers and producers of goods, aesthetes and activists, leisured and labourers, unionists and nationalists, rural and urban dwellers, militants and non-militants, Catholics and Protestants, males and females. By providing its audiences this variety, Dublin Suffrage Week enacted the larger philosophies of inclusion and tolerance that had heretofore allowed the sub-national project of women's suffrage to garner some measure of support, even as the Irish nationalists fighting for Home Rule placed increasing pressure on the suffragists to withdraw their agenda.

Unlike the incendiary activities of the militant Irish Women's Franchise League, the events of Dublin Suffrage Week went largely unnoticed by the mainstream press and were reported on in detail only by the suffragist paper, the *Irish Citizen*. Nonetheless, as a political spectacle, Dublin Suffrage Week presents a particularly rich opportunity to understand better one trait that typified the struggle for women's suffrage in Ireland: the way in which Irish suffragists exploited the theatricality of women in public to draw support from their audiences. Many Irish suffragists, such as Hanna Sheehy Skeffington and Margaret Cousins, were directly involved in the Irish Dramatic Movement and immediately recognised the ability of women on stage to inspire potent political effect among their audiences. In their public speaking campaigns to marshal support for suffrage, these women and others like them capitalised on the powerful association of feminism, nationalism, and dramatic performance in the public imagination to draw wide-scale attention to their quest for political representation. Their aggressive theatricality successfully engaged the interest of audiences who were otherwise hostile to women's suffrage or who considered suffrage secondary to the pursuit of Home Rule.

Remarkably, Dublin Suffrage Week purposefully distinguished between the theatrical and the political in its events, largely by providing a venue for each that clearly demarcated their differences.

IBSEN'S *ROSMERSHOLM*

The week opened with Elizabeth Young's production of Henrik Ibsen's 1887 social drama, *Rosmersholm*, which made its Irish debut at the Sackville Theatrical Club on December 8 and 9. This play depicted the failed efforts of the former pastor, John Rosmer, and his intellectual companion, Rebecca West, to develop further their 'emancipated' personal relationship and to secure public support for their unique social views. In this tragedy, which unfolds following the death of Rosmer's wife, Rebecca and Rosmer live and work together in his ancestral home, Rosmersholm. The community warily accepts this unconventional arrangement until the conservative Dr Kroll and the radical Peter Mortensgaard employ their respective newspapers to destroy Rosmer's reputation and undermine his platonic relationship with Rebecca. Unable to recalibrate their relationship in light of these disruptive events, Rebecca and Rosmer throw themselves into the estate's millrace. The play appears to stage radical new models for morality and freedom; however, society's rejection of these prototypes results in the tragic double suicide of its two free thinkers.

By 1913, Ibsen's work had become associated both with feminism and particularly with suffragism, so in some ways this play seems an appropriate choice for a suffrage conference designed to emphasise the international quality of the struggle for the vote. Rather than draw from Irish drama about women's issues, or even suffragist drama by Irish writers such as Francis Sheehy Skeffington and Susanne R. Day, the IWSF elected to stage a play set outside of the Irish context. The choice of *Rosmersholm* as the aesthetic centrepiece of Dublin Suffrage Week suggests that the organisers of this event believed that their audiences could adroitly move between the imaginative and the actual worlds. Set in nineteenth-century Norway, the play never explicitly addresses the concerns introduced by Dublin Suffrage Week or by the suffrage cause more generally. Nonetheless, it depicts themes that an audience member attuned to social and political issues associated with the suffrage cause could readily apply to the current situation in Ireland.

In particular, *Rosmersholm* echoed concerns voiced by the Irish suffragists about the importance of integrating the masculine public sphere and the feminine private sphere. Dr Kroll, the brother of Rosmer's dead wife, Beata, represents a conservative position in part because he considers the introduction of political issues an assault on the home. When Kroll discovers his two sons have subscribed to the radical newspaper, the *Beacon*, he bemoans the fact that 'dissension and revolt have crept into my own house – into my own quiet home! They have destroyed the peace of my family life!'[3] In Irish nationalist rhetoric, the home was considered the pedagogical counterinfluence to the English colonial school system, a space where the mother could maintain and instruct her children in the tenets of Irish nationalism. In *Rosmersholm*, Kroll's wife supports and even facilitates the intrusion of this paper extolling anarchic ideas into their home, while Kroll furiously objects to his wife and two sons subscribing to these views. Kroll tolerates Rebecca's exposure to the radical *Beacon* because, as he explains, all women are limited to a private, domestic role, and are inherently averse to participating in political frays. Yet the suffragists had consistently argued that Irish national health relied on the acceptance of the fact that women could be domestic and political, mothers and citizens, traditional and modern. For instance, one writer in the *Irish Citizen*, insisted women could be citizens and parents: 'The anti-feminist, of course, cannot realise that women are at once human beings and "the mothers of the race".'[4]

In addition, *Rosmersholm* advanced the ideal of uplift familiar from suffragist rhetoric. In its efforts to imagine how one might nurture and support an emancipated lifestyle, the play insists that individuals must work to influence and improve society. Rosmer describes the mass public as a fragmented population needing guidance from above; he imagines he can 'bring together men from both sides – as many as I can – and to unite them as closely as possible', if he devotes his life to 'the creation of a true democracy in this country'.[5] With his profound investment in conservative patriarchal and ecclesiastical hierarchies, Kroll resists this model of political equality and its utopian faith in the populace. Even for the insurgent Mortensgaard, the masses are merely lemmings best kept uninformed of the truth. Both Kroll and Mortensgaard, who represent extremes of the political spectrum, contend the masses cannot be transformed. Yet Rosmer's project of uplift is similar to the agenda espoused by Irish institutions ranging from the church to the Gaelic League to the suffragist reformers. He intends to 'make all the people in this country noblemen' by 'freeing their minds and purifying their wills'.[6]

This logic appealed to the feminist audience whose reforms were directed – as would be evidenced in the forthcoming Suffrage Week speeches – towards helping those forced into the 'mire' as factory workers, prostitutes, and Dublin slum residents.

The ideal of uplift – shared here equally by Rebecca and Rosmer – is especially important because the public sphere, the idea of rational discourse in a public forum mediated by print, is severely corrupted. Kroll's conservative *County News* and Mortensgaard's radical *Beacon* each seek to capitalise on Rosmer's name and his family history to promote their own political and social agendas. The *County News* regards the Rosmer name as a mark of traditionalism and integrity, while the *Beacon* hopes to capitalise on his affiliation with the church to lend credibility to its radical views. Despite their ideological differences, both papers are divisive and opportunistic. When Rosmer refuses to oversee the *County News* and privately shares with Kroll his conversion to radicalism, the *County News* distorts the information and publishes an incendiary editorial detailing Rosmer's apostasy, much to Rosmer's chagrin. In this world, a public sphere mediated by men alone lacks integrity and fosters divisiveness, the latter a particularly salient concern not only for women pursuing the vote, but also for those seeking a united Ireland and aware of increasing tensions between unionists and nationalists.

In the context of Dublin Suffrage Week, the play also seemed to encourage its audiences to regard the characters' quest for 'emancipation' as an effort to define a new kind of morality. Though he has little problem lying and betraying his friend Rosmer, Kroll is deeply invested in a middle-class morality; he claims to have 'no great faith in the morality that is not founded on the teachings of the Church'.[7] Through its evocative symbolism, including recurrent references to a ghostly white horse representing death, *Rosmersholm* stages a world rich with mysticism, one quite similar to that of Celtic spirituality. Yet this mysticism offers no redemption. The play similarly refuses to celebrate Rosmer's secular, purely rational mode of thought. Ultimately, it challenges viewers to seek a morality outside the constraints represented by Kroll and Rosmer and the self-seeking anarchism of Mortensgaard, and offers Rebecca's struggle for ethical practice as an ideal. In doing so, the play highlights an issue of intense concern for the suffragists and their audiences: sexual morality. After Kroll betrays Rosmer, he denounces Rebecca and Rosmer's 'emancipated' relationship as 'free love',[8] finding himself offended by the sight of Rebecca roaming about Rosmersholm in a dressing gown and her familiar use of Rosmer's first name. Kroll seems unable to distinguish between intellectual emancipation and sexual immorality, a conflation the suffragists critiqued in 'The Suffragist's Catechism' when they stated: 'There are other kinds of immorality besides sexual immorality; and there is nothing more immoral than robbing a human being of freedom to express herself and develop all her powers, which is what the present system is based on.'[9] Rebecca's heroism rests in her efforts to uncover a new morality that might serve as the grounding claim of a modern spirituality.

SUFFRAGE AND SEXUAL MORALITY

Despite their efforts to disentangle 'emancipation' and 'immorality', the suffragists regularly invoked sexual morality in their political discourse both to generate interest in their cause and to support their claims that female virtue could cure the corruptions of modern life. The public's fascination with sensational issues like prostitution, white slavery and the spread of venereal diseases was boundless, so the suffragists represented these perversions of normative sexuality as a spur for social reform. In doing so, they asserted an illogical causality between sexuality and politics. Of these specious arguments, the most notorious was the English suffragist Christabel Pankhurst's pamphlet that demanded a cure for the 'great scourge' of venereal diseases, a societal ill that would be cured with 'Votes for Women, Celibacy for Men'.[10] Yet an October 1913 editorial in the *Irish Citizen* propounded a similar link between women's oppression and sexual corruptions:

> Women's lack of political power leaves women a helpless prey to the sweating employer, and is therefore one of the causes of prostitution. Prostitution is the cause of venereal disease, the greatest scourge of our civilisation, and one which will finally sweep it away unless its ravages are checked. Therefore, suffragists, to awaken public conscience, and to show the urgent necessity of women's emancipation, are taking steps to enlighten women, and the public generally, on the subjects of Sweating, Prostitution, and Venereal Disease, with the direct causal relationship between the three.[11]

Rosmersholm repeatedly explores Rebecca's sexuality, providing a plot that hinges on the discovery of her incestuous affair with her stepfather, Dr West, and her disclosure of an erotic desire for Rosmer. The audience is asked to reconcile the play's concern with Rebecca's sexuality and the failure of Rebecca and Rosmer to redefine the home – and more pointedly, the failure of those from the outside such as Kroll to understand their efforts to change the domestic politics within it. The play suggests that if the public and private spheres were more integrated, if there were a space for the emancipated woman in an intimate relationship, then arguably the perversions that corrupted the world of Rosmersholm would not have occurred: Rebecca would not have been drawn into an incestuous relationship during her adolescence with Dr West, Rosmer's wife Beata would not have been compelled to commit suicide when convinced she was barren, Rosmer would be capable of embracing his passions and Kroll could tolerate the shifts in power and influence in his own home. By linking Rebecca's sexuality with public concerns, the play demonstrates the powerful (and perhaps arbitrary) links between sexual morality and politics, a point that would resonate powerfully with an Irish public that whispered about Maud Gonne's affairs and her 'adopted' daughter Iseult or watched Parnell's fall following his affair with the married Kitty O'Shea.

As a creative spectacle, *Rosmersholm* introduced themes – ranging from the role of politics in the home to the pernicious influence of the press to sexual morality – that resurfaced in the political rhetoric of the week's Suffrage Conference. This four-day conference featured panels addressing topics such as the current status of women's suffrage, work conditions for women in Ireland, women's trade unions and the vote, and the possible consequences of women attaining the vote. Staged in Dublin's Rotunda Concert Rooms from Tuesday 9 December to Friday 12 December, the Suffrage Conference provided the suffrage community an opportunity to create a civic domain in which their concerns reigned supreme. The speeches presented articulate and politicised feminists expounding their informed opinions in a public sphere, a space where women could engage in rational debate and hopefully obtain consensus from their audience.[12] Because they were the majority, their concerns about policy were presented to a sympathetic audience – a very different dynamic than the hostility many suffragists had encountered from audiences during their public speaking campaign across Ireland.

SUFFRAGE CONFERENCE

On Tuesday 9 December 1913, the IWSF opened their conference by setting out resolutions to ask for a government measure to extend the parliamentary franchise to women immediately, to convince the Nationalist Party that they should enfranchise women under any new government established in Ireland, to praise the Independent Nationalist Party for its support of women's suffrage, to congratulate the Unionist Council for its promise of enfranchisement in the Provisional Government and on admitting women to its Committee, and finally to petition the Unionist Council to use their influence with the Unionist Party in Great Britain to extend the franchise not just to the women of Ulster but to all women in the United Kingdom. This praise served as the overture to a series of speeches engaging broadly with women's issues in Ireland. In each of these speeches, the speakers, both male and female, largely avoided dramatic hyperbole and instead emphasised facts and figures to support their claims. For instance, Dr Mary Strangman, elected to Waterford County Council in 1912, detailed in her paper women's work in Waterford and was lauded for research 'admirably packed with facts and figures'[13] – even though the paper unfortunately went unread for lack of time. There was little, if anything, sentimental about the material presented in the oratory of Dublin Suffrage Week – a striking difference from the stump speeches previously presented by the suffragists across Ireland to enlist the support of the broader national audience, and an obvious contrast to the tragedy of *Rosmersholm*.

According to the *Irish Times*, Mary Ellen Spring Rice, President of the IWSF and prominent member of the Gaelic League, opened the conference by announcing that Dublin Suffrage Week 'had performed the feat of bringing North and South together to work amicably for the good of Ireland'.[14] Here, she cites one advantageous aspect of the fact that women's suffrage remains largely overlooked (or repressed) in nationalist rhetoric and practice: this quasi-invisible status allows an investment in women's suffrage to serve as a unique political device uniting north and south, unionist and republican. *Rosmersholm* had depicted a community divided by men, and now the conference celebrated a community united by women. Despite her insistence on the utopian potential for unification offered by these women, Rice noted that there were limits to what they could achieve through community formation alone since 'there were many societies of women working together for the good of the country, but they were seriously handicapped because they lacked the weapon by which they could most effectively help to bring about the reforms that they had at heart. That weapon was the vote'.[15] Even as she invoked martial metaphors, Rice relied upon a traditional and pacific model of feminist community to praise Irish women. Importantly, she also called attention to the limits of these communities. Her own experience of these limits may, in fact, explain her later role in the planning and execution of the 1914 smuggling of arms to the Irish Volunteers on board the *Asgard*.[16]

Susanne R. Day of the Munster Women's Franchise League opened the conference's first panel on the topic of 'The Present Position of Women's Suffrage'. Day announced that the vote for women was inevitable and went on to examine public anxieties about the women's franchise. Politicians and 'naturally timorous' men, she contended, withheld the vote from women because they did not know what women would do with it. One report quoted her telling the audience: 'Possibly nothing would happen when women got the vote – "I say possibly", added Miss Day, amid laughter – but possibly there would be a great though imperceptible change begun or perhaps there might be a complete social revolution'.[17] Nonetheless, Day cleverly recognised that she could make 'social revolution' more palatable if she represented it not as radical change, but rather as part of a natural cycle. This strategy explains her emphasis in this speech on the benefits of the pre-famine household and the villainies of the English and capitalism to which she attributes the current inequities in Irish society. She also called on the women of Ulster to ensure that the men of Ulster did not revoke their promise for women's suffrage following the instantiation of Home Rule.

Following Day's speech, Mrs Carson of the Lisburn Suffrage Society celebrated the advances in Ulster, namely the pledge by the Ulster Unionist Party that women should receive an equal share in any Provisional Government to be established. The next three speakers offered perspectives from the fight for suffrage being waged in England. In the panel's third speech, the 'partly Irish' Kathleen Courtney from the non-militant National Union of Women's Suffrage Societies (NUWSS) reviewed the status of women's suffrage in Great Britain. Courtney celebrated the 'great Pilgrimage' of suffragists, which had 'forced Mr Asquith to receive a deputation from them'.[18] She also underscored the international nature of the fight for suffrage. Next, Mrs Tanner of the militant Women's Freedom League observed that 'all suffrage societies were for the first time united on one demand, for a Government measure'.[19] She insisted colonial violence would not slow the process, citing instances of colonial unrest in India and South Africa, as well as the Phoenix Park assassinations in Ireland. She concluded by insisting: 'True womanliness could only develop in freedom'.[20] Finally, Mrs Kineton Parks of the Tax Resistance League condoned civil disobedience by championing tax resistance as a 'constitutional form of protest' for women.[21] Despite their different approaches to women and militancy, each of these speeches privileged community. That is, the success of suffrage hinged on the willingness of seemingly opposed parties – militant and non-militant, Irish and English, nationalist and unionist, male and female, coloniser and colonised – to work together for equality. In light of the divisive world portrayed in *Rosmersholm*, these speeches appear to offer the solution to the tragic fate of Rebecca and Rosmer. By reaching out to their community and working for consensus, these two characters might have circumvented their sufferings.

SUFFRAGE AND LABOUR

A special report published on the conference in the *Irish Citizen* summed up the contents of the remaining speeches presented during the final three days of Dublin Suffrage Week.[22] Entitled 'Women's Work in Ireland', the second panel examined the conditions of women's work in major Irish cities. These speeches focused on Belfast industrial workers, women who worked in the home, Limerick apprenticeships, the need for women factory inspectors in Dublin, and the necessity of healthier working conditions. In the panel's final speech, Dr Denham Osbourne cited low wages for women as a source of prostitution. According to Osbourne, the enfranchisement of women would 'forward the cause of morality by putting men and women on equal footing in the labour market and before the law'.[23] The third panel on the topic of 'Trade Unions and the Vote' drew a large audience. Likely, interest was due largely to the labour unrest that pervaded the country as James Larkin organised workers through the Irish Transport and General Workers' Union.[24] In this speech on poorly paid workers, Dr Marion Phillips of London observed that 'these women do not cease to feel the miserable conditions of their lives, because they are accustomed to such conditions; but they see no possibility of escape, and therefore resign themselves. It is this resignation that must be done away with. Women accept conditions which ought to be intolerable, not because they like such conditions, but because they see no hope of change'.[25] This passivity appears relevant not only to women workers, but also to the character of Rebecca West, who fails to see any alternative to suicide once she realises the limits of her relationship with Rosmer. Another speaker, Cissie Cahalan of the Irish Drapers' Assistants Union (and a member of the militant IWFL), held the decline of home industry responsible for the oppression of women in industry. She voiced scepticism about male charity, asserting: 'Women want not chivalry, but justice, and will obtain it through the vote'.[26]

SUFFRAGE AND THE FUTURE

The final panel on Friday, entitled 'If Women Had Votes', gave rein to the imaginative possibilities of a future in which women had the vote. The speakers concentrated on the role of female charity and invoked Christian ideals to promote unity among women. Mrs Webb Smithwick pleaded that women not judge one another and advised looking to motives to understand actions; and Miss Thirza Potts, a delegate from the National Union, urged the suffragists to join with the Women's Trade Unions. This final celebration of the power of female community stands in stark contrast to the isolation of Rebecca West at Rosmersholm. Further, these speeches suggested that the religious dystopia of the play might represent one cause of Rebecca and Rosmer's demise. Representing the Church League, Miss Stack 'made an earnest and religious appeal to her audience', while the Reverend Savell Hicks 'pointed out that neither homes nor nations can make true progress where men and women do not work as comrades, and go forward hand in hand'.[27] Mrs Tanner of the Women's Freedom League analysed the effects of women's suffrage in countries where it had been attained. She insisted: 'The general effect has been admittedly good, and has tended to purify politics, to promote temperance, and to further the cause of purity'.[28] Each of these claims would seem to fly in the face of the doctrinaire Christianity represented by Dr Kroll by advocating cooperation among citizens as the fundamental good.

DEBATE WITH THE ANTIS

The conference speeches each reflected a material reality that resonated with the themes appearing in *Rosmersholm*. Though this particular production of *Rosmersholm* received mixed reviews from its audience members, the conference was unilaterally well received according to the *Irish Citizen*, which reported: 'The speakers were listened to with marked attention, and were received with applause'.[29] By separating out political rhetoric and dramatic dialogue, these events could potentially reach different audiences while espousing the same message.

There was, however, one space amidst the conference activities in which the real and the theatrical merged. The Irish Women's Franchise League's (IWFL) 'Debate with the Antis', described by the *Irish Times* as the 'highest point of interest' of Suffrage Week, provided an event that staged current political issues but relied on dramatic conflict to attract audiences.[30] The *Irish Times* also noted that this debate attracted 'a large attendance in which there were not more than half a dozen gentlemen'.[31] Presided over by Dublin's Lord Mayor, the debate was waged between Mary Hayden, the first female professor of Modern Irish History at University College Dublin (who was also a member of the Irish Women's Reform League and one of the founding members of the IWFL), and the anti-suffragist Mabel Smith 'of London'. Smith was received with hisses from the Irish suffragist audience and was condemned for her praise of the British Empire. In particular, she was lambasted for her inability to debate and 'her aggressive and even offensive manner towards her audience . . . arousing almost as much hostility to her personality as to her cause. "What singularly unwomanly women all these prominent antis are!" was the reflection one heard uttered on every side'.[32] Meanwhile, Smith argued that: 'Militancy, so far, was only comparable to the militancy they had had from the lowest types of men – for instance, cattle-maiming. What the nation wanted were the manly man and the womanly woman'.[33] In response, Hayden invoked forward progress and change as ideals, stressing that 'there was a tendency towards [women's suffrage] all over the world, and in no instance had a step in that direction been retraced'.[34] Hayden unequivocally celebrated modernity and the suffragists' place in the global community, championing an 'emancipated' position akin to those espoused in *Rosmersholm*.

The *Irish Citizen* account of the debate focused largely on how the audience of about 500 responded to these women and in doing so revealed that the suffragists deployed tactics against the antis that they had gleaned from their own hostile audiences over the years. According to the *Irish Citizen*, the National League for Opposing Woman Suffrage (NLOWS) did itself a disservice when it 'emerged once more into the light of day in order to give its annual proof of existence' because 'it has also managed, incidentally and quite unconsciously to show two delighted and, I am afraid somewhat fearless, audiences that the "anti" is decidedly prone to lose her temper on a public platform on the slightest provocation'.[35] These women who opposed the vote, unlike the suffragists, did not benefit from public exposure and instead revealed themselves to be hysterical, out of control. As this account asserts: 'We have seen suffrage speakers pursue the even tenor of their way throughout a storm of missiles of many and varied descriptions – we have seen an anti lose her temper at every single question from the audience – verily, "by their signs ye shall know them".'[36] These performances, which are crucial given the mainstream press boycotts of the suffragists' work, allowed Irish audiences to see these political women as rational and well-behaved, a component of identity that eluded the anti-suffragists.

SUFFRAGE AND THE PRESS

Dublin Suffrage Week was notable for the wide range of social and political issues it addressed as well as for its capacity to unite Irish women to discuss their global and national status. In her summation of the week's events, Louie Bennett asserted that the IWSF had created a conference proving that: 'We Irishwomen cannot be accused of sentimentality or emotionalism in our work for the vote. Our Suffrage Week betrayed no hints of such characteristics'.[37] Yet it appears that this triumph of feminist rational discourse failed to reach a national audience. Bennett also took the Dublin press to task for ignoring 'the most prominent topic of the week ... woman's suffrage'.[38] She expressed doubt that the press could accurately represent the public by asking: 'Are we to believe that the press is sincerely endeavouring to cater for the Dublin public?'[39] She insisted that the Irish press had failed the public by featuring articles on the ladies' dresses at the Leopardstown race meeting rather than on facts about women's work and wages. In a regretful tone, Bennett closed her article: 'We should be sorry to believe that Dublin editors have accurately gauged the intelligence, the sympathetic imagination, or the good sense of the Dublin public.'[40]

Like the press in *Rosmersholm*, the press in real-life Ireland failed its constituency by ignoring or inaccurately reporting on the possibilities generated by the search for an emancipated lifestyle. The nationalist paper, *Sinn Féin*, offered absolutely no account of this conference. The *Freeman's Journal*, which held a more moderate nationalist position, granted attention to a number of public conferences and meetings, including the general meeting of the Dublin Central Branch of the Women's National Heath Association and a large charity benefit staged at the Gaiety where a 'very fashionable crowd' attended a set of entertainments including a *tableaux vivants*, but it provided limited coverage of Suffrage Week, printing only brief summaries of the speeches presented during the conference.[41] Excepting the *Irish Citizen*, the unionist *Irish Times* published the most extensive coverage of Suffrage Week, characterising the week's content with the headline: 'Militancy Not To Be Mentioned'.[42]

Dublin Suffrage Week offered a wide assortment of activities for those who wished to support women's suffrage, but the premiere of

Rosmersholm and the Suffrage Conference appear in the week's promotional material as the key events. These two events – one creative and one political – worked together during Dublin Suffrage Week to highlight concerns of importance to the Irish suffragists. Ironically, the conference speeches promised its audiences the possibility of a happy ending in real life, a world in which women could positively alter circumstance through political action. And the fictive drama ended in a tragedy of misunderstanding and thwarted good intentions by culminating in the suicide of its emancipated hero and heroine. Notably, the most lively and well attended event of the week was the debate between the suffragists and anti-suffragists, suggesting that perhaps the fusion of drama and information remained the suffragists most effective tool for attracting the attention – and eventually the support – of the Irish public.[43]

NOTES

1. *Irish Citizen* 6 December 1913; p. 237.
2. Rosemary Cullen Owens, 'Louie Bennett', in Maria Luddy and Fintan Lane (eds) Radical Irish Lives (Cork: Cork UP, 2001) p. 13. For a somewhat anecdotal but nonetheless enlightening account of Bennett's life, see R. M. Fox, *Louie Bennett: Her Life and Times* (Dublin: Talbot Press, 1958).
3. Henrik Ibsen, *Rosmersholm, The Lady from the Sea*, trans. Charles Archer (New York: Scribner's, 1912) p. 35. The Archer translation was used for this 1913 production of *Rosmersholm*.
4. M. E., 'Woman's Place in the World', *Irish Citizen* 2 August 1913, p. 85.
5. *Rosmersholm*, p. 60.
6. Ibid, p. 61.
7. Ibid, p. 86.
8. Ibid, p. 87.
9. 'The Suffragist's Catechism (IV)', *Irish Citizen* 7 June 1913, p. 19.
10. Christabel Pankhurst, *The Great Scourge and How to End It* (London: E. Pankhurst, 1913).
11. 'Free Speech on Sex', *Irish Citizen* 18 October 1913, p. 176.
12. The place of women in the public sphere has been written about often and well by feminist scholars who have documented, as Nancy Fraser describes it, 'the exacerbation of sexism characteristic of the liberal public sphere'. See Nancy Fraser, 'Rethinking the Public Sphere: A Contribution to the Critique of Actually Existing Democracy', in Bruce Robbins (ed.) *The Phantom Public Sphere* (Minneapolis: University of Minnesota Press, 1993), p. 6. In seeking to challenge the longstanding presumption that the public sphere was a purely masculine realm, a number of the studies of women and the public sphere have centred around suffragism, the route through which women sought to enter the public domain by demonstrating for the exercise of franchise. In doing so, Mary Ryan claims that historians who pursue this route of study have 'implicitly accepted a truncated definition of the public, focusing on but one manifestation of citizenship' which she claims has led women's history into the realm of 'political irony' because

women's suffrage was achieved at the very moment that electoral politics was losing its hold on the public. See Mary P. Ryan, *Women in Public: Between Banners and Ballots, 1825–1880* (Baltimore: Johns Hopkins UP, 1990), p. 9.

13. 'The Conference – Special Report', *Irish Citizen* 20 December 1913, p. 253.
14. 'The Suffrage Conference: Opening Day', *Irish Citizen* 13 December 1913, p. 244.
15. 'Women's Suffrage Conference in Dublin', *Irish Times* 10 December 1913, p. 10.
16. Sinéad McCoole, *No Ordinary Women: Irish Female Activists in the Revolutionary Years 1900–1923* (Dublin: The O'Brien Press, 2003) pp. 29–30.
17. 'The Suffrage Conference: Opening Day', *Irish Citizen* 13 December 1913, p. 244.
18. 'The Suffrage Conference: Opening Day', *Irish Citizen* 13 December 1913, p. 244–5.
19. 'The Suffrage Conference: Opening Day', *Irish Citizen* 13 December 1913, p. 245.
20. Ibid.
21. Ibid.
22. 'The Conference – Special Report', *Irish Citizen* 20 December 1913, pp. 253–4.
23. 'The Conference – Special Report,' *Irish Citizen* 20 December 1913, p. 253.
24. The famous strike during Horse Show Week in late August 1913 pitted William Martin Murphy and Larkin against each other, which culminated in Murphy staging a lockout that left some 25,000 families threatened by starvation. See Gary Granville (ed.) *Dublin 1913: A Divided City* (Dublin: O'Brien Educational Lmtd, 1978).
25. 'The Conference – Special Report', *Irish Citizen* 20 December 1913, pp. 253–4.
26. 'The Conference – Special Report', *Irish Citizen* 20 December 1913, p. 254.
27. Ibid.
28. Ibid.
29. Ibid.
30. 'Woman Suffrage: For and Against', *Irish Times* 12 December 1913, p. 6.
31. Ibid.
32. 'The Antis' Fiasco', *Irish Citizen* 20 December 1913, p. 252
33. 'Woman Suffrage Question: Public Debate in Dublin', *Irish Times* 12 December 1913, p. 6.
34. 'The Antis' Fiasco', *Irish Citizen* 20 December 1913, p. 252
35. 'The Bad-Tempered Anti', *Irish Citizen* 20 December 1913, p. 251.
36. Ibid.
37. Louie Bennett, 'Some Reflections on Suffrage Week', *Irish Citizen* 20 December 1913, p. 251.
38. Ibid.
39. Ibid.
40. Ibid.
41. See *Freeman's Journal* 10 December 1913, p. 9; and *Freeman's Journal* 11 December 1913, p. 9.
42. See *Irish Times* 10 December 1913: 10; *Irish Times* 11 December 1913, p. 6; *Irish Times* 12 December 1913: 6; *Irish Times* 13 December 1913, p. 9.
43. For further information on Dublin Suffrage Week, see Paige Reynolds, *The Audiences for Irish Spectacle: Drama and Modernism, 1890–1926* (Cambridge: Cambridge University Press, forthcoming).

CHAPTER FIVE

Publicising the Private: suffragists' critique of sexual abuse and domestic violence

LOUISE RYAN

Is it not time we had women on the bench and on the jury when such crimes as murderous and indecent assault receive nominal or no punishment?[1]

INTRODUCTION

This quote from the *Irish Citizen* refers to a court case involving a soldier accused of beating his wife with a poker and causing her serious injuries, the woman was still in hospital when the case went to trial and yet her husband only received a six month prison sentence. Suffragists such as L.A.M. McCracken and Marion Duggan were particularly concerned about domestic violence and sexual assaults on women and girls. They argued that the legal profession and the judiciary did not take such offences seriously. The fact that women were barred from practising as lawyers and could not sit on juries (until 1919) resulted in male dominated institutions that did not provide a system of justice for women and girls. Such was their mistrust of the legal system that a number of concerned suffragists set up a committee to monitor court cases involving girls and women. Reports of these cases were regularly published in the *Irish Citizen*. However, the women's presence in court, especially in cases involving 'indecency', was not always welcomed. Attempts to eject 'ladies' from some Dublin courts prompted the *Irish Citizen* to ask:

When will men realise that women are part of the public, that they are fully entitled to be present at all cases open to the public.[2]

In this chapter I examine the reports from the Watching the Court (WTC) committee and other articles about domestic violence and sexual assault that were published in the *Irish Citizen*. These articles are interesting not least because they highlight a hidden and secret aspect of Irish society in the early twentieth century. In addition, the articles also provide an important insight into the diversity of issues taken up by suffragists. This was far more than just a 'votes for women' movement. Critiques of legal institutions, and the male-defined morality that underpinned them, reveal sophisticated feminist analysis and nuanced negotiation of the 'secrecy' and 'publicity' that cross-cut the private and public spheres.

PUBLICISING THE PRIVATE

> Rather than viewing the vote simply as the key to enter a quite separate and distinct political sphere, suffragists sought to challenge both prevailing understanding of what it meant to be a woman, and the ideology that asserted the separateness of domestic and public life by arguing the significance of values associated with domestic roles for a reordering of society in general.[3]

Although Holton is referring to the British suffrage movement, I think her comments may also be relevant to the Irish suffrage movement. In early twentieth century Irish society the ideology of separate, gendered spheres, 'public man' and 'private woman', was propounded by all social institutions, especially the Catholic Church.[4] Women's proper sphere was within the confines of the home where she was under the 'protection' of her father or husband. The public world of politics, business, the law, higher education, the media, etc were the rightful domain of men. Arguing against female enfranchisement in 1892, the leader of the Liberal Party, William Gladstone, said that women must be 'saved' from the 'whirlpool of public life'.[5] However, the prevalence of the separate spheres ideology should not lead us to assume that this was an accurate distinction between 'public' and 'private'. Feminist historians are increasingly suggesting that the public/private dichotomy was an ideological tool that did not reflect the true levels of complex inter-connections between privacy and publicity.[6]

Because notions of public and private are so central to this argument, it is useful to begin the chapter by examining these concepts in some detail. From as early as the eighteenth century, feminists had engaged with the public/private dichotomy through a critique of 'separate spheres'. For writers like Mary Wollstonecraft and Anna Wheeler, women's sphere was too limited and constrained; instead, as Mary Cullen's chapter in this book demonstrates, they demanded a greater role for women in public life. In addition, as Jane Rendall[7] has argued, early feminist writers had a sophisticated understanding of how the public and private spheres were configured. 'Public' did not simply refer to formal political institutions, it also included public sociability and public spaces. In addition, 'private' did not simply mean the family, the home or the individual, it also referred to closed, exclusive associations with secret decision-making processes. Hence, the simple dichotomy between the private, domestic sphere and the public world outside can obscure the multiple meanings of 'public' and 'private'. Other factors such as class can also impact on how private and public are configured and experienced. For example, poor people had neither the level of personal privacy nor the level of access to public institutions enjoyed by the affluent classes.

In an attempt to make sense of these complex, shifting and over-lapping notions of public and private, some feminist historians have drawn upon the work of the German sociologist, Jurgen Habermas, in particular his notion of the bourgeois public sphere.[8] Habermas distinguishes the bourgeois public sphere from both the institutions of the state and those of the market place so that the public sphere is understood as truly 'public' where people come together, associate and generate public opinion. This bourgeois public sphere emerged from salons and coffee houses in the eighteenth century and grew with the spread of literacy. However, Habermas has been criticised for ignoring the gendering of the public sphere, especially in the eighteenth and nineteenth centuries when women were excluded from many aspects of public life. Nonetheless, Habermas's configuration of the public sphere may be useful in understanding the early women's movement. His notion of the public sphere as including literary culture, reading circles, newspapers and salons enables us to analyse the varied ways in which women have sought to gain access to and engage with the public sphere. As the WTC committee discovered, women's access to public spaces had to be carefully negotiated in complex ways.

'THE COWARDLY CONSPIRACY OF SILENCE'

On its front page in the June/July issue of 1919, the *Irish Citizen* carried the headline 'How Children are "Protected"'. The article, submitted by the WTC committee, included a list of the cases of indecent assault upon children that had come to court during 1918.

1. On 15th August a man aged 55 charged with indecently assaulting three girls between 7 and 12 years. Acquitted.
2. 30th March, in Belfast, soldier assaulted girl under 13; sentence: 1 month in the second division.
3. 6th September, man, aged 43, assaulted girl of 7 ½; sentence: 1 month's imprisonment, or fine of 40 shillings.
4. 10th March, soldier (married) assaulted girl of 5 ¾; acquitted on slight discrepancy in evidence.
5. 8th October, man, ship-steward, aged 27, assaulted girl of 5, died in prison.
6. 30th November, man (married) assaulted girl of 11 ½; sentence: 3 months' imprisonment (most unusual sentence).[9]

The article concluded that these men deserved the pillory of public opinion, instead of which their light sentences 'practically condone the offence'.

The WTC committee originally began under the auspices of the Irishwomen's Reform League in May 1914; however, in March 1915 it was reorganised to facilitate greater participation by members of other suffrage societies, most notably the Irish Women's Franchise League. The committee deliberately remained small with between 10 and 20 dedicated members, based in Dublin, undertaking to 'watch' cases at the Four Courts, Assizes and Recorder's Court. Its objectives were:

> To show by their presence in court that women demanded, both as a right and a duty, to be admitted to the administration of justice, on equal terms with men, as police, jurors, solicitors, barristers, magistrates and judges . . . To collect evidence bearing on the above demands, and on any other legislative reforms needed for the protection of women and children, together with accurate information as to moral conditions.[10]

The committee grew out of the particular interest and expertise of Marion Duggan, a law graduate who, because of her sex, was unable to practise as a lawyer. At the meeting on 1 March 1915 she was elected as honorary secretary and treasurer. Other members of the committee included: Margaret Connery, Hanna Sheehy Skeffington, Mrs Hoskin, Miss McGlade, Miss G. Manning, Mrs Nolan, Miss O'Brien and Mrs

Wilson. However, there is little doubt that Duggan was the driving force behind the committee. In her weekly reports to the *Irish Citizen* she vividly described the masculine world of justice as experienced by women and girls.

In the summer of 1914, members of the WCT observed a case involving a man named Madden who was accused of raping a 7-year-old girl:

> Scene: Green Street Courthouse, packed with people; row upon row of men and women gaze down. Twelve men far away in a box, a big man in a strange wig, another above strangely clad, at the table a timid girl, terrified, shy. The scene lasts a minute and ends; the Crown have withdrawn the charge against Madden, ex-free labourer for having infected a child, barely 7 with a foul disease, on the grounds that she is too young to answer questions.[11]

Duggan argued that this court environment was totally unsuited to the needs of a child. There should be a children's court with women police and a woman barrister to speak to the child in a friendly way. As well as changing the court environment, there was also a pressing need to transform the attitudes of the judiciary, who simply did not view the abuse of children as a serious crime.

The Madden case occupied the committee for several months. Despite the silence about this case in the press, the *Irish Citizen* managed to stir up some interest and there were several letters and articles written to the paper about the case. One article proclaimed that the protection of women and girls 'can only be won by publicity' and demanded an 'end to the cowardly conspiracy of silence' surrounding indecent assaults on children in Ireland.[12] This is an interesting reversal of the usual association between protection and privacy. Women and children were assumed to be 'protected' within the privacy of the domestic sphere. This article argued that privacy and silence only protected the abuser. The only real protection against indecency was not secrecy but publicity.

In an attempt to uncover more information, the WTC committee persuaded an MP, Charles Duncan, to ask a question in parliament about why the Crown had dropped its case against Madden. Obviously, the fact that women were excluded from parliamentary politics meant that they needed a sympathetic male representative to negotiate this space on their behalf. The official response to the parliamentary question was that there had been insufficient corroboration of the child's story.[13]

Duggan expressed her frustration that such corroboration was deemed necessary even though the child was confirmed to have contracted a sexually transmitted disease, gonorrhoea, and Madden's wife was known to have contracted the same disease shortly after her marriage to him in 1913. As will be discussed below, venereal disease was one of the many 'taboo' issues that the WTC committee regularly confronted.

In addition to the Madden case, the WTC committee focused on another 'indecency' case, involving a Mr Jones, during the summer of 1914. Jones received six weeks' imprisonment after being found guilty of indecent assault upon a child. As Duggan pointed out, somewhat sarcastically: 'How lucky he didn't break a window or steal of pair of boots' because these crimes would have resulted in a much harsher sentence.[14] Although Jones had received a six-week sentence, it was later discovered that he was released from prison after just two weeks.[15] In a subsequent article, Duggan reported on information received from the Under-Secretary to the Lord Lieutenant, the representative of the Crown in Ireland.[16] It seemed that Jones had been a model prisoner and so had received remission on his six-week sentence. Thus a man found guilty of indecent assault on a child served only two weeks in prison.

As war in Europe began to occupy people's minds, Duggan reminded readers that, while much attention was being paid to 'German outrages', it was important not to overlook outrages closer to home. The police authorities had informed the WTC committee that thirty-eight cases of criminal assault on children had been investigated during the previous six months and that twenty-four of these had been convicted with sentences ranging from one month to three years.[17]

'SEX, SEX, SEX!': WOMEN AND MORAL PURITY

In many of the cases reported by the WTC committee, barristers and judges, and probably the juries also, excused male behaviour on the grounds that men could not help acting on their natural urges, especially if women had encouraged them in any way. For example, in a 'seduction' case, Mr Justice Dodd reminded the jury of the 'natural and irresistible impulses animating the man'.[18] The committee also investigated reports that a city magistrate had dismissed an assault case against a man on the grounds that his 15-year-old victim actually looked 16.[19] This notion that men's sexual urges were natural and irresistible, Duggan argued, explained the apparent sympathy and tolerance towards men who committed 'outrages' on children.[20]

In a breach of promise case the defending counsel, Mr Chambers KC, excused his client's behaviour on the grounds that 'it was right and manly for the defendant, even if engaged, to flirt with the girls'.[21] Duggan castigated this 'double standard of morality' that viewed 'man as a hapless victim' of 'human nature', but saw it as 'utterly wrong' for any girl to 'throw herself at a man'. She described Mr Chambers as a 'silly buffoon'. 'Sex, sex, sex! To the men of the Chambers type that is what men and women were created for'. Duggan argued that these men were utterly unsuited to make judgements in 'sexual cases where the deep interests of women are at stake'. Duggan concluded the article by saying she made her protest 'in the name of Purity'.[22]

The subject of morality, moral purity and double moral standards were regularly discussed by Irish suffragists, as Paige Reynolds' chapter in this book also shows. Articles on these controversial topics also appeared on a regular basis in the *Irish Citizen*.[23] Under the heading 'Morality – conventional or otherwise', Margaret Connery argued that 'in all ages men have been great sticklers for the observance of a code of conventional morality – on the part of women'. Of course, men did not inflict such an exacting code of morality on themselves. Thus women were expected to uphold strict moral standards, while men's immoral behaviour was tolerated and even condoned. Connery declared that: 'In Ireland, as elsewhere, public morals must continue in an unhealthy state while we tolerate the shameful double moral standard'.[24]

In seeking to eradicate double moral standards, suffragists like Connery and Duggan sought to create a new moral standard by which both men and women would abide. In an article in the *Irish Citizen* in July 1919, Connery once again referred to 'corrupt double moral standards'; she pointed out that for certain types of men sex had become an obsession, a disease. 'Sex and all that appertains to it is enveloped in a veritable fog of obscurity, obscenity and vulgarity.' Men had restricted women's sphere of activities to the mere exercise of the sex function: 'which in practice results in denying her a human status and reducing her to a condition of pure animalism'. Connery argued that there was no form of slavery 'so debasing, so destructive of everything fine and spiritual in the human soul as this slavery of sex'. Women's economic dependence on men meant that they were also vulnerable to sexual exploitation. As well as being sexually abused and exploited by individual men, women were also abused by the male-dominated systems in society.

It is not for nothing that judges, juries, lawyers, magistrates and
police are of the same sex as the offenders in these kind of cases,
and that such offenders are regarded with an indulgent tolerance
that to thinking women turns the administration of justice into a
ghastly joke.[25]

In this article Connery used the familiar argument that 'any considerable
improvement in our moral standards must inevitably keep pace with the
growth of women's power and influence in the public life of the
community'.[26] Women's economic and political freedom would lead to a
'revolution in our moral standards'. Thus, the only solution to the sexual
abuse and exploitation of women and children was empowerment for
women. This would in turn bring about a higher form of morality that,
instead of seeking sexual freedom, advocated a protection from sex.

   While the British suffragette, Christabel Pankhurst, famously called
for 'votes for women, chastity for men', campaigns for 'moral purity' were
undertaken by feminists in several countries during that period.
Feminists in Britain,[27] Canada[28] and Australia[29] challenged double
standards and campaigned for an improvement in public and private
morality. Feminists in many countries sought to raise moral standards by
publicising and rooting out all forms of immorality, vice, disease and
abuse. As Lucy Bland has argued:

> Their wish to transform the public world for the benefit of all,
> though especially, of course, for women, was rooted in a wider
> feminist vision in which women had freedom of movement in all
> spheres of society and the issue of men's behaviour towards women
> was squarely on the political agenda. One part of their work
> entailed campaigning for women's entry into government – at both
> local and national levels. Another part of their work involved
> addressing issues of sexual violence – providing support to victims
> of male assault and campaigning for changes in unjust laws.[30]

Issues of mobility and access were crucial to this moral crusade.
Feminists used a range of strategies to negotiate and traverse public
spaces from which they had been traditionally excluded. This meant that
feminists frequently found themselves in unfamiliar places confronting
shocking and taboo issues such as prostitution, venereal disease and
sexual abuse. Thus, when Irish feminists such as Connery and Duggan
expressed views such as 'we suffragists demand perfect moral purity from
men and women alike',[31] they was very much in line with the stand
taken by many feminists in other countries.

As mentioned in the Madden case above, the subject of venereal disease was an on-going concern for the WTC committee. Writing in September 1915, Duggan said that 'dangerous disease is the inevitable result of sexual laxity'. However, she was particularly critical of the double moral standard that punished women for sexual laxity but accepted men's philandering as natural.

> Is immorality in men a sin or a physical necessity? Does man's nature compel him to live a life that brings pain and degradation upon himself, his wife and family – and, above all, ruins, morally and physically, the woman whom his bodily needs employ. Men's answer through the ages has been that men must yield, but that the women who comply are vile sinners. This is most unfair.[32]

Duggan argued that there were two possible solutions to this dilemma. Either men must learn to conduct themselves in a responsible and moral way or else prostitution must be recognised as an honourable and indeed entirely necessary profession. Venereal diseases had been of concern to feminists since the mid-nineteenth century.[33] Husbands passed the disease from prostitutes to wives and through wives to their unborn babies. However, rather than blaming prostitutes for the spread of such dangerous diseases, Duggan, like many other feminist campaigners, argued that it was not prostitutes but the men who created the demand for their services who were to blame for the spread of such diseases.

Of course, in addition to sexual diseases the other great threat that sex posed to women and girls was pregnancy outside of marriage. Although suffragists were generally very critical of childbirth outside of marriage, they were even more critical of the fact that the 'unmarried mother' bore all the costs and difficulties, while fathers could not even be sued for maintenance. This matter was taken up by Mrs E. Sanderson who had 'watched' her first court case in 1915. The article gives a detailed report on a seduction case against a married businessman from Greystones, Co. Wicklow. His affair with a young 'shop girl' had gone on for months; however, not until the birth of her baby was the girl's family aware of her condition. The girl, who had worked in her mother's flower shop, died in childbirth and her mother was now suing the businessman for 'loss of service'. Mrs Sanderson commented that, as a suffragist, she found it shocking that this businessman was under no legal obligation to support his child and so the only way the dead girl's family could sue him was for loss of her 'service' in the flower shop. The defending counsel argued that the mother knew of her daughter's on-going affair and she was to blame for permitting it to continue. In the end, the jury found for the plaintiff and awarded the dead girl's mother £500. Mrs Sanderson used this case to develop some of her own views.

> It struck me how appropriate a jury of men and women would have been on this and on many a similar case. Women . . . in many cases are in a better position than men to judge fairly. No mention was made of the amazing self-repression practised by the dead girl in concealing her condition. Only a woman could visualise and sympathise with that nine months' torture . . . It is only a natural sequence of other justices to women that we should take our share in administering justice. Perhaps it is not too much to hope that someday . . . we may not only have women jurors, but women counsel and women judges, too.[34]

SECRECY VERSUS PUBLICITY: INCEST AND WIFE BEATING

In 1915, the *Irish Citizen* published its editorial under the heading: 'Ladies and Children to leave court'.[35] In a case of indecency against two girls aged 7 1/2 and 9 1/2 years, the Lord Chief Justice asked ladies to leave the court. Members of the WTC committee refused to leave and had to resist police threats to physically remove them. The matter was taken up by the committee's own counsel, Messrs Cochrane. Because women, even those with law degrees, could not represent themselves in court, they had to rely upon men, such as Mr Cochrane, to mediate this space on their behalf.

The WTC committee accrued considerable legal expense in defending their right to attend court cases and resisting attempts to have them ejected on the grounds that some cases might be too shocking for ladies. It was often the cases that they most wanted to highlight which were shrouded in such secrecy. As Jane Rendall argues, feminists' attempts to gain access to public spaces illustrates the complex intersections of 'the open and the secret, the public and inaccessible'.[36] Like feminists in other contexts, the WTC committee was not merely seeking to publicise and scrutinise what went on inside the privacy of the home but also the secrecy surrounding male-dominated institutions such as the courts. They sought access to what had previously been inaccessible, secret and hidden. This shows the intersections between 'private home' and 'public institutions' and the ways in which feminists used the public sphere both through their own mobility and through the press to challenge the abuse that such secretiveness sought to perpetuate.

In response to Messrs Cochrane's intervention, Lord Chief Justice Cherry agreed that the committee members could remain in court for all cases except incest, which was held in camera. The editorial highlighted this irony:

> One fails to grasp why, if public morality is such that these crimes take place, it can best be served by hushing them up and attempting to give the impression that such offences are unheard of in our Christian civilisation.[37]

The other issue that was usually relegated to the secrecy of the domestic sphere was wife-beating:

> An age-long tradition prevails that in matrimonial affairs what transpires in the home must be carefully concealed from the world without. The quarrels and differences, ranging from 'incompatibility of temper' to wrangling, to physical violence and giving of 'black eyes' must be kept strictly secret, particularly on the wife's part if she is the one ill-treated.[38]

In this lengthy article, L.A.M. Priestley (Mrs McCracken) argued that it was natural for people to want to keep their domestic hearth private; home life was sacred and should be kept inviolate. However, such privacy gave a sense of security to the husband who ill-treated his wife. Priestley stated that 'wife-beating' was 'of common occurrence and is suffered for the most part in silence by the victim'. For the sake of their children and their financial security, women in most cases put up with abuse by their husbands. But attempts by the women to 'keep up appearances' only enabled the abuse to continue unchecked. Although the first blow may have been struck in the heat of argument and regretted later on, it had set a precedent and gradually it became easier for the husband to use his fists to control or repress his wife.

But when a woman plucked up the courage to take her abusive husband to court she rarely received any sympathy or support. Most magistrates left the husband off with a light fine. Men were rarely incarcerated because it was believed that the family needed them as a breadwinner and could not survive without them. However, Priestley argued that this attitude gave tacit encouragement to wife beaters. Men who abused their wives should be given a long term of hard labour and their families should be supported through public funds.

What touches the public purse stamps itself well upon the public imagination, and if the community pays in this way there would be more hope of working a reformation in husbands. Unhappily there are subtle influences towards condoning the dastardly offence of wife-beating.[39]

She then cited a recent court case in which the defendant's counsel sought to defend his wife-beating by saying 'the woman provoked her husband beyond measure' and by arguing that some women 'do not deserve anything but harshness'. In summing up the evidence the judge said that it was very trying for any man when his wife turned out to be troublesome but it took a good deal of troublesome behaviour 'to justify personal violence'. Priestley asked if we were to infer from this statement that corporal punishment was justified if a woman was very trouble-some. She stated that a man could mistreat his wife in a way that he dare not, with impunity, treat any other person. Yet, she argued, wife-beating was the most monstrous of crimes. For a man to woo and win a young, trusting girl and then after marriage to beat and abuse her 'seems the very negation of personal honour and morality'. As this article was written after women had been enfranchised, Priestley appealed to women to use their voting rights to address such issues:

It is surely the duty of enfranchised women to seek to have the personal safety of the wife adequately and effectively secured, and every deterrent that an educated and Christian opinion, and heavy penalties upon the offender can enforce, imposed upon ill-tempered and brutally disposed men until the relation between husband and wife shall be that of civilised and independent human beings not that of ruthless tyrant and hapless victim.[40]

CONCLUSION

Research from many countries suggests that feminists in the late nineteenth and early twentieth centuries had a double agenda; firstly, to protect the health and well being of women within the private sphere and, secondly, to raise standards of morality in the public sphere. However, these were not separate campaigns, their interconnectedness demonstrated the overlapping of these two spheres. In order to protect the sanctity of their homes and the well being of their families (both moral and physical), women needed to come out of the seclusion of the private, domestic sphere and work to purify the public sphere. Women's exclusion from formal institutions such as parliament and the judiciary meant that they had to rely on men to mediate these spaces on their behalf. Undaunted, the women used their growing mobility, knowledge, experience and confidence to access as many public arenas and forums as possible so that they could scrutinise and publicise abuse and violence and then lobby for reforms. This is why Habermas's concept of the public sphere, as a forum that exists somewhere in the middle between the formal institutions of the state and the domestic sphere of the home, is very useful in understanding the strategies adopted by suffragists. From their position within this 'public sphere', the women sought to scrutinise both the domestic space and the formal, male-dominated, structures of the state.

In this chapter I argued that Irish suffragists had a sophisticated and nuanced understanding of the interactions and overlaps between the so-called private and public domains and that they engaged with this ideological construct in three key ways. Firstly, these suffragists revealed how the notion of 'privacy' could be used to mask violence and abuse not just within the private domestic sphere but also in many male-dominated institutions, such as courtrooms, where 'privacy' was used to exclude outsiders and draw a veil of secrecy over proceedings. Secondly, campaigns such as Watching the Court illustrate how suffragists challenged the prevailing ideology about the proper sphere of women. These suffragists called for women's entry into 'public life' not just as a right but also as a duty of citizenship. Only by gaining access to public institutions could women have a role in publicising and improving the conditions affecting all women and children throughout society. Thirdly, the reports of court cases in the *Irish Citizen* provided suffragists with a forum in which to challenge the prevailing double standards of morality that dictated one code of behaviour for women but tolerated and excused very different behaviour in men. So long as women could not or would not take their rightful place in public life, abuse, degradation and immorality would continue to go unchecked. Men simply could not be relied upon to improve the social conditions of women and children.

Court reports by the WTC committee aimed to shatter the 'conspiracy of silence' around sexual crimes in Irish society. At a time when cultural nationalism and the Catholic Church were constructing Irish society as the bastion of morality and clean living in contrast to the decadence of England, reports of incest and other child sexual abuse cases were shrouded in secrecy. Hence, the work of the WTC committee and the regular reports in the *Irish Citizen* offer an important counter-narrative to the dominant discourses about Irish society in the early decades of the twentieth century. In addition, as I have argued throughout this chapter, the work of groups like the WTC committee reveal the range of issues taken up by the suffrage movement in Ireland and so demonstrate the extent to which this was far more than a single issue, votes for women, movement.

NOTES

1. *Irish Citizen*, February 1919.
2. *Irish Citizen*, 19 June 1915.
3. Holton, S. 'The suffrage and the average woman', *Women's History Review*, 1, 1 (1992), pp. 9–24, p. 13.
4. See, for example, Murphy, C. 'The Religious Context of the Women's Suffrage Campaign in Ireland', *Women's History Review*, 6, 4 (1997) pp. 549–65; Ryan, L. 'Traditions and Double Moral Standards, the Irish Suffragists' critique of nationalism', *Women's History Review*, 4, 4 (1995) pp. 487–503; and *Gender, identity and the Irish Press, 1922–37: Embodying the Nation* (New York: Edwin Mellen Press, 2002).
5. Cited in Offen, K., *European Feminisms 1700–1950: a political history* (Stanford: Stanford University Press, 2000), p. 223.
6. Rendall, J. 'Women and the Public Sphere', *Gender and History*, 11, 3 (1999), pp. 475–88, and Ryan, M. *Women in Public: between ballots and banners* (Baltimore: John Hopkins University Press, 1990).
7. Rendall, op cit.
8. See the work of Nielson Varty, C. 'A career in Christian Charity: women's benevolence and the public sphere in a mid-nineteenth century Canadian city', *Women's History Review*, 14, 2, (2005) pp. 243–64 as well as Rendall and M. Ryan op cit.
9. *Irish Citizen*, June/July 1919.
10. *Irish Citizen*, 13 March 1915.
11. *Irish Citizen*, 18 July 1914.
12. *Irish Citizen*, 15 July 1914.
13. *Irish Citizen*, 22 August 1914.
14. *Irish Citizen*, 18 July 1914.
15. *Irish Citizen*, 29 August 1914.
16. *Irish Citizen*, 12 September 1914.
17. *Irish Citizen*, 26 September 1914.
18. *Irish Citizen*, 11 July 1914.
19. *Irish Citizen*, September 1916.
20. *Irish Citizen*, 4 September 1915.
21. *Irish Citizen*, 26 June 1915.
22. Ibid.
23. For an overview of this discussion, see Louise Ryan, *Irish Feminism and the Vote: an anthology of the Irish Citizen Newspaper* (Dublin: Folens, 1996).

24. *Irish Citizen*, November 1917.
25. *Irish Citizen*, July 1919.
26. ibid.
27. Bland, L. *Banishing the Beast* (London: Penguin, 1995).
28. For a discussion of similar issues in Canada, see 'A Career in Christian Charity' and Mackintosh, P.G. 'Scrutiny in the modern city: the domestic public and the Toronto Local Council of Women at the turn of the twentieth century', *Gender, Place and Culture*, 12, 1 (2005) pp. 29–48.
29. For a discussion of the campaigns in Australia, see Lake, M. 'The Inviolable Woman: feminist conceptions of citizenship in Australia, 1900–45', *Gender and History*, 8, 2 (1996), pp. 197–211.
30. *Banishing the Beast*, p. 122.
31. *Irish Citizen*, 26 September 1914.
32. *Irish Citizen*, 4 September 1915.
33. See *Banishing the Beast* for a full discussion of early feminist campaign work around venereal diseases.
34. *Irish Citizen*, 19 June 1915.
35. *Irish Citizen*, 14 August 1915.
36. Rendall, p. 485.
37. *Irish Citizen*, editorial, 14 August 1915.
38. *Irish Citizen*, September 1919.
39. ibid.
40. *Irish Citizen*, September 1919.

CHAPTER SIX

'Great Gas' and 'Irish Bull': Humour and the Fight for Irish Women's Suffrage

CLÍONA MURPHY

P.S. – Mary Longfield rang me up on the telephone about an hour ago. She said she could not sleep until she knew what an "unsexed female" was. I said: "Of course, a new breed of Irish Bull!"[1]

INTRODUCTION

Many are familiar with humorous portrayals of women looking for the vote. The cartoons and stereotypes are often thrown into history textbooks as a way of attracting interest. Indeed, there are plenty of examples in the literature of the international women's suffrage movement. However, the humour had many layers and was not as superficial as a cursory glance through a book or chapter on suffrage would imply. It was practised just as enthusiastically by the suffragists as well as the anti-suffragists or Antis, and Ireland was no exception to this phenomenon.

Humour here has a very broad definition and ranges from funny to satire to parody to sarcasm to clever word play. It involves insight, verbal skill, and being very precise about what one is saying to get one's point across. While humour may have been a way of belittling the opposition (either pro or anti suffrage, depending upon one's perspective), it was also a strategy for drawing attention to a point of view. People were far more likely to remember something and tell others if it gave them a chuckle, had them puzzled for a moment before they saw the joke, or had a sharp cruel edge to it. Moreover, 'humour' was used to get points across a lot more quickly and succinctly than long, rambling treatises and mundane pieces of prose. Sarcastic humour allowed individuals to deal with unpleasant situations, like the suffragists who went through gruelling prison sentences. Overall, humour had a dramatic quality that made one think, smile, smirk or laugh out loud depending upon the sentiment involved. The humour available to historians is the written and visual humour. The former either reported oral humour or was deliberately written with a reader in mind. The latter captured images and stereotypes that struck a chord with their contemporary readers.

Perhaps, the effort to find humour in a serious civil rights issue might be found irreverent by some – then and now. However, the individuals involved in the suffrage movement, and those against it, were rounded, multi-dimensional individuals who were not always serious, and who were not simply synonymous with their 'cause'. They could recognise a humorous situation, could make jokes about serious issues, or could use imagery to demonstrate the absurdity of their opponents' opinions. These attempts at humour are revealing for historians as they provide an alternative view of concerns and perspectives, a view that captures attitudes normally lost in historical documentation.

The fight for suffrage was a very serious topic to the women involved in the cause. There were those who were prepared to break the law, go to jail and hunger-strike. For some, the fight for the vote was the main focus. For others, it was one of a number of serious concerns like domestic abuse, the white slave trade, inequity before the law, temperance, the right to enter the professions and so on. Being a suffragist in the West at the turn of the twentieth century was a pretty bleak prospect with only a few rays of hope coming from parts of the world that were enfranchised like New Zealand, Australia, and a few states in the United States.

Yet, humour was prevalent wherever suffragists appeared. The English science fiction writer and noted author of *War of the Worlds* (1898), H.G. Wells, had fun with the English suffragettes in his novel *Ann Veronica* (1909).[2] This is the story of a young woman who, for a while, joins the suffragettes in London, but eventually settles back into domesticity. During the process, Wells introduces the reader to the various stereotypes of the suffragists and anti-suffragists alike. In *The Strange Death of Liberal England* (1934), historian George Dangerfield portrays the suffragettes as frustrated and sex-deprived, and was of the opinion that 'it would be ingenious to suppose that the suffragette was ultimately concerned with anything so remarkable as suffrage'.[3] Cartoons in magazines like *Puck*, in the United States, portrayed both the changing role of women and the fears of those who opposed that change. One such cartoon made fun of an Irish policeman in New York telling an Italian immigrant to treat his wife better; when he goes home he is served hand and foot by his own wife who is glad he stood up for the Italian woman. She is oblivious to the irony of the situation.[4]

The same stereotypes and allusions are to be found in Ireland, and link the Irish movement to the international movement. Phrases like 'shrieking sisterhood', 'unsexed females', 'howling viragoes' seeped in from British and American culture. They were meant to ridicule the suffragists by making them appear strident and unfeminine. However, there were also distinguishing characteristics regarding humour and the Irish suffragists that reflect political, cultural and social differences in Ireland. Irish women were accused of being part of an English movement, and of being anti-nationalist. Along with that, there was, to some, the comical reality of them belonging to a suffrage movement which had no native parliament to demand the vote from. It was reiterated over and over again that they should focus on getting an Irish parliament before going after the franchise.

Readers of this volume will be either aware of, or have access to, the histories of the movement in Ireland.[5] The early women's suffrage movement started in the 1870s with the founding of the Irish Women's Suffrage and Local Government Association by the Haslams. Carmel Quinlan's book title, *Genteel Revolutionaries*, backs up the general perception of this organisation's genteel yet determined nature.[6] For a number of diverse reasons, explored elsewhere, suffragists in Ireland became much more active at the beginning of the twentieth century. Several different organisations were formed reflecting diverse shades of religious and political opinion. A branch of the League for Opposing Women's Suffrage also was formed. Hence, the demand for women's suffrage was 'out there' and, consequently, we find increasing coverage of the topic, humorous and otherwise.

The area where we have the greatest concentration of available and apparent humour is connected with the most active group, the Irish Women's Franchise League (IWFL). The two couples who founded this group, Frank and Hanna Sheehy Skeffington and James and Margaret Cousins, were well educated, insightful, and articulate, all ingredients that enhance and promote the expression of humour. None of the four was averse to making a joke about themselves or their situation, and they were all the butt of others' joking, ridicule, and sarcasm, especially the men. However, as shall be seen, they were well able to counter the witticisms of their often seemingly less-intelligent opponents.[7]

Their newspaper, the *Irish Citizen*, founded in 1912, has been the subject of study by numerous historians, especially over the last twenty-five years.[8] It contains all aspects of humorous intercourse: the absurd statements of the anti-suffragists; the hilarious antics of suffragists travelling about the country; their encounters with their countrymen; quips from politicians and churchmen; cartoons; caricatures; and humorous and satirical observations of people and incidents abroad. All this can be found in between very serious and sometimes mundane but thorough, small-print coverage of regional, national and international meetings, goings on in parliament, book reviews, and, as Louise Ryan's chapter shows, reports from the courts. This may be why sometimes, then and now, the humour can seem funnier than it actually was.

Humour was more prevalent in the years before 1916. The combined factors of the ongoing war, and its related Irish deaths (documented in detail in the *Citizen*), the emigration of the Cousins to England and then India (although they still occasionally wrote for the *Citizen*), and the murder of Frank Sheehy Skeffington in May 1916 certainly dampened spirits thereafter. Nevertheless, we do see a little uplift in humour after the vote was granted.

HUMOUR ALL AROUND

There was humour within the movement itself about the difficulty of its task, about its opponents, about the court cases, sentencing, and even about hunger striking. A number of the suffrage leaders and prominent members were very good writers, as can be seen from the columns of the *Irish Citizen*, where an excellent and informed standard of writing prevailed. Some of the Irish suffragists and their supporters were actual writers, whose literary skills brought an added punch when they attempted humour. These included L.A.M. Priestley, Edith Somerville, Susan Day, Frank Skeffington, James Cousins, and George Bernard Shaw. The latter was often quoted since he was given to succinct humorous observations that could be easily inserted here and there. The *Irish Citizen* was not the only forum for suffragist humour. It also appeared in reminiscences, autobiographies, short stories, poems, novels, plays, and letters to newspapers.

However, the suffragists were not the only ones enjoying a joke. Segments of Irish society were bemused and sometimes much amused by the women's suffrage 'phenomenon', and joked good (and not so good) humouredly about the suffragists. As elsewhere, those opposed to

1. Mary had a little bag, from the *Lepracaun*, 1912, reproduced
in *Did Your Granny Have a Hammer* (Attic Press)

the suffragists expressed their misgivings on what was going to happen
to women, the family and society if there was female enfranchisement.
These misgivings, made in seriousness, were found by some, then and
now, to be highly amusing. The more outlandish the misgivings, the
more the speaker or writer felt he or she made their point, and, perhaps,
the more absurd or funny they now seem. John Dillon, the deputy leader
of the Irish Parliamentary Party, told a deputation of Irish suffragists:
'Women's suffrage will, I believe, be the ruin of our Western
Civilization. It will destroy the home, challenging the headship of man
laid down by God. It may come in your time – I hope not in mine'.[9] The
Cork Constitution was not so concerned. One of its articles saw the
solution in simpler terms. It recommended that the government give the
suffragists an island 'at present chiefly occupied by such chattering birds
and animals as cockatoos and monkeys, in order that the Suffragettes
may have a parliament of their own . . . '[10]

Newspapers not only provide a record of events, they also leave a
valuable record of attitudes, opinions, tensions and biases. According to
the *Irish Citizen*, the media's failure to report ordinary behaviour, like

2. Biff, Bang Bash, from the *Lepracaun*, 1913, reproduced
in *Did Your Granny Have a Hammer* (Attic Press)

holding a peaceful meeting, was also indicative of their prejudice.[11] Instead, the raucous, the absurd and the comical was what made news regarding the suffragists. Whether or not the media reflected the prevalent humour surrounding the movement or helped create it, probably does not have a clear answer. Perhaps each depended upon the other.[12]

The militancy of the suffragists was very alluring for the cartoonists. It provided the possibility of exaggerating the stereotype of the mentally deranged women in the movement, and, at the same time, making the women's behaviour seem ridiculous. For example, cartoons portrayed tough looking women with hammers and paraffin, and in the act of breaking windows. Rosemary Cullen Owens has drawn attention to the cartoons in The *Lepracaun*, a satirical magazine, in her book *Smashing Times* and her educational packet, *Did your Granny have a Hammer?* These cartoons contained little ditties and sketches lampooning the women, particularly their militant behaviour. In 1912, one appeared which portrayed a constable leading a suffragette with a hammer sticking out of a bag that says 'Vote for Women'. It was accompanied by the following verse:

Mary had a little bag
And in it was a hammer
For Mary was a suffragette
For votes she used to clamour
She broke a pane of glass one day,
Like any naughty boy
A constable came along,
And now she's in Mountjoy.[13]

The following year another cartoon showed women attacking Dublin Castle shouting:

Sing "Biff! Bang! Bash!!"
With a right good smash.
Heave ho, with a one two, three.
A big stone dash
Through a window crash!
Then, hurrah for liberty![14]

The *Citizen* countered with their own series of cartoons on why some men should not have the vote. There was a sequence of cartoons where a drunk, a gambler, and two physically inferior men were portrayed. All cartoons had the same question: 'Should men have the vote?'[15] Other cartoons ridiculed the establishment's paranoia that all women were possible militant suffragists.[16] For example, in May 1913, the *Citizen* had a cartoon with the heading 'The Suffragette Scare in Dublin'. It shows two policemen, one terrified and perspiring profusely, interviewing a bedraggled onion seller holding her baby. The caption states: 'Discovery by the Intilligence [sic] Department of a Disguised Militant Selling Bombs'.

Just as in the cartoons, humour in prose resorted to contemporary stereotypes about the women who became suffragists. The *Catholic Bulletin* published a short story in 1912 called 'Kitty's Fight for Freedom'. The protagonist's friend, Sophia Moore, had joined the suffragists and was a 'spinster of uncertain age'. 'The firelight that showed the curves of Kitty's rosy cheeks, and the soft masses of her brown hair' revealed 'her friend as thin and hatchet faced'.[17] Such caricatures of suffragists abound and can be found internationally. In H.G. Wells' *Ann Veronica*, Miss Miniver is described in the stereotypical fashion of the time that was deemed to be amusing and acceptable:

When she gets it, what will she do with it?

3. Ballot Box, reproduced in *Did Your Granny Have a Hammer* (Attic Press)

Miss Miniver looked out on the world through large emotional blue eyes that were further magnified by the glasses she wore, and her nose was pinched and pink and her mouth was whimsically petulant. Her glasses moved quickly as her glance travelled from face to face . . . On her lapel was an ivory button bearing the words "Votes for Women".

Ann Veronica, just like Kitty above, eventually left the suffragettes and made a 'respectable' marriage.

In her study, *The Spectacle of Women*, Lisa Tickner quotes from the *Daily Mirror* in 1914, which asserted: 'There is no longer any need for the militants to wear their colours or their badges. Fanaticism has set its seal upon their faces and left a peculiar expression which cannot be mistaken'.[18] Du Bois and Dumenil would seem to agree when they assert, referring to the American situation, that 'ridicule is a means for dealing with changes in gender patterns'. They state that many jokes in the American magazine, *Puck*, rested 'on stereotypes of women, from the mannish middle-class suffragist to the culturally backward female immigrant'.[19] This underscores that, contrary to general opinion, humour was not always funny and was frequently cruel.

The Irish suffragists were well aware of the prevalent view of their members not conforming to feminine ideals. There is an account of a short imaginary conversation in the *Irish Citizen* in 1914, entitled 'A Railway Dialogue', which takes place in a train carriage. The participants are John Redmond, leader of the Irish Parliamentary Party, a suffragist, T.W. Russell, MP, and a 'Womanly Woman'. The 'Womanly Woman' does not say much, except to advise Mr Redmond not to 'enter into a dispute' with the suffragist. Clearly her inclusion in this little skit, and her very label, is an indication that the author appreciates, and is amused by, the fact that the anti-suffragists do not see herself and her ilk as very 'womanly'.[20] However, Tickner, in her work on England, states the definition of 'womanly woman' was one that both sides fought over.[21] Her assertion is reinforced by the *Citizen*'s complaint about the *Evening Herald* 'being hypnotised by the ancient caricatures of the "masculine" and viragoish type of suffragists'. The *Citizen* went on to claim that the 'most essentially "womanly" women feel most keenly the wrong inflicted on their sex'.[22]

Frank Sheehy Skeffington may have sought to undermine the unattractive suffragist stereotype in his one-act comedy, *The Prodigal Daughter*, a humorous portrayal of Irish society's reaction to the suffrage movement. It is interesting that he gave the play the subtitle 'a comedy', and did not make it a serious drama which, judging by its subject matter, it could well have been. The play is about a young suffragette, Lily Considine, who has just been released from Mountjoy prison, and is arriving home in the 'country' facing the reaction of friends and family. Lily is portrayed as a practical young woman, spontaneous and full of life, much more level-headed and appealing than Miss Miniver or Sophia Moore, described above.

The play is replete with caricatures of those opposed to women's suffrage: a befuddled local priest; a slightly intoxicated father; and a prim and proper anti-suffragist married sister ('It's well Maggie's married; Arthur Rafferty would never have looked at her if this had happened before the wedding'). Her mother declares: 'Och, there's no end to the worries this unfortunate girl is bringin' on us with her sufragettin' [sic].' The play makes fun of attitudes which deemed being a suffragist as ruining one's chances for a happy life, including marriage: 'No decent man in Ballymission will ever look at her.' It also takes a few stabs at nationalists like the Ancient Order of Hibernians and their attempts to disrupt the suffragists.[23]

The script of the play was published in the *Citizen* in 1914.[24] Despite being a comedy, it can be considered as an interesting primary source on

4. Gambler, from the *Irish Citizen*, June 14, 1913

the IWFL at that point in time. A commentary on the play appeared in the *Citizen* two months later which was close to the mark when it stated:

> There is hardly a sentence of the play that will not a century hence require, as footnote an extract from the "Irish Times" or "Freeman's Journal", in order to carry proof to an awakened posterity that men and women in the first decade of the twentieth century were the fools they were when brought up against the touchstone of a great principle like woman suffrage as embodied in the deeds and words of Lily Considine, a forerunner of the coming race of free women.[25]

So, even though Frank Sheehy Skeffington called it a 'comedy', its content is as valuable to the historian as a serious portrayal of the movement. This underscores that comedy/humour should not be taken lightly as a historical source!

BEING RIDICULED IN PUBLIC

Suffragists in the IWFL sought to counter the stereotypes in the media by distributing the *Irish Citizen* and by public speaking. In *The Prodigal Daughter*, Lily declared:

I mean to say I am going to wake up Ballymission – or, at all events, the women of Ballymission. I'll canvass them from house to house, and sell the suffrage papers. I'll get father to sell them in the shop as well. And I'll ride into Malmoy on fair days and sell them there.[26]

Her brother responds: 'That'll be great gas, Lily.' And, for some, it was 'great gas'. KSCO'B talks about her amusing experience selling the *Irish Citizen* in Sligo. One of the copies she sold 'after much bartering, found its way into the hold-all of a farmer's wife, who asseverated that she didn't understand what I was saying, but that she would take the paper, because her husband always liked to know what was going on – an excellent example for doubtful purchasers!'[27]

Indoor and outdoor meetings were held throughout the country. The extent of the movement is evident from 'The Suffrage Map of Ireland' printed in the *Citizen* in 1913.[28] Clearly, promoting a radical cause in public for women's suffrage anywhere was bound to prompt ridicule. In Ireland, where it conflicted with nationalist sentiment, the Catholic Church and a conservative rural public, that reaction was sometimes quite vocal. It is debatable whether the suffragists' public appearances contradicted or supported the caricatures. Their own reports of their public inter-actions are a combination of self-congratulation on what a good job they were doing, and descriptions of their boisterous and sometimes hilarious encounters.

Margaret Cousins states in her joint autobiography that these meetings around the country 'forced us to do things for which we had no training, pushing us into dreaded and undesired publicity; bringing ridicule, scorn, misrepresentation'.[29] Obviously, public speaking did not always come naturally, and Margaret Cousins rehearsed open-air speaking, in what is now a much quoted image, 'in a field behind our house with only an ass for my audience'.[30] Lily, in Sheehy Skeffington's play, wondered where she might hold open-air meetings: 'Well, I'll just have to speak from the wall of the chapel yard, after Mass the same as the United League organiser does.' She does admit: 'I'm very nervous about public speaking, and I want some more coaching. But, maybe again, it might be as well for me to plunge into it at once.'[31] Such enthusiasm for 'plunging in' suggests that those who ventured out to do public speaking were the types who were also ready to have some fun.

Humorous banter was often part of the interaction when the suffragists faced the public, with women gaining expertise in responding to jokes, jeers and taunts the more often they occurred. Apparently,

" Ma dear fella, we cann't give Votes to Women. They are physically and mentally
our inferiors."

5. Physically and Mentally Inferior, from the *Irish Citizen*, September 6, 1913

going to women's suffrage meetings (whatever side one was on) became a form of entertainment: 'On November 5th the various speakers at big demonstrations in Cavan were subjected to severe heckling, the crowd hugely enjoying the apt retorts of the women. . . .'[32]

Further south the same year, 1913, students from UCC went to a Munster Women's Franchise meeting at the Council Chamber in the City Hall ' . . . with the obvious intention of making a noise; but they abandoned the intention when Mrs Park rose to speak, and instead listened quietly to what she had to say'.[33] Whether the speaker was an American, like Mrs Park, or was Irish or English, it was just as entertaining.

When the leader of the English WSPU, Mrs Pankhurst, spoke at the Cork City Hall, despite the largely favourable audience, there was some noise at the back of the hall. According to the *Cork Free Press*, this was due 'to the potency of Irish whiskey'. On a visit to Longford the following year, Hanna Sheehy Skeffington had a similar experience. She was amused that 'one interrupter who essayed dubious jests was sternly quelled, and we were apologetically informed that he was "no Longfordman", an excuse which seems all sufficient to the native'.[34] In

the same article, she also reminisces about her visit to Carrick where
there was:

> A howling raging mob, led by a drunken virago. In spite of Lent,
> in spite of the proximity of the church, they paraded the space
> before the hotel, creating a pandemonium for over two hours with
> motor-bombs, savage yells and obscene jeers, mock "suffrage"
> orations and wild charges across the street.

Such public spectacles were probably not so funny at the time. It is
interesting that Sheehy Skeffington used the word 'virago' to deride her
female opponents, a word usually used to denounce suffragists.

Susanne R. Day, suffragist, writer, and poor law guardian lampooned
the attitudes of people in a small town outside Cork in her quasi-
fictional book, *The Amazing Philanthropists*. When a suffragist was due
to speak to the local Young Men's Society, its governing body was
assured that she was not a fit or proper person to address the young men
of Ballybawn: 'the innocent lambs who . . . would never recover, religion
would be abjured morals blasted, the society disrupted'.[35] The protagonist of the book writes in jest to her friend, Jill, attempting to portray
what she believed to be the absurd sentiments of those around her:

> And, my child, deeply as it grieves me to say it, we now know that
> all Suffragists are children of the Scarlet Woman; they violate the
> sanctity of the home; invite men to become members of their
> leagues in order to encourage – well, let me quote Miley –
> "shocking immorality among women is becoming a marked feature
> of the movement"; they are freaks, degenerates, "unsexed females".

She concludes her letter to Jill by writing:

> P.S. – Mary Longfield rang me up on the telephone about an hour
> ago. She said she could not sleep until she knew what an "unsexed
> female" was. I said: "Of course, a new breed of Irish Bull!"[36]

Day's participation in an actual suffrage meeting in Kerry, in 1913,
suggests the audience she encountered were not exactly docile like the
men of Ballybawn:

> In Killorglin there was the largest crowd. A thick mass of men and
> women standing at the back, and chairs filled, with the exception

6. Scarem Skirt, from the *Lepracaun*, 1912,
reproduced in *Smashing Times* (Attic Press)

of the front row. They inclined to be facetious at first, and "out for
a lark" many of them. . . . The inevitable "local celebrity" sat
prominently in the front row, shouting approbriation, but a quiet
"please don't interrupt" from the platform was taken in good part,
and he too, composed himself to listen.[37]

For some hecklers the appearance of male suffragists or supporters was
a further reason to have a joke. Even George Bernard Shaw, who was a
supporter of the Irish Women's Suffrage Movement, and whose
witticisms are often quoted in the *Irish Citizen*, participated in the
humour: 'I have seen that miserable domestic pet, the male suffragist,
hauled to the platform between stalwart females, and made to sit up on
his hind legs and beg.'[38]

James Cousins put it another way:

When I stayed away from your Phoenix Park meetings for a while,
I became aware of the fact that it was quite clear to a section of
your audience that I stayed away because my wife compelled me.
When at last I turned up to be exhibited as a specimen of the tame
husbands of the Irish Women's Franchise League, it was quite

" Mr. Judge said the movement was one in which there was no room for the ladies.
They would want at least two million pounds, and the ladies could form a
society, and collect money for that, and put their hearts and souls into it. (Cheers)."
—" Irish Volunteer."

7. Irish Volunteer Fund, from *Irish Citizen*, May 16, 1914

evident that that section had settled, in the thing it regards as its
mind, that I had come because my wife had compelled me![39]

The heckling did not deter the suffragists and, indeed, they were like
missionaries forging ahead with a zeal to bring the 'good news'. In a
little article called 'Dreamy Roscommon', the *Citizen* commented that:
'If the West is awake, some of the western midlands would seem to be
still in a dreamy condition.' It was referring to a recent meeting of the
'Board of Guardians' where it was suggested that two women be 'co-opted
on the Board'. This was objected to because 'we want no hatchet throwers
in the Boardroom' (a referral to a hatchet being fired at Asquith in Dublin
in 1912). Two men were co-opted instead. The *Citizen* asked: 'What
suffrage society will undertake the task of waking up Roscommon?'[40]

RIDICULING THE ANTIS

The suffragists also enjoyed dealing with their opponents. The Antis in
Ireland were nowhere near as well organised, or as numerous, as in

8. Angel of Freedom, from the *Irish Citizen*, March 15, 1913

England. However, they did start to become more public in 1912. As has already been argued in the English case:

> It was possible that the anti position was more powerful when unarticulated; that as a set of *a priori* assumptions passed off as common sense it was hard to contest. Shrewder suffragists welcomed the advance of their opponents as "the best thing that has yet happened in England". Once anti-suffrage opinion was organised publicly it was obliged to mobilise residual prejudice into rational argument, and in doing so it helped to clear away any indifference, which in the suffragists' view was the most serious obstacle to their own campaign.[41]

When suffragists went to anti-suffragist meetings, they experienced what it was like to be at the other side of the platform, being entertained. One such meeting occurred in May 1913. According to the *Irish Citizen*: 'The Anti-Suffrage meeting in Dublin on Tuesday was delightful. Miss Morton, in a burst of candour, said it reminded her of *Alice in Wonderland*. Mrs Greatbatch elicited loud applause by the statement that many suffragists thought the Antis ought to be in the Ark or the British Museum. It was a fairly accurate summing up.' The *Citizen* went on to comment:

> The Molesworth Hall, which holds about 300, was about one-third full: and fully half the audience were suffragists who had come for a night's entertainment. They certainly got it. . . . There were about ten people on the platform, and at most thirty or forty sympathisers in the body of the hall. We fancy that about exhausts the strength of anti-suffragism in Dublin – outside the brothels.[42]

It seems clear that women suffragists, not surprisingly, believed the anti-suffragists had little sense of humour, and the suffragists appeared to enjoy ridiculing and caricaturing them. The *Citizen* wrote: 'We can cordially commend the *Anti Suffrage Review* to suffragists as a great help in propaganda. The cartoon also is worth the penny!'[43] The *Citizen* frequently published spoofs of the anti-suffrage mentality, and also actual pieces about or by anti-suffragists that they thought were funny. These included snippets with anti-suffrage punchlines. Under the heading, *Sancta Simplicitas*, the following insert was published in March 1913:

> Extract from a school essay by a boy of 14, striving to be impartial on the question of Votes for Women: "To this great question as to all great questions, there are two sides: first, there is the woman's side, then there is the side of humanity and common-sense".[44]

On May 22 1915, 'M.E.' in the *Citizen* composed a mock 'Examination in International Affairs' for male anti-suffragists. Female anti-suffragists were advised that they need not take it since, according to Antis, they were allegedly 'incapable of grasping' international affairs. The 'Exam' contained five essay questions, among which included:

1. Justify the policy of consulting Australia (where women vote) as to Imperial affairs and refusing to enfranchise English women.
2. Use adjectives to differentiate between (a) an English soldier who seduced an English girl and (b) a German soldier who outraged a Belgian girl. In each case describe the character of the girl as the press would see it.[45]

The Irish personification of anti-suffragism was John Redmond, the leader of the Irish Parliamentary Party. The *Citizen*, in an article in 1913

MR. JOHN REDMOND "We may differ about the independence of Irish men, but we are agreed on the
MR. F. E. SMITH subjection of Irish women."

9. Subjection of Irish Women, originally in the *Lepracaun*, 1913,
reproduced in *Smashing Times* (Attic Press)

entitled 'Wedding Presents', observed that the newspapers 'published long lists of the wedding presents received by Miss Johanna Redmond, on her marriage to Mr Max Green, chairman of the Irish Prisons Board'. According to the *Citizen*, the lists were not complete: 'No mention was made of certain interesting and ingenious reminders of Votes for Women which were received by the bride's father on the morning of the wedding.'[46] Redmond was the subject of 'Our Special St Patrick's Day Cartoon' in the *Irish Citizen* in 1913. He was portrayed by 'EK' as 'The Angel of Freedom' equipped with great big wings and holding a banner stating:

> Hurro! For
> Liberty!!!
> No Irish Woman need Apply
> No Votes for Women
> By order
> The New
> Liberator

One of his feet is on top of a prostrate, bound, woman who has dropped her copy of the *Irish Citizen*. Home Rule appeared to be stamping on women's suffrage. While not straightforwardly funny, the cartoon illustrates what a foe to their cause they believed Redmond to be.[47] Shortly after, according to the *Citizen*:

> The cartoon was seen by all the Dublin Press; but its caustic meaning escaped them until, two months later, the London correspondent of both the "Freeman" and "Telegraph" discovered that it was "offensive". With delightful naivete both papers set out in words the subject of the cartoon – for all the world to see and realize its truth. The oily "Freeman" suppressed the name of this paper for fear of advertising us but its evening brother made up for it by reproducing the cartoon, thus making itself an accessory to the offence and adding to the boom in the *Citizen*. We quite agree that the cartoon is offensive. It shows up one of the most glaring political offences of all time; and we remember the profound words of Holy Writ: "Woe to him by whom the offence cometh".[48]

It is interesting that the St Patrick's Day cartoon two years later was much more optimistic. It shows a benevolent St Patrick with a 'Votes for Women' sash across his chest. The snakes that are being chased out of Ireland carry captions such as 'sham patriotism' (Mr Redmond?), 'municipal corruption', 'white slavery', 'gambling' and other issues seen as undesirable by the suffragists.[49]

As late as 1918, Redmond was still on the minds of the suffragists, and he appears almost to have taken on demonic proportions. Lucy Kingston concluded that 'antagonism to woman suffrage seems to have been inextricably melted into Mr John Redmond's system by some malign fairy'.[50] It was not just Mr Redmond's system. Those who sat in parliament, too, were contaminated. In response to George Bernard Shaw's statement, 'There are some men to whom age brings golf instead of wisdom', Margaret Connery replied: 'There must be an astonishing number of the species in the House of Commons!'[51] Another writer in the *Citizen*, in April 1913, observed: 'Parliament is at present convulsed by a grave problem, on the proper solution of which the comfort of its members, and therefore the stability of the Empire, depends – namely, whether members should be permitted to have sausages with their tea.' The writer concluded: 'No wonder there is no time to attend to women's claims, when thoughts of legislators are engrossed by this all-important question.'[52] In a similar vein, two years later, *The Cork Weekly Examiner* quoted Tom Kettle in the 'House, on the occasion of the reading of one of the numerous Women's Suffrage Bills'. Kettle's wife, Mary, was a prominent suffragist and was the sister of Hanna Sheehy Skeffington:

"Mr Speaker," he cried in his rich Dublin accent and almost drawling intonation, "they say that if we admit women here as members the House will lose in mental power." He flung a finger round the packed benches: "Mr Speaker," he continued, "it is impossible." The house roared with laughter. "They tell me that the house will suffer in morals. Mr Speaker, I don't believe that either." The applause rang out again at this double hit. Rarely has the House had a more appealing picture than that of this tall dark-haired boy defending the women's cause with all the gallantry and wit of his race.[53]

Despite this light hearted banter, Margaret Connery concluded that it 'would be futile to look for a saving sense of humour amongst the quaint fossils who control the machinery of the British House of Commons'. Because:

We have the preposterous proposal embodied in the Speaker's Electoral Reform Scheme now before the House to confer the Parliamentary Franchise on women – with a limitation imposing an age barrier of 30 or 35! British women will wake up one of those days to find that English Law has solemnly ordained that a woman only reaches years of discretion after she has passed middle age. This scheme is on the level of intelligence with the enactment passed for Ireland last Autumn, that Irish clocks should be put forward twenty-five minutes ahead of the sun. Britons apparently are not going to want to be content to rule the waves, they also want "a place in the sun".[54]

Not surprisingly, the British Prime Minister, Herbert Asquith, too, was a long- running joke in the *Citizen* until party leadership was taken over by Lloyd George in 1916. Ever since his visit to Dublin in 1912, where he was attacked by two English suffragists, the *Citizen* had fun talking about him, from finding it humorous that Mrs Asquith wanted the hatchet that was thrown into her husband's carriage[55] to observing changes in Irish public opinion towards him. In October 1914, in a little article entitled 'The Fickle Mob', the *Citizen* quotes a suffragist distributing leaflets outside of Asquith's meeting who noticed a difference from Asquith's previous meeting in 1912:

On the Asquith night in 1912, a typical street-boy came up to me and said, "Suffragettes! You should all be ducked in the Liffey" –

amid the general approval of the crowd. This time, a youth of the same type approached me and said, "Asquith and Redmond ought to be shot, the pair of them". The *Citizen* concluded "So time brings its revenges".[56]

A few months later, in another little article called 'A Happy Atmosphere', *The Citizen* could not keep itself from sarcasm when speaking about the British Prime Minister, eight months into the First World War:

> Mr Asquith, speaking in the House of Commons on Monday, said that "it would be most unpatriotic to revive the spirit of controversy in place of the happy atmosphere in which we have lived during the last few anxious months". If Mr Asquith were an Irishman, this collocation of happiness and anxiety would be called a bull. But perhaps Mr Asquith means that this time, though anxious for people of keen sensibilities and imagination, is a happy one for him, inasmuch as he is spared all trouble from rebellious suffragettes and others. Doubtless he is quite right.[57]

The *London Opinion* was quoted in 1915 as describing Asquith's attitude 'on things in general' as follows: 'I cannot understand how anything I may or may not have said could have given anyone any impression whatever.' The *Citizen* retorted: 'On one point, however, Mr Asquith has revealed a surprising and unprecedented definiteness: he intends to continue drawing his present salary, and regards any attempts to tamper with Ministers' or members' salaries as "highly controversial". Woman, as usual, to "pay up and shut up".'[58] Later the same year, the *Citizen* turned its sardonic eye from the British Parliament westwards to events in the United States. In a piece entitled 'The Latest Anti Argument', the *Citizen* lamented that:

> It is a pity we have no coloured population in these countries. American Antis discover that the reason they cannot give the vote to white women is that some black women might get it; apparently the male negro voter doesn't worry them half as much ... One can imagine Mr Asquith explaining to a deputation how eagerly he would enfranchise white women, but that he feared giving the negro population preponderance! But here at home politicians have to invent other bogeys: Home Rule or Clericalism, Woman's innate Conservatism or Woman's rampant and equally innate Radicalism. A negro population would be much simpler.[59]

The *Citizen* observed wryly that the situation was much simpler in Mexico where, according to a quote in the 'Maryland Suffrage News', equal suffrage 'may be said to prevail to a large extent. The women are not permitted to vote and the men are afraid to.'[60]

THE VOTE

After the vote was granted, albeit in a limited manner, there was some humorous coverage about the 1918 election, on both sides. The *Saturday Herald* had a cartoon of a feisty looking woman with a hammer in hand, leaning on a ballot box. Underneath is a jug of paraffin. The caption states: 'When she gets it, what will she do with it?'[61] That question would not be answered fully for a while. When women finally could vote in the December 1918 election, the following tongue-in-cheek account of the election in the *Irish Citizen* reveals that while the worst fears of the Antis were not realised, the humour had survived:

> The election passed quietly is[sic] Ireland, and the women destroyed once again many pleasant male illusions about them, the disappointing creatures. Babies were washed and husbands were fed on Election day just as they are Washing Day or at spring cleaning. The Police Court returns showed no increase in domestic strife, such as was predicted by the duties if a wife voted against her husband's favourite. Women's presence, as usual, raised the tone and purified the atmosphere. There was practically no drunkeness or disorder. Babies were wheeled along to booths and police looked after them while mothers voted – sometimes fathers even condescended to the task.[62]

NOTES

1. Susanne R. Day, *The Amazing Philanthropists*, (London: Sidgewick and Jackson, 1916) p. 21.
2. H.G. Wells, *Ann Veronica* was first published in 1909. (The edition referred to here was published by Virago, London, 1980.)
3. George Dangerfield, *The Strange Death of Liberal England 1910–1914*, (New York: Capricorn Books, 1961, 10th edition), p. 147. The book was first published in 1934, close enough to the time of the suffrage movement to reflect some viewpoints from the time.
4. Reproduced in Carol Ellen DuBois and Lynn Dumenil, *Through Women's Eyes: An American History with Documents* (Bedford: St. Martin's Press, 2004), p. 394.

5. For studies on the suffrage movement, see, for example, Rosemary Cullen Owens, *Smashing Times: A History of the Irish Women's Suffrage Movement, 1889–1922* (Dublin: Attic Press, 1984); Cliona Murphy, *The Women's Suffrage Movement and Irish Society in the Early Twentieth Century* (Hertfordshire: Harvester, 1989); Margaret Ward, *Hanna Sheehy Skeffington: A Life* (Dublin: Attic, 1997); Louise Ryan, *Irish Feminism and the Vote* (Dublin: Folens, 1996).
6. Carmel Quinlan, *Genteel Revolutionaries* (Cork: Cork University Press, 2001).
7. See in particular Margaret Ward, *Hanna Sheehy Skeffington: A Life* (Dublin: Attic Press, 1997); Leah Levenson, *With Wooden Sword* (New York: Syracuse University Press, 1983) and James and Margaret Cousins, *We Two Together* (Madras: Ganesh, 1950).
8. See, for example, the work of Rosemary Cullen Owens, Dana Hearne, Maria Luddy, Cliona Murphy, Louise Ryan and others cited elsewhere throughout this book.
9. Hanna Sheehy Skeffington, 'Reminiscences of an Irish Suffragette', in A.D. Sheehy Skeffington and R. Owens, *Irish Women's Struggle for the Vote* (Dublin: Arlen House, 1975), p. 18.
10. *Cork Constitution*, April 1912, p. 4.
11. *Irish Citizen*, June 22 1912, p. 34.
12. I go into a lot more detail on press coverage in my book, Cliona Murphy, *The Women's Suffrage Movement and Irish Society in the Early Twentieth Century* (Brighton: Harvester Press, 1989), pp. 122–6.
13. *The Lepracaun*, 1912, reproduced as postcard in, and cover of, *Did Your Granny have a Hammer*, Rosemary Cullen Owens (ed), Attic Press, 48 Fleet Street, Dublin 2.
14. *The Lepracaun*, 1913 *Ibid.*
15. See the following issues of the *Irish Citizen*: 17 May 1913, 14 June 1913, 6 September 1913 (all front page).
16. *Irish Citizen*, 31 May 1913, front page.
17. Nellie O'Connor, 'Kitty's Fight for Freedom', *The Catholic Bulletin*, 1912, pp. 290–301, p. 290.
18. See Lisa Tickner, *The Spectacle of Women* (Chicago: University of Chicago Press, 1988) p. 167.
19. DuBois and Dumenil, p. 393.
20. *Irish Citizen*, 20 June 1914, p. 34.
21. Tickner, p. 167.
22. *Irish Citizen*, 8 June 1912, front page.
23. Murphy, pp. 129–30.
24. Frank Sheehy Skeffington, 'The Prodigal Daughter: A Comedy in One Act', the *Irish Citizen*, 7 November 1914, pp. 196–8.
25. *Irish Citizen*, 26 January 1915, p. 43. The play was performed for a few nights in November 1916. *Irish Citizen*, November 1916, p. 232.
26. Frank Sheehy Skeffington, *The Prodigal Daughter*, p. 197.
27. *Irish Citizen*, 25 October 1913, p. 182.
28. *Irish Citizen*, 23 August 1913, p. 109.
29. James and Margaret Cousins, *We Two Together* (Madras: Ganesh and Co., 1950), p. 166.
30. Ibid.
31. *The Prodigal Daughter* p. 197.
32. *Irish Women's Franchise League Report*, 1913 p. 6 Also quoted in Luddy, p. 277.

33. *Irish Citizen*, 20 December 1913, p. 255.
34. Hanna Sheehy Skeffington, 'Votes for Women in the West', *Irish Citizen*, 14 March 1914. The full article for those interested is in Louise Ryan's *Irish feminism and the vote: an anthology of the Irish Citizen newspaper, 1912–1920* (Dublin: Folens, 1996).
35. Susanne R. Day, *The Amazing Philanthropists* (London: Sidgewick and Jackson, 1916), p. 20.
36. Day, *The Amazing Philanthropists*, p. 21.
37. S.R. Day, 'Touring in Kerry' *Irish Citizen*, 20 September 1913, p. 143 (also in Ryan p. 38).
38. Quoted in Murphy, p. 117.
39. *Votes for Women*, 27 January 1911, p. 271. See also Margaret Ward, Chapter 5 for more on Frank Sheehy Skeffington's public role in the movement.
40. *Irish Citizen*, 8 February 1913, p. 298.
41. Tickner, p. 99.
42. *Irish Citizen*, 31 May 1913, p. 12.
43. *Irish Citizen*, 5 October 1912, front page.
44. *Irish Citizen*, March 1913, p. 322.
45. *Irish Citizen*, 22 May 1915, p. 3.
46. *Irish Citizen*, 18 January 1913, p. 774.
47. *Irish Citizen*, 15 March 1913.
48. *Irish Citizen*, 24 May 1913, front page.
49. *Irish Citizen*, 20 March 1915, front page.
50. Lucy Kingston, 'The Irishwoman's Outlook', *The Englishwoman*, 37, (January– March 1918), quoted in Maria Luddy, *Women in Ireland, A Documentary History, 1800–1918* (Cork: Cork University Press, 1995), p. 287.
51. *Irish Citizen*, April 1917, p. 257.
52. *Irish Citizen*, 26 April 1913, p. 386.
53. Quoted in *Irish Citizen*, October 1916, p. 230. Kettle was a supporter of women's suffrage, and husband of prominent suffragist Mary Kettle (formerly Sheehy). However, he irked members of the IWFL when he decided the struggle for Home Rule should come first. For more on Kettle, see Murphy, *The Women's Suffrage Movement*, pp. 183–4. See also Ward, p. 78.
54. *Irish Citizen*, April 1917, p. 257. The muddled reference to time here was in connection to the 1916 law where Greenwich Mean Time was extended to the whole of Ireland in 1916.
55. *Irish Citizen*, 5 October 1912, p. 155.
56. *Irish Citizen*, 3 October 1914, p. 154.
57. *Irish Citizen*, 20 March 1915, p. 340.
58. *Irish Citizen*, 25 December front page.
59. *Irish Citizen*, 21 August 1915, front page.
60. *Irish Citizen*, 28 August 1915, front page.
61. *Saturday Herald*, 14 December 1918 (in *Did your Granny have a Hammer?*).
62. *Irish Citizen*, January 1919, front page.

CHAPTER SEVEN

Suffragettes and the Transformation of Political Imprisonment in Ireland, 1912–1914

WILLIAM MURPHY

INTRODUCTION

Ireland's brief militant suffrage campaign occupies a central place in the narrative of the Irish female suffrage movement. This has ensured that suffragette prisoners are better served by historians than many other Irish political prisoners. The accent of the extant scholarship on suffragette prisoners has naturally emphasised their role in the suffrage movement,[1] but these women have not been accorded the pivotal place they deserve in the narrative of political imprisonment in Ireland. The suffragettes were not the first Irish political prisoners to protest their prison treatment. For some nationalists in the nineteenth century the prison became an arena of conflict and a source of propaganda, transforming imprisonment into a political opportunity.[2] However, the suffragettes employed concerted levels of prison militancy which were unprecedented in an Irish context. This chapter charts the progress of the suffragette crisis in Irish prisons through four distinct phases – each marked by particular attitudes and tactics – and draws some conclusions as to the legacy of this struggle.

CONTEXT

The Prisons Act of 1877, which established the General Prisons Board (GPB) to control prisons in Ireland, provided for a category of convict called first class misdemeanants, restricted to all those convicted of sedition, seditious libel, or contempt of court.[3] This was the only class in Irish penal law which catered for those who might be regarded as political prisoners. Essentially it facilitated the separation and better treatment of respectable people who had committed respectable crimes. The status was accorded to rare prisoners, almost always men of status and influence. In the opening years of the twentieth century the prison authorities coped comfortably with these occasional individual convicts.

In Britain fundamental changes were taking place. The English prison system became a political battleground as suffragettes mounted a militant campaign in favour of 'Votes for Women'. Quickly, the status of suffragette prisoners and their treatment began to receive attention.[4] The judiciary, penal administrators and politicians were mired in confusion. They dithered when considering the women's prison classification; some were designated first class misdemeanants while many were associated with regular convicts in the second or third divisions. This facilitated the suffragettes in bringing militancy into the prisons by providing a cause around which they generated conflict and publicity.

The conflict escalated in Britain in July 1909, when various members of the Women's Social and Political Union (WSPU) adopted the tactic of hunger strike. In September the authorities responded by beginning to artificially, or forcibly, feed many of those on strike, but again they were inconsistent in their approach. Upon his appointment as Home Secretary in February 1910, Winston Churchill attempted to bring some clarity to the issue of suffragette prison treatment. Wilfrid Scawen Blunt, a former Home Rule MP and land war prisoner who was related through marriage to Lady Constance Lytton, a WSPU prisoner, encouraged Churchill to create a status of 'political prisoner'.[5] Following the advice of Home Office officials, Churchill did not create an actual legal status of 'political prisoner', but *de facto* provided for such a status by empowering the Home Secretary to grant first class misdemeanant conditions to 'prisoners (in the Second Division) who are persons of good antecedents, and who have been convicted of offences which do not involve dishonesty, cruelty, indecency, or serious violence'.[6] Prison rule 243a, or the 'Churchill rule' as it became known, facilitated the improved treatment of many suffragettes, but failed to neutralise prison treatment as a suffragette cause as it did not apply to prisoners given sentences in the third division or with hard labour.

Although the Irish executive did not then face a suffragette campaign, in October 1910 they introduced a similar rule.[7] The first prisoner afforded the benefits of the Irish version of the Churchill rule was not jailed for suffrage activity. On 4 July 1911, Helena Moloney protested against the visit of George V to Dublin by throwing a stone at a portrait of the King and Queen displayed in the window of an optician's shop. She later recalled that: 'At the time no well brought up girl would dream of throwing stones in public, for any purpose whatever. The Suffragettes had not yet gone into real action for their cause, and we would have thought it undesirable – if we had paused to think at all.'[8] When Moloney refused to pay a fine, she was sentenced to a month in prison, but was allowed all the privileges under the Churchill rule.[9] She was released after five days when an anonymous donor – described by Rosamund Jacob as 'some fool' and later identified as Anna Parnell – paid her fine.[10]

In November 1908, Hanna Sheehy Skeffington and Margaret Cousins, along with their feminist husbands, Francis Sheehy Skeffington and James Cousins, founded the Irish Women's Franchise League (IWFL) to pursue a more assertive suffrage policy in Ireland. A vanguard of committed activists quickly emerged. In November 1910, six IWFL members, including Margaret Cousins, were imprisoned in England when they participated in protests organised by the WSPU.[11] On that occasion, Leila Gertrude and Rosalind Cadiz – otherwise known as Margaret and Jane Murphy – excused themselves at the last moment and were not jailed, causing friction with the IWFL for the first, but not the last, time.[12] Several other IWFL members were imprisoned for militant activity in England.[13] 'Prisoners' Nights', when IWFL women recounted their experiences, were a regular feature in the organisation's programme of events by late 1911.[14] Early in the summer of 1912, the IWFL resolved to take militant action within Ireland. On the morning of 13 June 1912, eight women threw stones through the windows of various government offices in Dublin and were arrested. They were Hanna Sheehy Skeffington, Margaret Murphy, Jane Murphy, Marguerite Palmer, Marjorie Hasler, Kathleen Houston, Maud Lloyd and Hilda Webb.[15] The Irish prison system now faced the immediate prospect of suffragette convicts.

CONCILIATION

On 20 June 1912, Sheehy Skeffington, Palmer and the Murphys were convicted and sentenced to one month in prison and a further month on refusal to pay a fine. The *Daily Mail* reported that Sheehy Skeffington stated 'she would personally like to go to Mountjoy Prison, because she wanted to see how political prisoners were treated there, and she would insist on her rights in that respect'.[16] In passing sentence, Judge Swifte indicated that he would have liked to place the women in the first division, but felt that their status was a question for the prison authorities. Sheehy Skeffington later noted that 'no-one in prison ever felt it in their power to grant privileges, but everyone always felt competent enough to withdraw those privileges'.[17] Nonetheless, the authorities' primary impulse was to conciliate and avoid conflict. Without delay, Dublin Castle sanctioned those privileges allowed under the Churchill rule.[18] Other minor matters were addressed; Sheehy Skeffington's and Margaret Murphy's cells were repainted when they complained that the whitewash caused a glare which hurt their eyes. New gas burners were fitted to their cells and they were permitted light until late in the evening.[19]

The women were not satisfied, however, and demanded extended rights to visits and letters, the right to associate during exercise and work, and to be allowed to pursue their professions. Often, when faced with militant political prisoners demanding a status or treatment which could not be accommodated within their world order – the regulations – prison officials were possessed by premonitions of anarchy; however, this had to be balanced against the politic and pragmatic. At first, the GPB argued against extending privileges beyond the Churchill rule.[20] Despite this, the Lord Lieutenant, Lord Aberdeen, ordered the GPB to concede all three points.[21] Within days the Murphys sought further privileges, including access to their own 'lady doctor', Dr Katherine Maguire.[22] Margaret was allowed to see Maguire because she couched the request in terms of medical necessity and not as a right due as a political prisoner.[23] Jane was not allowed to see Maguire; she continued to demand the visit as a right.[24]

The prisoners, especially those who had been jailed in Britain, were impressed by the Irish prison system. Marguerite Palmer's 'Mountjoy Jottings' was typical. She asserted that: 'In Ireland the prison officials seem to have found the art of tempering necessarily strict discipline with kindness – whether it be by an occasional smile, a kindly word, or even a look – there is a distinctly human feeling in the place'.[25] In this phase of protest, the *Irish Citizen* was generally complimentary of the Irish authorities: 'Irish Officialdom, both high and low, has come well out of this first test of its attitude towards suffragist prisoners as compared with the officials on the other side of the Irish Sea.' A week later the paper speculated that 'public opinion is better trained in these matters in a country many of whose foremost politicians passed through prison to prominence'.[26]

On 12 July, Hasler, Houston, Lloyd and Webb were given sentences of six months, but on this occasion the judge specified that they should be treated as first class misdemeanants.[27] What must have seemed like a helpful direction became a complicating factor when the new prisoners immediately sought association with their suffragette colleagues.[28] Under prison rules, the second group – as first class misdemeanants – should not have been associated with the first group, who were classified as ordinary prisoners, even if very privileged ones. Now a growing advocate of flexibility, Major A.F. Owen Lewis, governor of Mountjoy, supported the women's request, arguing that it made both practical and principled sense. Given his staff numbers it was illogical to have two sets of segregated prisoners and, he argued, the principled purpose of segregation was to save this type of prisoner from the indignity of associating with the criminal class. On 15 July, Dr Edgar Flinn, medical member of the GPB, encouraged a decision to allow the new group to associate among themselves, but simply re-iterated the rule on the matter of association between classes of prisoners. Nonetheless, on 16 July, the Lord Lieutenant approved the association of all eight women.[29] This suggests that the impulse to avoid conflict was even stronger among the political authorities in Dublin Castle than it was among the prison officials.

The authorities in general were very publicity conscious. James Dougherty, Under-Secretary of State for Ireland, suppressed a number of the letters which the prisoners sought to send to the press, stating that 'it would form a serious precedent'.[30] On another occasion, Sheehy Skeffington was allowed to see her son, Owen, in her cell rather than in a public reception room when he began to cry loudly: the superintendent feared that the child's tantrum might be reported in a way which would reflect negatively on the prison regime.[31] The politicians were highly motivated to avoid the political difficulties of defending any seemingly harsh treatment of the women. These political sensitivities are emphasised by the Lord Lieutenant's insistence on making the decisions arising from the prisoners' memorials while the Chief Secretary's office insisted on having as much information as possible on the day-to-day situation in Mountjoy.[32] The impact of social standing and influence cannot be ignored. That Sheehy Skeffington was the daughter of David Sheehy, MP, must have heightened sensitivities around these imprisonments. David Sheehy was not well inclined towards suffragism;[33] nevertheless, membership of such a prominent family undoubtedly impacted on the authorities' attitude towards Sheehy Skeffington and her colleagues.

A final factor, which contributed to the authorities' accommodating approach, was the attitude of the suffragettes. In general, these early IWFL prisoners – with the occasional exception of the Murphy sisters – were not confrontational. Owen Lewis described them as 'quiet and orderly',[34] while the *Irish Citizen* reported that prison officials

> . . . who were looking forward to the custody of suffragists with some apprehension, have been agreeably surprised to find them women who, while calmly determined to insist on their right as political prisoners, are perfectly reasonable and perfectly courteous to the official whose duty it is to carry out the regulations.[35]

This led to sympathy for Hasler, Houston, Lloyd and Webb as their longer sentences stretched on. Sir John Irwin, the chairman of Mountjoy's visiting committee, advised the women to petition for early release, indicating that this might be favourably received. The women refused as it was their view 'that having been awarded full political privileges, they ought to serve out their entire sentences without complaint'.[36] Despite this, Irwin wrote to the Lord Lieutenant seeking an early release, stressing that the women were 'exceptionally well behaved'. In early November, Max Green, the new chairman of the GPB, noted that although the prisoners were not entitled to remission – as first class misdemeanant prisoners they had not done the work required to gain remission – the board believed the Lord Lieutenant would want them to be released early. On the following day they were released, over a month before their sentences expired.[37]

CONFLICT

Everything seemed under control until the WSPU intervened, disrupting life for the authorities and for the IWFL. On 18 July 1912, Prime Minister Herbert Asquith visited Dublin. Irish suffragist groups organised a number of peaceful protests; the IWFL prisoners wore black rosettes on the day.[38] The WSPU, however, sent emissaries – Mary Leigh, Gladys Evans, and Lizzie Baker (whose real name was Jennie Baines)[39] – with more radical intentions. They succeeded in throwing a hatchet at Asquith and John Redmond and attempted to set the Theatre Royal ablaze.[40] The relationship between the authorities and these representatives of the WSPU was altogether more fractious. Both sides comported themselves in a much less conciliatory manner. The women were more obdurate and the authorities were sterner.

Initially, all three were remanded to Mountjoy on 19 July.[41] Even before conviction, Leigh was cautioned for persistent whistling[42] and had to be forcibly lifted into the van which arrived to take her to court.[43] The authorities feared a hunger strike; as early as 27 July the medical officials in Mountjoy consulted with doctors in Birmingham prison where Leigh had been forcibly fed in the past.[44] The women were convicted on 6 and 7 August and the sentences were harsh. Baines was convicted of conspiracy and given a sentence of seven months with hard labour. Leigh and Evans were convicted of conspiracy, arson, and explosives charges and were given five years' penal servitude each.[45] On 8 August, all three sent memorials to the Lord Lieutenant, seeking to be treated as political prisoners, and on the same day the eight IWFL prisoners sent memorials, seeking to be associated with the WSPU women.[46] As hard labour and penal servitude prisoners, however, they neither qualified for special status under the first class misdemeanant rules nor the Churchill rule. While the authorities dithered, the three women went on hunger strike on 14 August.[47] This caused a crisis for the authorities, but also for the IWFL prisoners.

From the beginning, the authorities noted a marked difference in attitude between the Murphys and their IWFL colleagues. On one occasion, Jane demanded 'an answer within three days, as after that, I have no alternative but to resort to the Hunger Strike'. The prison authorities characterised the Murphys' more aggressive approach as indicative of 'neurotic tendencies',[48] but the Murphy sisters made their suffragette colleagues equally nervous. In June 1912, IWFL policy ruled out hunger strike and so the Murphys' threats were a cause of concern to the other prisoners. On 19 June, over seventy WSPU members imprisoned in Holloway had embarked on a mass hunger strike.[49] Sheehy Skeffington later complained:

> The prison policy fixed and discussed before militancy was not adhered to, the badge of the league was replaced by that of the WSPU. The Misses C. blamed the league for not catering for them while in prison, repudiated its policy, treated its secretary and members with insolence and discourtesy. They communicated to the WSPU offering to hunger-strike with the English prisoners then in Holloway if the WSPU so desire.

In the event, the WSPU told the Murphys to adhere to the policy of the Irish organisation.[50]

The strike by Leigh, Evans and Baines re-opened this rift. Immediately, the Murphys joined the strike on 14 August. None of the other IWFL prisoners joined the strike on the first day. Then on the afternoon of the second day, Sheehy Skeffington and Palmer – who were due for release on 19 August – joined, but the other four IWFL women did not.[51] Sheehy Skeffington's accusation that the Murphys made the 'situation for the other Irish suffrage prisoners difficult and trying' and acted with a complete 'want of judgement' is certainly derived from her irritation that they had been hurried into hunger strike by the Murphys' actions. There was a lingering bitterness; after release it was with great reluctance that the other IWFL prisoners agreed to share a reception with the Murphys[52] and the sisters were expelled from the IWFL on 4 February 1913. This triggered some sympathetic resignations[53] while the sisters attempted to sue the IWFL over their expulsion; the case was thrown out on the grounds that they were all 'engaged in a criminal conspiracy'.[54]

In prison in August 1912, the authorities quickly removed the privileges of the four striking IWFL women, but simultaneously sought a compromise. On 17 August, Owen Lewis offered concessions to the English women; if they ceased to strike while the government considered their memorials, they would be allowed associate, wear their own clothes and remain in the prison hospital on a hospital diet. Leigh and Evans refused. Owen Lewis reported Leigh as saying:

> If the Government will undertake to give votes to women, I will take my food, and I will gladly do my sentence of five years or longer, but under no other circumstances. You can kill me if you like, and I will gladly die, but I won't give in.

Baines proved less assured. She stated that her hunger strike had the attainment of treatment as a political prisoner as its purpose. Owen Lewis immediately offered her association with the IWFL women and the privileges of a first class misdemeanant if she stopped striking, while stating he could not make this offer to Leigh and Evans as they were penal servitude prisoners. Momentarily, Baines relented. Owen Lewis reported:

> After I left, I am informed that she drank a cup of tea and took some of the jelly, and then dropped the plate on the floor and burst into tears, saying she was a traitor to the cause, and would take no more. I have since had a long talk with her and she persists in her determination to continue the hunger strike.

She vomited most of the tea and jelly she had consumed during her brief waivering.[55]

On 19 August, Baines was released on health grounds along with the four IWFL women who had completed their sentences.[56] Margaret Ward has no doubt that the decision to begin forcible feeding of Leigh and Evans was delayed until the Irish hunger strikers had departed Mountjoy. She is certainly right that the authorities were 'dreading the public furore if Irish women were known to be undergoing forcible feeding'.[57] The GPB sought outside medical opinion from Dr Joseph O'Carroll, who first examined the women on 17 August and did not then advise forcible feeding. After a second visit on 20 August, O'Carroll altered his opinion.[58] That O'Carroll's second visit was delayed until 20 August was surely not an accident.

During the hunger strike, the Irish administration was inundated with petitions from Ireland and Britain, seeking the release of the women or the granting of political status.[59] The Irish Office waged a constant battle in the press to present their side of the situation. They informed the press of the offer of ameliorated conditions made to the prisoners. On 7 September, the *Irish Citizen* published a letter, which stated that the English women could not accept these terms, as they did not include visits or letters, ensuring that the prisoners were still incommunicado and therefore their position might be open to misrepresentation.[60] In what looks like a direct response, on 9 September Edgar Flinn offered Leigh and Evans improved access to newspapers and letters in addition to the previous offer. They reiterated that they would stop when promised the vote.[61]

Forcible feeding was a traumatic process, particularly in the case of Leigh, who resisted. Evans was fed in her own cell, in her own chair, unrestrained, and through the mouth. She gave 'every assistance, placing her own fingers in her mouth to prevent her teeth closing on the tube . . . She has retained all her food'. Leigh was entirely uncooperative. She had to be restrained and fed through the nose. When the doctors discovered that she would immediately vomit, they restrained her in a reclined padded chair for two hours after each feeding.[62] Leigh was released on licence, on 20 September, when the medical officers became alarmed at her health and Evans followed, on 3 October, when Raymond G. Dowdall, medical officer in Mountjoy, reported that she was close to a nervous breakdown.[63] The *Irish Citizen* expressed the opinion that: 'Irish officialdom – shall we add, the Irish Judiciary? – has been taught a terrible lesson'.[64] The GPB certainly reconsidered its policy in the aftermath of the crisis.

ISOLATION

Until Leigh and Evans left Ireland, on 21 December 1912,[65] the GPB faced the real prospect that they might be re-committed for a lengthy period. Upon contemplating this possibility, the GPB suggested a new approach, incorporating three major changes. Firstly, Leigh and Evans should not be held in Mountjoy but Tullamore, a provincial gaol, where they would be isolated from other prisoners, supporters and the press. Secondly, he proposed a reversion to a policy of conciliation. Leigh and Evans should be held in the prison hospital, given a reasonable hospital diet, and treated as patients; 'borderline insane cases'. They should be given a room each, a common sitting room, and 'all possible latitude consistent with safe custody' with the intention of depriving them of any 'ground for considering themselves treated with harshness or indignity'. Finally, he proposed that they should not be forcibly fed and instead warned that they would be 'allowed to starve themselves to death if they so desire'.[66]

On 23 November, Max Green argued that in future not only Leigh and Evans, but all suffrage prisoners, should be held in Tullamore prison. In his opinion, continuing to hold suffragettes in Mountjoy involved 'grave consequences to Prison discipline' while Tullamore provided a location where the suffragettes could be quarantined from a public which was potentially disruptive and a prison population which was potentially disgruntled.[67] At no point did Green allude to a possible problem. Tullamore prison had become infamous in the 1880s when many Land League activists were imprisoned there. Most controversially, John Mandeville died shortly after release from Tullamore, leading an inquest jury to ascribe his death to 'the brutal and unjustifiable treatment he received in Tullamore Gaol'. The GPB cannot have been unaware of these resonances, particularly as the father of the new Vice-Chairman of the board, The MacDermot, had represented Mandeville's next of kin.[68]

Green's theories were put to the test. On 28 January 1913, Margaret Connery, Margaret Cousins and Barbara Hoskins were each given a month with hard labour for smashing windows in Dublin Castle.[69] Once more the judiciary provided the prison authorities with an awkward problem, as hard labour prisoners were excluded from the ameliorations available to first class misdemeanants and under the Churchill rule. The women were despatched to Tullamore on the day after conviction, where they insisted that they be afforded the same privileges as earlier IWFL prisoners.[70] They were granted a series of ameliorations, but these fell far short of the women's demands.[71] On 5 February, Mabel Purser joined them in Tullamore prison. Purser was convicted on 30 January and given a two month sentence, but her removal to Tullamore was delayed by a slight chill. Purser shared the others' dissatisfaction with the extent of the ameliorations granted. When she arrived in Tullamore she had been on hunger strike since 3 February and found that her colleagues had adopted the same policy on 2 February.[72]

For the first time, Irish suffragettes had embarked on a hunger strike in Ireland which was not symbolic. The prison authorities had a significant problem and they delegated Edgar Flinn, on 6 February, to assess the women's attitude. He reported that they were determined to pursue the strike until afforded the rights of 'political prisoners'. No attempt was made to forcibly feed the women, but neither could the authorities contemplate allowing Irish women to starve. On 8 February, Hoskins was released.[73] On the same day, Owen Lewis, who had been promoted to inspector of prisons, was despatched to talk to the women. He told them that if they made specific requests rather than a general claim to a status, he would guarantee a quick decision. They effectively demanded all the privileges given to the first group of women and called off the strike when the authorities decided to grant these.[74]

The change in policy had proved successful in many respects. The decision to not forcibly feed and to return to a policy of compromise had been vindicated, even in the face of a hunger strike. Again, when Connery and Cousins were released they informed the newspapers that they had found 'the Irish prison system more humane than the English'.[75] In her memoir, Cousins repeated this point, stating that we 'were addressed by our names, not by numbers as in Holloway' and recalling that we 'felt very well pleased that Ireland had come through its test so humanely and had not stained its history, as England had stained hers, by forcibly feeding suffrage prisoners'.[76] A somewhat speedier compromise, however, might have seen a hunger strike avoided entirely and starved the suffragettes of much publicity. In an article in the *Irish Independent* published on her release, Cousins celebrated the fact that the suffragettes had fought for their rights in Tullamore just as John Mandeville and William O'Brien had in the past.[77]

The attempt to isolate the prisoners was a mixed success. The authorities had succeeded in cutting the women off from other prisoners, but not from their supporters. Throughout their imprisonment, representatives of the IWFL stayed in Tullamore. They convinced Tullamore

Urban District Council (UDC) to pass a resolution calling for political treatment and hosted a large public meeting in the town.[78] The women became exotic celebrities in Tullamore. At the end of the strike, as a victory present, the Chairman of Tullamore UDC, A. Lumley, sent feather pillows to the prison. Once eligible for daily visits, the women not only received family and colleagues from the suffrage movement, but also the great and good of Tullamore and surrounding countryside. Among those who called were Mr and Mrs Lumley, Mr Crean, the local chief inspector of the RIC, Mr Rogers, a local solicitor, Mrs Bradshaw, wife to the district school inspector, Mrs and Miss Bready, wife and daughter of a visiting justice, Reverend Kirkwood, the local Methodist minister, and Douglas Hyde, who was in town on a speaking engagement. On their release, Connery and Cousins were released a few hours early to facilitate their attendance at a send off breakfast in the town hosted by Kirkwood.[79]

That the authorities felt Tullamore jail and surrounds had become something of a circus during the imprisonment of these women is indicated by their treatment of Marguerite Palmer, Dora Ryan and Annie Walsh. In the early hours of 11 May 1913, they smashed the fanlight over the door of the United Irish League's offices in Dublin and cracked windows in the nearby home of John Dillon.[80] They were jailed in Tullamore where they were given the full raft of privileges with the exception of having daily visits and letters.[81] Perhaps the authorities hoped to prevent the daily arrival of curious Tullamore people and IWFL day-trippers from Dublin. This quickly became a matter of tension. On 5 June, the IWFL sent a letter to the editor of the *Freeman's Journal* in which they raised this grievance.[82] Two days later, the *Irish Independent* reported that a hunger strike was likely if these privileges were not extended.[83] Emotions were high as, on 4 June, Emily Wilding Davison had martyred herself at the English Derby. The women went on hunger strike on 13 June and were released on 18 June.[84] The policy of isolation then had various results but the benefits of Tullamore were highlighted in November 1913 when Hanna Sheehy Skeffington was jailed in Mountjoy. On Saturday, 29 November, suffrage activists protesting outside Mountjoy became embroiled in clashes with the police and with football supporters on their way home from Dalymount Park.[85]

EXPULSION

By the second half of 1913 the imprisonment of suffragettes in Ireland entered a new phase, for two important reasons. Firstly, in September

1913 the WSPU decided to organise in Ireland, sending Dorothy Evans to Belfast to take charge.[86] The WSPU added bite to a northern militant campaign which radical elements within the indigenous Irish Women's Suffrage Society (IWSS) had begun.[87] From this moment the locus of suffragette protest in Ireland switched to Belfast and its environs and when these women were arrested they tended to adopt instant disruptive tactics, denying the legitimacy of courts or laws while they remained disenfranchised. Importantly, they consistently went on hunger strike at their very imprisonment rather than in protest at their treatment, making debates about convict status and treatment irrelevant. Secondly, in April 1913, parliament had radically altered the circumstances surrounding hunger strike by passing the Prisoners (Temporary Discharge for Ill-health) Act, more commonly known as the Cat and Mouse Act. This allowed the prison authorities to temporarily release a hunger-striking prisoner on the condition that she returned on a specified date to complete her sentence. Understandably, suffragettes complained that this was a cruel form of torture likely to lead individuals to conduct damaging serial hunger strikes. In Ireland, this did not transpire, as the authorities rarely insisted on the return of released prisoners. Instead, they sought to utilise the Cat and Mouse Act as a means of ridding themselves of these troublesome dissidents. The dissidents were not easily shaken, however, and consistently re-offended.

Palmer, Ryan and Walsh were released under the Cat and Mouse Act in June 1913. The IWFL quickly indicated that the women had no intention of returning to prison and the authorities did not pursue them.[88] A similar stance was taken with Sheehy Skeffington in December. Suffragists feared, however, that a different attitude would be adopted towards prisoners associated with the WSPU. On 11 April 1914, Mabel Small was given a two month sentence for breaking windows in Belfast. She was granted a whole series of special privileges despite being a hard labour prisoner, but she went on hunger strike in protest at her conviction and was released, on 14 April, under the Cat and Mouse Act.[89] While at liberty, Small was informed that the Lord Lieutenant could not respond to a memorial seeking her unconditional release until she was back in prison,[90] but an informal indication that her application would be treated sympathetically had obviously been given because she voluntarily returned to prison on 30 April.[91] She was immediately given privileges, did not hunger strike, and her sentence was commuted after five days.[92] On the next day, Kathleen Houston was released from Mountjoy while on hunger strike.[93] She had been jailed five days earlier when she broke windows in protest at the use of the Cat and Mouse Act to re-commit Small.[94] Marguerite Palmer explained Houston's actions by stating that the IWFL would not stand by while suffragettes were tortured in the North.[95] Houston's release was not under the Cat and Mouse Act, but an unconditional release on medical grounds.[96]

Also in April 1914 Dorothy Evans and Madge Muir (an assumed name for Florence McFarlane) were arrested in Belfast on charges of possession of explosive substances.[97] The Irish administration was now dealing with a new level of militancy; the northern-based suffragettes had launched a significant arson campaign.[98] Evans and Muir heckled and threw objects at the judge until their trial was suspended.[99] While on remand in Belfast prison, they went on hunger strike.[100] On 12 April, after four days, they were released under the Cat and Mouse Act.[101] When an attempt was made, on the morning of 22 April 1914, to burn down Annadale House, Ballynafeigh, Evans and Muir were re-arrested on new charges rather than under any provision of the Cat and Mouse Act, resumed hunger striking and this time were released after three days. The manner of their second release was farcical and indicative of the prison authorities' desperation to be rid of these wearisome women. Chief Warder Griffith reported that he gave both women copies of the terms of their release before they were driven off in a car. In a melodramatic account, Muir and Evans claimed to have been locked into the car and sped from the prison – by 'the Governor's myrmidons' – before they had time to look inside the envelopes, containing the terms of their release.[102]

The suffragettes and authorities appear to have engaged in a contest where the suffragettes did everything in their power to enter jail and the jailors ejected them as quickly as possible. Evans became a persistent nightmare for the authorities. During an imprisonment in July she was transferred to Tullamore. When John Boland, governor of Tullamore, attempted to release Evans, she refused to be discharged into the care of her friends, insisting that it was the government's responsibility to transport her to Belfast. In response, Boland had her lifted from the prison to a car and taken to the local hospital. Promptly, the car returned with the prisoner and a hospital official, who explained that she had refused to enter and demanded to be returned to the prison. Finally, Boland gave Evans a coupon for the train to Belfast and returned to his office, no doubt devoutly praying never to see her again.[103]

In early August, Evans was arrested again with Joan Wickham, Dorothy Carson and Lilian Metge and charged with causing an explosion in Lisburn Cathedral.[104] When they went on hunger strike they were released on 12 August. Wickham and Carson refused to leave and had to be ejected.[105] They immediately went to the post office on Donegall Square and broke windows. Wickham told the arresting policeman: 'I want to go to jail' and they complained to the court that 'they had been "flung out of jail with great violence" on the previous day. They felt it was very cruel and brutal treatment, and as a protest went and smashed the windows deliberately'.[106] That Muir, Wickham and Carson were jailed twice while Evans was imprisoned three times in the space of a few short months illustrates the ping-pong nature of the prison campaign in its final months. In addition, the polite if determined approach of the IWFL had receded. The rhetoric used suggests that a genuine animus developed between the prison officials and these later prisoners. When Muir accused the medical officer in Belfast of ill-treatment,[107] his response – not unusual among prison officials faced with aggressive suffragettes – was to suggest that she was mentally ill, adding that 'before committal it is alleged she was partly attired in male clothes'.[108]

LEGACY

The period of suffragette militancy ended in August 1914, but suffragette prison militancy was adopted as a template – with varying degrees of alacrity – by other Irish protest groups. The militant suffrage campaign was ongoing when first they were flattered by imitators during the Dublin lock-out of 1913. James Connolly – who had publicly expressed his support for the female suffrage campaign on several occasions[109] – began to hunger strike when committed to Mountjoy during the lock-out. Connolly's daughter recalled that he insisted: '"What was good enough for the suffragettes to use . . . is good enough for us." He was never ashamed or afraid to admit from what source he took his methods or his plans'.[110] Several jailed labour activists adopted hunger strike at this time, including Frank Moss[111] and James Byrne.[112] On 9 June 1915, Francis Sheehy Skeffington was given a six month sentence with hard labour for making a speech likely to be prejudicial to recruitment. Given his intimacy with the suffrage movement it was not a surprise when he announced from the dock: 'I will eat no food from this moment and long before the expiration of the sentence I shall be out of prison, alive or dead'.[113] An unsympathetic Birrell felt that Sheehy Skeffington would be glad to become a martyr and 'make his equally mad wife . . . a joyful widow',[114] but this was averted by Sheehy Skeffington's release on 15 June.

Shortly afterward, Hanna received a letter from Desmond FitzGerald, expressing satisfaction at Francis' 'fine stand . . . and the way he beat the authorities in spite of their unlimited power'.[115] Within months, FitzGerald, a leading Irish Volunteer, was prosecuted under the Defence of the Realm Act. He was accused of a similar offence and given a similar sentence. He did not hunger strike, however, and in his memoir described hunger strike as 'morally indefensible . . . completely illogical and undignified . . . To hunger strike seemed to me to suggest that I was surprised and horrified at what my action had brought me, whereas I had acted with open eyes'.[116] Such qualms remained even as the nationalist movement escalated its use of such tactics. For some, this reluctance was augmented by the association of prison protest with the suffrage movement. As tensions between convicts of the 1916 Rising and the prison authorities climbed in Lewes prison in the spring of 1917, the chaplain expressed the anxiety that the prisoners would 'descend to the level of the suffragettes'.[117] In the event there was serious trouble in Lewes, but the convicts did not hunger strike; according to one convict, they did not wish to be seen to copy the suffragettes.[118] Of course, nationalist prisoners copied the suffragettes and did so ever more frequently. As with the English suffragettes in 1909, hunger strikes were at first instigated by individual activists rather than encouraged by the leadership. By the summer of 1917, however, the tentative tactic was given effective and menacing shape. This culminated in the death of Thomas Ashe after forcible feeding on 25 September.[119] The *Irish Citizen* expressed 'horror and condemnation' and reminded the readers of the hunger strike's suffrage heritage.[120]

If the *Irish Citizen* was anxious to draw attention to suffragette precedent, then the Irish Volunteer hunger strikers seem to have been less anxious to do so. The Bureau of Military History (BMH) contains six witness statements by men who participated in the Ashe hunger strike.[121] None of these men refer to the fact that their actions mimicked those of the suffragettes. Una Stack, whose husband Austin was a leader of the strike, is an exception in acknowledging the suffragette inspiration.[122] It is difficult to avoid the suspicion that this is because the men were sensitive to any accusation of using the 'women's weapon', as Kevin O'Higgins would later describe it with disparaging intent.[123] Perhaps as importantly, Irish nationalists might have worried that to acknowledge that they had learned the tactic from suffragettes would taint their protest with English associations.[124]Once nationalists had acquired a hunger strike martyr in the person of Ashe, he became the inspiration for future nationalist strikers. As martyrs accumulated with the deaths of Terence MacSwiney, Michael Fitzgerald and James Murphy in October 1920, nationalists became more assured in their ownership of the hunger strike and soon one might imagine that they had invented this most dangerous and torturous of prison protests.

CONCLUSION

The impact of suffragette imprisonment lingered. The Churchill rule went some way towards democratising political imprisonment and the suffragette campaign demonstrated that, when challenged, authority was flexible in its treatment of political prisoners. During their campaign, the suffragettes proved the effectiveness of militancy within the prison system. They emphasised that an organised body of prisoners could make the imposition of penal discipline almost impossible and could be a constant political menace. They extracted more than the limited propaganda value which attached to merely going to jail. Constant conflict within the jails ensured consistent dividends in publicity. Most obviously, they introduced to Ireland the tactic which has become synonymous with Irish political imprisonment from Ashe to Bobby Sands: the hunger strike. The novelty of their campaign and its subsequent influence upon political imprisonment in Ireland should not be underestimated. Although their inheritors did not always acknowledge the debt owed to the suffragettes, these women contributed to the transformation of political imprisonment in Ireland.

NOTES

1. Rosemary Cullen Owens, *Smashing Times* (Dublin: Attic Press, 1984); Cliona Murphy, *The Women's Suffrage Movement and Irish Society in the Early Twentieth Century* (Hertfordshire: Harvester Wheatsheaf, 1989); Margaret Ward, *Hanna Sheehy Skeffington: A Life* (Cork: Attic Press, 1997).
2. Jeremiah O'Donovan Rossa, *Irish Rebels In English Prisons* (New York: P.J. Kennedy, 1882); Beverly A. Smith, 'William O'Brien, Mr Balfour's prisoner', in *Éire-Ireland, xviii* (1983), pp. 72–96.
3. Sections 48 and 49 of An Act to Amend the law relating to Prisons in Ireland, 1877, in 40 & 41 Victoria.
4. In the region of 1,050 suffrage campaigners were jailed in Britain between 1905 and 1914. For slightly varying figures see Martin Pugh, *The March of Women* (Oxford: Oxford University Press, 2000), p. 212; June Purvis, '"Deeds, Not Words": Daily life in the Women's Social and Political Union in Edwardian Britain,' in June Purvis and Sandra Stanley Holton (eds), *Votes For Women* (London: Routlege, 2000), pp. 135–6; Andrew Rosen, *Rise Up, Women!* (London:

Routledge, 1974), p. 271. In Ireland there were thirty-five separate jailings during this campaign, but only twenty-seven women were imprisoned as several were imprisoned on more than one occasion.

5. Wilfrid Scawen Blunt to Winston Churchill, 25 February 1910, in CHAR 12/4/2–12/4/12A in Winston Churchill Papers in Churchill Archives, Cambridge. See also Wilfrid Scawen Blunt, *My Diaries: Being a Personal Narrative of Events, 1888–1914* (London: M. Secker, 1932), pp. 859–65.

6. Edward Troup, Under-Secretary of State, Home Office, to Winston Churchill, 4 March 1910 in HO 144/20098 in Home Office Papers, TNA.

7. Copy of new rule, 24 October 1910, in GPB 1913/7451 in GPB, NAI.

8. Witness Statement of Helena Moloney, WS 391 in BMH, NAI.

9. J.S. Gibbons, chairman of GPB, to Major A.F. Owen Lewis, governor of Mountjoy, 6 July 1911, in Folder 26, Box 4 in GPB Suffragette Files in GPB, NAI; John Mulhall, vice-chairman of GPB, to James Dougherty, Under-Secretary of State for Ireland, 24 June 1912, in File A, Box 1 in Suffragette Files in GPB, NAI.

10. Rosamund Jacob Diary, 5 and 10 July 1911, in Ms 32,582 (22) in Rosamund Jacob Diaries, NLI; Margaret Ward, *Unmanageable Revolutionaries* (London: Pluto Press, 1983), p. 79.

11. James and Margaret Cousins, *We Two Together* (Madras: Ganesh, 1950), p. 178.

12. Statement by Hanna Sheehy Skeffington explaining the expulsion of Leila and Rosalind Cadiz from the IWFL, undated but most likely from early 1913, in Ms 21,639 (i) in Sheehy Skeffington Papers, NLI.

13. For further information on these women and their experiences see *Irish Citizen*, 25 May 1912; *Irish Citizen*, 22 June 1912; Index of Suffragette Prisoners in England, 1906–14, in HO 45/24665 in Home Office Papers, TNA.

14. IWFL Programme of Events for October to December 1911 in Ms 21,639 in Sheehy Skeffington Papers, NLI.

15. Prisoner Record Sheets in File A, Box 1 and File C, Box 1 in Suffragette Files in GPB, NAI.

16. *Daily Mail*, 21 June 1912.

17. Margaret Ward, *Hanna Sheehy Skeffington*, pp. 86–7 and p. 95.

18. Memo by John Mulhall, 27 June 1912, in File A, Box 1 in Suffragette Files in GPB, NAI.

19. Hanna Sheehy Skeffington to Lord Lieutenant, 21 June 1912, and Memo by Sir John Irwin, chairman of the Visiting Committee, Mountjoy, 25 June 1912, in File A, Box 1 in Suffragette Files in GPB, NAI.

20. Memo by John Mulhall, 27 June 1912, and John Mulhall to James Dougherty, 24 June 1912 in File A, Box 1 in Suffragette Files in GPB, NAI.

21. Major A.F. Owen Lewis to Frank Sheehy Skeffington, 25 June 1911, in Ms 21,623 (ii) in Sheehy Skeffington Papers, NLI.

22. John Mulhall to James Dougherty, 28 June 1912, and Margaret Murphy to Lord Lieutenant, 1 July 1912, in File A, Box 1 in Suffragette Files in GPB, NAI. Katherine Maguire had a practice at 67 Merrion Square, Dublin. She, like Margaret Cousins, was from Boyle, Co. Roscommon and it seems likely that they knew each other. Thanks to Margaret Ó hOgartaigh for this information and for further detail see Margaret Ó hOgartaigh, *Far From Few: Professional Women in Ireland, 1880–1930* (UCD, PhD, 1999). The Murphys cannot have known Maguire very well as they referred to her as Kathleen Maguire in letters sent to the *Evening Mail*, 10 July 1912, in GPB 1914/7451 in GPB, NAI.

23. A memo by Lord Lieutenant, Aberdeen, 9 July 1912, and a note to Aberdeen, 9 July 1912, in File A, Box 1 in Suffragette Files in GPB, NAI.

24. Note by Governor of Mountjoy, 20 August 1912 in File C, Box 1 in Suffragette Files in GPB, NAI.
25. *Irish Citizen*, 7 September 1912.
26. *Irish Citizen*, 6 and 13 July 1912.
27. Max Green, chairman of GPB, to James Dougherty, 7 November 1912, in File C, Box 1 in Suffragette Files in GPB, NAI.
28. Hasler, Houston, Lloyd and Webb to Lord Lieutenant, 14 July 1912, in Folder 10, Box 2 in Suffragette Files in GPB, NAI.
29. Major A.F. Owen Lewis to J.S. Gibbons, Chairman of GPB, 14 July 1912, and Dr Edgar Flinn, medical officer of GPB, to Edward O'Farrell, Assistant Under-Secretary of State for Ireland, 15 July 1912, and Edward O'Farrell to GPB, 16 July 1912 in Folder 10, Box 2 in Suffragette Files in GPB, NAI.
30. James Dougherty to S.H. Douglas, secretary of GPB, 15 July 1912, in File A, Box 1 in Suffragette Files in GPB, NAI.
31. Hanna Sheehy Skeffington, 'Reminiscences of an Irish Suffragette', in Andrée Sheehy Skeffington and Rosemary Cullen Owens (eds), *Votes for Women: Irish Women's Struggle for the Vote* (Dublin: 1975), p. 20; Ward, *Hanna Sheehy Skeffington*, p. 91.
32. T.P. Le Fanu, private secretary to the chief secretary, to Edward O'Farrell, 26 June 1912, in Folder 27, Box 4 in Suffragette Files in GPB, NAI; Edward O'Farrell to GPB, 26 June 1912, in File A, Box 1 in Suffragette Files in GPB, NAI.
33. Ward, *Hanna Sheehy Skeffington*, p. 90.
34. A.F. Owen Lewis to J.S. Gibbons, 27 June 1912, in File A, Box 1 in Suffragette Files in GPB, NAI.
35. *Irish Citizen*, 6 July 1912.
36. *Irish Citizen*, 12 October 1912.
37. Sir John Irwin to Lord Lieutenant, 3 October 1912, and Max Green to James Dougherty, 7 November 1912, and GPB Note, 8 November 1912, in Folder 10, Box 2 in Suffragette Files in GPB, NAI.
38. *Irish Citizen*, 27 July 1912.
39. For biographical detail on Sarah Jane (Jennie) Baines see Elizabeth Crawford *The Women's Suffrage Movement* (London: UCL Press, 1999), pp. 24–6; Judith Smart, 'Jennie Baines: Suffrage and an Australian connection' in Purvis and Stanley Holton (eds), *Votes for Women*, pp. 246–66.
40. Cullen Owens, *Smashing Times*, pp. 57–8.
41. Report by R.G. Dowdall, medical officer of Mountjoy prison, 15 September 1912, in File C, Box 1 in Suffragette Files in GPB, NAI.
42. Major A.F. Owen Lewis to Max Green, 30 July 1912, in Folder 17, Box 3 in Suffragette Files in GPB, NAI.
43. Major A.F. Owen Lewis to Max Green, 1 August 1912, in Folder 9, Box 2 in Suffragette Files in GPB, NAI.
44. B.J. Hackett, assistant medical officer of Mountjoy prison, to J. Mahern, medical officer of Birmingham Prison, 27 July 1912, in File C, Box 1 in Suffragette Files in GPB, NAI.
45. Record of suffragette crimes and sentences in Folder 2, Box 2 in Suffragette Files in GPB, NAI.
46. Baker, Leigh Evans, Sheehy Skeffington, Margaret Murphy, Jane Murphy, Palmer, Hasler, Houston, Lloyd and Webb to the Lord Lieutenant, 8 August 1912, Folder 12, Box 2 in Suffragette Files in GPB, NAI.
47. Report of R.G. Dowdall, 20 August 1912, in File C, Box 1 in Suffragette Files in GPB, NAI.

48. Jane Murphy to Lord Lieutenant, 21 June 1912, and memo by John Mulhall, 27 June 1912 in File A, Box 1 in Suffragette Files in GPB, NAI.
49. Rosen, *Rise Up, Women!*, p. 166.
50. Statement by Hanna Sheehy Skeffington explaining the expulsion of Leila and Rosalind Cadiz from the IWFL, undated but most likely from early 1913, in Ms 21,639 (i) in Sheehy Skeffington Papers, NLI.
51. *Irish Citizen*, 24 August 1912.
52. Statement by Hanna Sheehy Skeffington explaining the expulsion of Leila and Rosalind Cadiz from the IWFL, undated but most likely from early 1913, in Ms 21,639 (i) in Sheehy Skeffington Papers, NLI.
53. Kathe Oldham to Hanna Sheehy Skeffington, 11 February 1913, and Maud Lloyd to Hanna Sheehy Skeffington, 7 February 1913, in Ms 33,603 (18) in Sheehy Skeffington Papers, NLI.
54. *Times*, 18 July 1913.
55. Major A.F. Owen Lewis to Max Green, 17 August 1912, in Folder 17, Box 3 in Suffragette Files in GPB, NAI.
56. Major A.F. Owen Lewis to Max Green, 19 August 1912, in Folder 9, Box 2, in Suffragette Files in GPB, NAI.
57. Ward, *Hanna Sheehy Skeffington*, p. 95.
58. Dr Joseph Carroll to GPB, 20 August 1912, in File C, Box 1 in Suffragette Files in GPB, NAI.
59. Petitions in Folder 14, Box 3 in Suffragette Files in GPB, NAI.
60. *Irish Citizen*, 7 September 1912.
61. Dr Edgar Flinn to James Dougherty, 9 September 1912, in File C, Box 1 in Suffragette Files in GPB, NAI.
62. Report of R.G. Dowdall, 29 August 1912, in File C, Box 1 in Suffragette Files in GPB, NAI.
63. R.G. Dowdall to Max Green, 20 September 1912, and Dr C.J. Nixon and Dr Thomas Myles to Max Green, 20 September 1912, and R.G. Dowdall to Max Green, 2 October 1912, and Dr Edgar Flinn to Max Green, 2 October 1912, in File C, Box 1 in Suffragette Files in GPB, NAI.
64. *Irish Citizen*, 12 October 1912.
65. Telegram from Dublin Metropolitan Police to Scotland Yard, 21 December 1912, in HO 144/1223/227166 in Home Office Papers, TNA.
66. Max Green to James Dougherty, 19 October 1912, in File C, Box 1 in Suffragette Files in GPB, NAI.
67. Max Green to James Dougherty, 23 November 1912, in Folder 6, Box 2 in Suffragette Files in GPB, NAI.
68. *Mandeville Inquest: Copy of Transcript of Shorthand Notes of Proceedings* in British Parliamentary Papers (1888), lxxxiii.
69. *Irish Independent*, 29 January 1913.
70. C.A. Munro to Max Green, 29 January 1913, and Margaret Cousins, Margaret Connery and Barbara Hoskins to Max Green, 28 January 1913, in File F, Box 1 in Suffragette Files in GPB, NAI.
71. Dr Edgar Flinn to John Boland, 29 January 1913, John Boland to Max Green, 31 January 1913, The MacDermot, vice-chairman of the GPB, to James Dougherty, 4 February 1913, in File F, Box 1 in Suffragette Files, GPB, NAI.
72. John Boland to Max Green, 5 February 1913, and Mabel Purser's Prison Record Sheet, and report by R.G. Dowdall, 3 February 1913, in File F, Box 1 in Suffragette Files in GPB, NAI.

73. Dr Edgar Flinn to Max Green, 6 February 1913, and John Boland to Max Green, 8 February 1913, in File F, Box 1 in Suffragette Files in GPB, NAI. Hoskins, according to the *Irish Independent*, was not released into medical care but given a shot of brandy and helped into the cold third class carriage of the Dublin train, which sat in Portarlington for a half an hour *en route* to Dublin. It states that she suffered a heart attack. See *Irish Independent*, 15 February 1913.

74. John Boland to Max Green, 1 March 1913 in Folder 15, Box 3 in Suffragette Files in GPB, NAI; Major A.F. Owen Lewis to Max Green, 9 February 1913, in File F, Box 1 in Suffragette Files in GPB, NAI.

75. *Freeman's Journal*, 28 February 1913.

76. Cousins, *We Two Together*, pp. 192–4.

77. *Irish Independent*, 28 February 1913.

78. *Irish Citizen*, 1 and 15 February 1913.

79. Reports by John Boland to the GPB, 16, 19, 20, 21 and 23 February 1913, in Folder 15, Box 3 in Suffragette Files in GPB, NAI.

80. *Daily Express*, 17 May 1913.

81. Dr Edgar Flinn to James Dougherty, 9 June 1913, in File G, Box 1 in Suffragette Files in GPB, NAI.

82. *Freeman's Journal*, 5 June 1913.

83. *Irish Independent*, 7 June 1913.

84. Dr Kennedy, medical officer at Tullamore prison, to Max Green, 15 June 1913 and John Boland to Max Green, 18 June 1913, in File G, Box 1 in Suffragette Files in GPB, NAI.

85. *Irish Times*, 1 December 1913; *Irish Citizen*, 6 December 1913.

86. Monica Whately, 'Dorothy Evans: The Story of a Militant', in *Dorothy Evans and the Six Point Group* (London: 1944), p. 44.

87. Diane Urquhart, *Women in Ulster Politics 1890–1940: A History Not Yet Told* (Dublin: Irish Academic Press, 2000), pp 29-30.

88. *Evening Herald*, 19 June 1913; *Irish Citizen*, 12 July and 9 August 1913.

89. Max Green to James Dougherty, 14 April 1914, and Mabel Small to Lord Lieutenant, 14 April 1914, and Order by Lord Lieutenant, 14 April 1914, in File K, Box 1 in Suffragette Files in GPB, NAI.

90. GPB Memo, 29 April 1914, in Folder 21, Box 4 in Suffragette Files in GPB, NAI.

91. Captain William Barrows to Max Green, 1 May 1914, in File K, Box 1 in Suffragette Files in GPB, NAI.

92. Journal entry of Dr Stewart, medical officer of Belfast prison, 1 May 1914, and Captain William Barrows to James Dougherty, 30 April 1914, and GPB Memo, 4 May 1914, in Folder 21, Box 4 in Suffragette Files in GPB, NAI.

93. Order by Lord Lieutenant, 5 May 1914, in Folder 22, Box 4 in Suffragette Files in GPB, NAI.

94. *Irish Independent*, 2 May 1914.

95. *Freeman's Journal*, 2 May 1914.

96. *Daily Express*, 6 May 1914.

97. *Freeman's Journal*, 9 April 1914.

98. Urquhart, *Women in Ulster Politics*, p. 36.

99. *Freeman's Journal*, 9 April 1914.

100. *Irish Independent*, 11 April 1914.

101. Order by Lord Lieutenant, 12 April 1914, in File K, Box 1 in Suffragette Files in GPB, NAI.

102. Memo by Chief Warder Griffith, Belfast prison, 25 April 1914, and Dorothy Evans and Madge Muir to Captain William Barrows, governor of Belfast prison, 26 April 1914, in Folder 20, Box 4 in Suffragette Files in GPB, NAI.

103. John Boland to Max Green, 26 July 1912, in Folder 24, Box 4 in Suffragette Files in GPB, NAI.
104. Prisoners' Record Sheets in File O and File P, Box 1 in Suffragette Files in GPB, NAI.
105. Captain William Barrows to Max Green, 12 August 1914, File P, Box 1 in Suffragette Files in GPB, NAI.
106. *Belfast Newsletter*, 14 August 1914.
107. Madge Muir to Lord Lieutenant, 4 June 1914 in Folder 23, Box 4 in Suffragette Files in GPB, NAI.
108. Minute by Dr Stewart, medical officer of Belfast prison, 4 June 1914, in Folder 23, Box 4 in Suffragette Files in GPB, NAI.
109. Murphy, *The Women's Suffrage Movement*, pp. 119–21.
110. Witness Statement of Ina Heron, WS 919 in BMH, NAI.
111. See extensive correspondence in Folder 8, Box 2 in Suffragette Files in GPB, NAI.
112. *Times*, 5 November 1913.
113. *Irish Times*, 10 June 1915; Leah Levenson, *With Wooden Sword: A Portrait of Francis Sheehy Skeffington, Militant Pacifist* (Dublin: Gill & MacMillan, 1983), p. 177.
114. Augustine Birrell to Sir Mathew Nathan, Under-Secretary of State for Ireland, 10 June 1915, in Ms 449 in Sir Mathew Nathan Papers in Bodleian Library, Oxford.
115. Desmond FitzGerald to Hanna Sheehy Skeffington, 25 June 1915, in Ms 33,604 (ix), Sheehy Skeffington Papers, NLI.
116. Desmond FitzGerald, *The Memoirs of Desmond FitzGerald* (London: Routledge, 1968), pp. 95–6.
117. Dr A.J. O'Loughlin, chaplain of Lewes prison, to Art O'Brien, Irish National Relief Fund, 30 March 1917, in Ms 8443 in Art O'Brien Papers, NLI.
118. Memo by Colonel J. Winn, prison inspector, 8 June 1917, in HO/144/1453/311980 in Home Office Papers, TNA.
119. Memo by Max Green, 29 September 1917, in '(A) Main File re Prison Treatment of DORA prisoners, June to Oct 1917', in GPB DORA Box One in GPB DORA, NAI.
120. *Irish Citizen*, October 1917.
121. See Witness Statements by Michael Brennan (WS 1068), Eamon O Duibhir (WS 1511), Peter Howley (WS 1379), Art O'Donnell (WS 1322), Seán Murnane (WS 1048), William McNamara (WS 1135) in BMH, NAI.
122. Witness Statement of Mrs Austin Stack, WS 418 in BMH, NAI.
123. *Parliamentary Debates Dáil Éireann*, iii, 438–9 and 526, 25 April and 2 May 1923. See Jason Knirck, '"Ghosts and Realities": Female TDs and the Treaty Debate', in *Éire–Ireland*, xxxii–xxxiii (1997–8), p. 176.
124. In his account of republican prison protest, Tim Pat Coogan suggested that the hunger strike was 'peculiarly Irish', entirely ignoring the immediate inspiration which the suffragettes provided for Ashe and Terence McSwiney while instead suggesting that the Gaelic weapon of honour, starvation, as practiced hundreds of years earlier, provided their template. See Tim Pat Coogan, *On The Blanket: The H Block Story* (Dublin: Ward River, 1980), p. 15. The title of the more recent Sean O'Mahony, *The First Hunger Striker – Thomas Ashe* (Dublin: Elo Publications, 2001) speaks for itself.

I would like to acknowledge the assistance of the Irish Research Council for the Humanities and Social Sciences, Catherine Cox, Mary E. Daly and Paul Rouse.

CHAPTER EIGHT

'Rolling up the Map of Suffrage'[1]: Irish Suffrage and the First World War

MARGARET WARD

FEMINIST REACTIONS TO WAR

For many suffragists, England's declaration of war on Germany on 4 August 1914 confirmed for women, in the words of Hanna Sheehy Skeffington, that they were 'aliens in their own land, powerless to stem the tide of barbarism'.[2] The focus of this chapter is an examination of the impact of the First World War on the different groups that made up the Irish suffrage movement, using, as far as possible, the testimony of suffragists themselves to events that 'turned the world upside down', as Maud Joynt described her reaction to the declaration of war.[3]

Jo Vellacott has identified three stages within the development of the suffrage movement. Firstly, a drive to access power that remains defined in male terms; secondly, a celebration by women of their 'difference' through promoting the value of women's caring role in health and welfare; thirdly, a deconstruction of the ideological binaries of patriarchal –bellicose and maternal–pacific and a replacement with an internationalist socialist feminism. Sharon Ouditt emphasises the fact that all three stages 'over-lapped and co-existed prior to and during the First World War'. In that context, 'the fight for the vote in collision with the fight against the nation's enemies sorted women out into warrior mothers, servants of the state and radical pacifists'.[4] Irish feminists fitted into all these categories, alongside their suffragist sisters throughout the world.

A section of suffrage activists throughout Europe and America were determined to continue to campaign for the vote, in addition to anti-war campaigning, so that women would in future be 'given a voice in the councils of the nations, that they may exercise a salutary check upon male aggression and militarism'.[5] This was, however, a minority sentiment, as a wave of patriotic enthusiasm swept over the feminist movement. In the pre-war years the suffrage movements of Britain and Ireland, both ruled by the same male élite in Westminster, had fought a united campaign for women's right to vote. All the British organisations had links with Irish groups, and strong friendships and alliances had been forged. The responses of the various groups, British and Irish, to the reality of war reflected their wider ideological standpoints.

Although it had been decades since any European war had been fought, the Boer War in Africa had come to an end only twelve years previously, and feminists like Millicent Fawcett, who had supported the British imperial effort then, were strongly in support of this new war. The largest of the British suffrage organisations, the non-militant National Union of Women's Suffrage Societies (NUWSS), led by Fawcett, announced its suspension of suffrage activities in order to concentrate on war-time relief work. Many middle class women were happy to give up suffrage campaigning because war relief work promised what Sylvia Pankhurst (while anti-war in her views) recognised as offering 'undreamt-of opportunities . . . a great unlocking of their energies'.[6]

The most extreme reaction was that of the Women's Social and Political Union, led by Emmeline and Christabel Pankhurst, formerly the most militant of all suffrage organisations, and illustrated by the re-naming of their paper, *The Suffragette*, as *Britannia*. Christabel declared that the war required 'national militancy' and offered the services of the WSPU to the government. In return for the ending of suffrage militancy, all suffrage prisoners were released. The WSPU had established an 'Ulster Centre' in September 1913 in order to pursue its campaign to persuade Ulster Unionists to support the women's cause. From that time until the start of the war, the focus of WSPU activity had been in the north of Ireland. WSPU members had travelled over to Ireland and local women had deserted their suffrage groups in order to join the Pankhurst organisation. With war came orders for all the regional offices of the WSPU to close down. From Crumlin Road jail in Belfast two of the WSPU prisoners, Joan Wickham and Dorothy Carson, issued a joint statement: 'In view of the present crisis in which our country is involved, we hereby undertake not to commit any further militancy, while the policy of the WSPU remains as at present, conditional on our release and being sent home without abuse'.[7] In England and Scotland all remand prisoners were released and their cases dropped. As the bloody reality of war had not yet penetrated, Margaret Cousins felt free to comment: 'It is glorious to think of our suffrage prisoners being free. I don't think a European war was too big a thing to bring them . . . '[8] By 22 August, 5 College Square East, the Belfast office of the Ulster Centre of the WSPU, was empty as the WSPU pulled out of Ireland. There were some who disagreed strongly with that decision. Dorothy Evans, one of the last of the suffrage prisoners, was one who did not agree with the patriotic pro-war stance of the Pankhursts. She stayed in Ireland until 1915.[9]

Not all concurred with this new direction and in England members resigned both from the WSPU and the NUWSS. Some joined anti-war suffrage groups such as the Pethick-Lawrences' United Suffragists. Other feminists continued to work both for the vote and for an end to war in organisations like the Women's Freedom League (whose President, Charlotte Despard, would move to Ireland during the War of Independence, devoting the rest of her life to Irish causes) and Sylvia Pankhursts' East London Federation of Suffragettes, which devoted energy to campaigning for working class families, for better pensions and allowances for soldiers and sailors' wives and for equal pay for those women now involved in industrial employment, who replaced men conscripted into the army but who received only half the male wage.

The Irish situation had an additional complexity. The majority of suffragists sided with Britain and with the need to give support to the war effort, and called a halt to their campaign for the vote, at least temporarily. However, although the prospect of Home Rule had receded with war, because the war was being fought on behalf of 'small nations' like Belgium, advanced nationalists regarded this as an opportunity to persuade the international community that Ireland had the right to take its place on the world stage. Most combined this view with an anti-war perspective that derived not from pacifism but from hostility to British rule over Ireland. Suffragists within the Irishwomen's Franchise League were pacifists, but also strongly pro-Irish. They were a small, albeit prominent minority within the suffrage movement.

A pro-war attitude was most evident amongst members of the Munster Women's Franchise League, who included women with a strong attachment to the continuation of the union with Britain. The writer Edith Somerville, who came from the ascendancy class, was a member. Their immediate response to war was to declare that they would raise funds to send an ambulance to Belgium, prompting nationalists like Mary MacSwiney to resign membership. According to Rosamund Jacob, this initial enthusiasm for war work was short-lived: 'Ambulance work is slackening off a bit. Miss Farrington says it was Miss Somerville and Miss Day who were responsible for starting it and neither of them is in Cork now.' Jacob, who was from Waterford, could find no sign of suffrage activity in her home town: 'They never show themselves in public much during the summer.' She imagined that they were 'making socks etc'.[10]

A more moderate view was represented by the Irish Women's Suffrage and Local Government Association. Thomas and Anna Haslam, the elderly founders of the IWSLGA, were pacifists and unionist in their political sympathies and did engage in war work, but not to the exclusion of continued suffrage work. Mrs Haslam's war-relief work consisted of fundraising for a bed for wounded soldiers, used by the Red Cross Hospital in Dublin Castle.[11] Their biographer, Carmel Quinlan, finds no evidence that they engaged in 'bellicose language – the war is "terrible", not glorious, Germans are not vilified'.

The strongest anti-war relationship between British and Irish groups centred around the personal and political relationship of Emmeline and Frederick Pethick-Lawrence and Hanna and Frank Sheehy Skeffington. The IWFL very quickly sent a message of support to Emmeline Pethick-Lawrence, who was touring America in an effort to establish a peace party that would reinforce American neutrality and bring pressure to bear on the warring nations.[12] By 1915 Emmeline was writing to Hanna: 'We should be very glad to consider the possibility of your suggestion of having a meeting in Dublin . . . I feel that the positions of ourselves and of you and your husband are identical'.[13]

Margaret and James Cousins, co-founders of the IWFL, were living in England at this time. Margaret, although homesick for her old comrades, remained an active feminist and confident that the war would provide 'a great chance for educational propaganda all over the country'. To her amazement she discovered that the Pankhurst's support for the government meant that the WSPU was 'closing up shop'. Writing of her 'shock', she described the situation of British militants to her close friend Hanna Sheehy Skeffington:

> Called at Edinburgh WSPU offices, long chat with Mary Allen, organiser there, and disappointed to hear of remittance of sentence only to those in prisons – not untried prisoner. Two days later . . . called in at Liverpool WSPU offices and found them packing. No paper being published till after the war and Miss Jollie and organisers given notice. Don't get even half pay or a cent till the work is taken up again after the war – Christabel's tactics confound me for the first time. I will be glad if you can throw any further light on them. I can well imagine you and Mr Skeffington feeling sick at the pro-English sentiments current in Ireland now.[14]

In the wake of the WSPU pulling out of its office in Belfast, the IWFL hoped that Margaret McCoubrey, who worked for the Co-operative Movement, would be able to recruit women into a northern branch of the IWFL. L.A.M. Priestley McCracken, feminist author and well-known Belfast suffragist, wrote to Hanna Sheehy Skeffington to say that Mrs McCoubrey was coming to see her to talk about the winter's programme. She was pessimistic about any outcome: 'Dreadfully difficult to get women to be interested in anything beyond knitting socks or sewing shirts for soldiers.'[15]

KEEPING 'SUFFRAGE FIRST'

The Irish Women's Franchise League, having spent the previous three years locked in battle with government and politicians, was determined to maintain women's campaign for citizenship, regardless of popular feeling. However, enthusiasm for the war was far greater than they had expected. The first of their summer series of outdoor meetings to take place after the outbreak of war occurred in the genteel surroundings of Kingstown (now Dún Laoghaire). The report in the *Irish Citizen* declared that 'war fever' had spread to the town. Although it was the largest crowd they had addressed that year (presumably there was interest in finding out what suffragists had to say on the issue of war), 'martial feeling' was the dominant sentiment. In her speech Hanna Sheehy Skeffington was forthright in her justification for the women's refusal to give up their campaign: 'Militancy by women was condemned but no one thought of denouncing the far greater militancy of the present war.' She condemned the war 'because of the terrible sacrifice of human life' and urged her audience to support women's right to vote. They would have to pay a high price in war 'as they suffered the loss of their men folk and struggled with rises in food prices', so they should have the same voice in deciding 'whether a nation should plunge into these horrors or not'.[16]

Marguerite Palmer, a former IWFL prisoner, was expecting a baby within weeks and spending her enforced inactivity in fundraising to maintain production of their paper. She understood immediately the effect that war would have: 'I need to revise all my carefully laid plans about the ads: no one will advertise this winter I fear.' In trying to cajole money from women who had always been strong suffrage supporters, she found them 'overflowing with sympathy for men and none to spare for women just now', but she hoped that she had steadied them with 'another point of view'. Keeping the *Irish Citizen* in production in war conditions was essential: 'The paper must be sold at all costs to keep suffs free from war panic and straight on suffrage – they all seem terrible wobblers!' In writing of her thoughts regarding political and organisational priorities, we are left with a clear picture of the difficulties facing those who refused to accept that women's demand for citizenship should be ignored because of the advent of war:

> I feel strongly that we have got to keep the motto of "suffrage first" well before the League. Or we are done as a League – they are so scared by the war that they are prepared to drop suffrage altogether if we let them. I am writing Miss Maxwell about paper-selling too and shall concentrate on money-grubbing while I'm laid up. Headquarters must be kept, secretary must be kept and paper must be kept. These seem to me to be our first three needs.[17]

Frank Sheehy Skeffington, editor of the *Irish Citizen*, had responded to the news of war with a defiant poster, 'Votes for Women Now – Damn Your War!', which he insisted on sticking to the gatepost of the Sheehy Skeffington home, despite protests from neighbours. Some of the street sellers of the paper feared they would be mobbed if they displayed the poster, but the paper reported that the brave souls who took to the streets encountered 'no unpleasantness'.[18] That might have been the case, but many suffrage societies objected to the stand taken by the *Citizen*, which up to this point, because it had always covered all suffrage activities (despite political differences between militants and non-militants) was regarded as a suffrage paper for the whole movement. In October the Irishwomen's Reform League announced that it was suspending selling the paper for the next three months because the 'Damn Your War' poster was not a 'neutral position'.[19] Miss Browning, representing the Irishwomen's Reform League, had already been engaged in heated debate within the *Citizen*, supporting Christabel Pankhurst's love of 'her Empire' and accusing Irish militants of inconsistency for condemning men for using militancy to preserve the nation while they used militancy for their own ends.[20]

Despite the ceasing of hostilities between government and suffragists, women continued to be denied opportunities to voice dissension by a government who remembered too clearly the disruptive effect they had had upon public meetings. For example, when Prime Minister Asquith visited Dublin in October 1914 as part of an army recruitment drive, women found – as during the suffrage years – that they were not admitted to the rally and all streets leading to the Mansion House were blocked off by police. Hanna Sheehy Skeffington and Margaret Connery were arrested for addressing a protest meeting and detained in College Street police station for two hours, without charges being made. As this was the first occasion when their detention had not led to charges been laid, their conclusion was upbeat: 'Dublin has greatly changed to suffs since 1912, the crowds are friendly if puzzled.'[21] Such treatment engendered support for the militants, provoking the non-militant Mary Hayden to agree to speak at an IWFL protest meeting and to write a letter to the *Freeman's Journal* in their support. However, the 'paper wall' that had prompted the birth of the *Irish Citizen* two years previously still existed. Her letter was not published. [22]

Louise Ryan, in her invaluable compilation of articles from the *Irish Citizen*, concludes that the paper, 'while allegedly representing all suffrage groups in the country was, in fact, out of step with most of the other suffrage societies on the subject of the war'. Despite this, the paper continued to publish all articles submitted, whether or not they supported the anti-war views of the editor. [23] Some suffragists, while immersing themselves in war relief work, did support those who continued to give priority to the women's cause. Hanna Sheehy Skeffington's correspondence contains several letters from women who continued their subscription to the *Irish Citizen*, seeing their war work 'as extra and independent of suffrage work', as Marion Holmes wrote from Essex, naively asking if there was a 'special fund for Irish regiments – I want to help the Irish and Ireland – obliged for information'.[24] Dana Hearne, surveying the various attitudes taken by suffrage groups in Ireland towards the war, concludes that the pacifists, while undoubtedly significant, 'were greatly outnumbered by women who, when the crisis came, supported the nationalist agenda over the feminist agenda'.[25] In her analysis, 'nationalist' included both those who sided with Britain over Germany and those who gave priority to Irish self-determination, founding a women's auxiliary organisation, Cumann na mBan, in 1914, which came in for much criticism within the pages of the *Citizen* for its role as an 'animated collecting box' for men.[26]

THE CHIVALRY OF WAR

Hanna Sheehy Skeffington's immediate response to war had been a powerful article, 'The Duty Of Suffragists', which praised the stance taken by the International Suffrage Alliance, 'the fine solidarity of organised womanhood' in speaking 'bravely and firmly' against war. This recognition of the unique character of the international solidarity of women was shared by many pacifists within the suffrage movement. Catherine Marshall, a leading British pacifist and an important figure in the NUWSS, wrote in 1915: 'In former great wars there was no organised women's movement to give expression to the passion of horror in the women's hearts, to be fired by it to co-operative action. Today there is such a women's movement, organised, articulate in almost all the belligerent and most of the neutral countries.'[27] It was a significant feminist milestone, as Sheehy Skeffington made very clear. Although women had been ignored by male statesmen 'eager to let loose the yelping dogs of war at one another's throats', their protest had been registered, and 'united womanhood has intervened for the first time on a great issue and her message will be remembered when the shouting is over'. She was farsighted in many ways, not least in her understanding of the gendered nature of women's war effort and the danger this posed for women's struggle for citizenship in the future: 'Some of these tasks are noble, some ignoble, but all end for suffragists in a cul-de-sac. When the war is over we shall be gently but firmly put back in our place once more – on our pedestals.' Suffragists should not engage in war work: 'It is not for us to mitigate by one iota the horrors of war,' she declared, because to do so would be futile, 'fiddling with symptoms while the disease rages unchecked'. What women wanted was not 'mopping up the blood and purifying the stench of the abattoir, but (at) clearing away the whole rotten system. Until then it is our duty to press on with unabated energy, to increase our activities at this crisis, to preach peace, sanity and suffrage'.[28]

For some women, this was too radical a stance. Her friend Violet Crichton wrote to protest that it was an 'inhumane stand', as the wounded had to be tended and women were needed to fill the places of men who had gone to the front.[29] This was the popular view. The Irishwomen's Suffrage Federation (which consisted of all suffrage groups except for the IWFL), following an emergency meeting, decided to form a Suffrage Emergency Council, nominating Dora Mellone as secretary. She admitted: 'Only grave reasons can justify a suffrage organisation in slackening its propaganda for the sake of relief work,' and explained to the readers of the *Irish Citizen* why the Federation had agreed to this course of action: 'To help save the nation we take our share in the war.' There would be a specific feminist focus to the work, so that suffragists would not 'lose their identity and be swamped in the flood of workers'. She recognised that this work was likely to be unrewarded 'when medals are given and rewards distributed', so that although they were engaged in war relief work for the present, 'in the future we will again throw our whole energy in the work for votes for women'.[30] Not all Federation members agreed with this attitude. Louie Bennett, who had been a founder member of the Irishwomen's Reform League and the Federation, now found she had more in common with the IWFL. She wrote gloomily to Hanna Sheehy Skeffington, with whom she previously had had many public disagreements, that all women's organisations 'had gone to pieces', except the IWFL. She admired its 'stability', adding: 'I suppose when the necessity of knitting socks is over the order will be 'Bear sons' and those of us who can't will feel we had better get out of the way.'[31] Providing clothing for soldiers appeared to be a favourite occupation for many middle class women. Marion Holmes, before realising the depth of the resistance to women engaging in war work, had asked Sheehy Skeffington: 'Does the IWFL approve of sewing ourselves or does it condemn amateurs taking work from unemployed women?'[32]

Margaret Connery considered the issue of women's war work in an impassioned denunciation of the 'unmitigated evil' of war. It was her conviction 'that feminism and militarism are natural born enemies and cannot flourish on the same soil'. There could be no affinity between 'women struggling for freedom and the forces responsible for precipitating the present horrible catastrophe. Therefore, it had to be 'those who have plunged the nation in war' who had to 'shoulder the full responsibility for their deed'. Suffragists would not yet 'resurrect the domestic mop (true emblem of our enslaved condition)!', she declared. It was the duty of the state:

> If the State must drive men forth like "dumb driven cattle" to be slaughtered, let it at least have sufficient humanity to make provision against want for the homes it has desolated, for the widows and orphans its policy has made. For groups of private individuals to attempt to cope with a condition of distress so far-reaching and complex is on a level with the labours of the historic lady who strove out the tide with a broom.[33]

This view accorded closely with that of Sylvia Pankhurst, who was busily organising in the East End of London, mobilising women's organisations and trade unions to press for better allowances and pensions for the women whose sole source of income was now what the state paid them in recompense for the fact that their men had been conscripted into the army. Sylvia was due to speak at a public meeting in Dublin in March 1915. There was great interest in this well-known figure's visit and the IWFL were able to sell tickets to a wide range of women, including the Irishwomen's Reform League, who indeed sold tickets themselves on behalf of the IWFL. It appeared to offer an opportunity for groups to get together over an issue that all would be able to agree upon. Disappointment and considerable annoyance was expressed privately amongst the membership of the various groups when Pankhurst pulled out at the last minute, telegramming 'paramount importance of political situation prevents my leaving'.[34] The IWFL, urged by Pankhurst, decided to hold the meeting as planned, returning ticket money to anyone dissatisfied with that arrangement. Hanna Sheehy Skeffington read out Pankhurst's statement condemning the Board of Trade's proposals for the industrial conscription of women, while Margaret Connery and Frank Sheehy Skeffington proposed and seconded a resolution for the meeting which was carried unanimously.[35] Later, Pankhurst explained in more detail the urgency of the situation: 'I was disappointed not to be able to speak in Dublin, but it seemed to me that the very vital importance of securing that women shall not be exploited in the present crisis came before any number of mere propaganda meetings.' Her aim was to ensure that women would receive 'equal pay for equal work' and for women to be given representation on the various tribunals being set up to regulate the war industries. A few days later (having caused L.A.M. Priestley McCracken some agitation over whether she would travel or not), Pankhurst spoke at a meeting for northern suffragists. The issue of support for the war effort was even more delicate in Belfast, which explains why McCracken, in writing of the event, told Sheehy Skeffington: '(Miss Dowling) and I agree that the *Irish Citizen* should lay some stress upon the fact that so many representatives of different societies – militant and non militant – were here to meet Miss P. at my home.'[36]

One year later in Belfast, Margaret McCoubrey addressed the Ulster Socialist Party on the subject 'The Chivalry of War'. It was a long and wide-ranging speech, rooted in analysis of working class women's experiences of war. It was reproduced in two parts in the *Irish Citizen*, providing powerful argument for the trade union movement to give support to women's demand for equal pay for equal work and arguing fiercely against the sexual double standard that continued to blight the lives of women. She was outspoken in her condemnation of the Contagious Diseases Act, which many feared would be re-introduced to curb prostitution:

Why should the chivalry of war decree that those women should be victimised and harried when the men who make their existence possible are not checked or restricted in any way. If some of our gallant defenders are found to be unable to control themselves, why not confine them to barracks, instead of penalising and court-martialling women?

She was bitterly resentful of the consequences to women of an atmosphere engendered when 'the dogs of war awaken the beast and lust runs riot in his veins'. The result was that: 'Since the outbreak of the war many of our magistrates have been so chivalrous (to men) that they have acquitted perpetrators of shameful assaults on little girls, on the grounds that the man had joined, or would join, the Army.' Feminist concern for the consequences of unbridled male sexuality had always been a central issue of the suffrage movement, articulated most famously in Christabel Pankhurst's 1913 polemic *The Great Scourge and How To End It*, with its slogan 'Votes for Women, Chastity for Men'. Walter Carpenter, representing the Irish Labour Party, had spoken at a meeting on the regulation of prostitution organised by the IWFL in November 1914. He disagreed with the Contagious Diseases Act but favoured regulation of prostitution on the grounds that: 'It is her trade, should be regulated because dangerous to the community, but it is bread and butter and therefore an economic question about society.' He was surprised to be asked to speak, because Hanna Sheehy Skeffington, who had extended the invitation, had previously stated it was not a question for men but for women.[37] Her change of view was an indication that women recognised the need for strong allies in the changing situation.

McCoubrey's speech highlighted the mounting concerns of suffragists regarding the impact of war and the increase in the numbers of soldiers on the lives of women. Women's patrols were instituted in Dublin, with the signed approval of the Lord Lieutenant and the Chief Commissioner of the Dublin Metropolitan Police. The *Irish Citizen* published accounts of the patrols, initiated by the Irishwomen's Suffrage and Local Government Association, with a total of twenty women's patrols having been formed by 1915. Another initiative was the 'Women Watching the Courts Committee', which reported on cases involving sexual assault and seduction. Anna Haslam hoped that the women's patrols would become part of a police force. This occurred in Britain, but in the context of post-independence Ireland, all that happened was that the 'Dublin Women's Police Force' dwindled away as its members reached retirement age.[38]

UNITING FOR PEACE

Anti-German feeling, an inevitable consequence of war, was viewed with concern by many feminists. It threatened the unity of the international women's movement and ran counter to what many had experienced in their travels abroad. Pre-war, the German women's movement had been regarded as one of the most significant, possessing leaders of the eminence of Clara Zetkin, yet now women were making statements similar to that of Laura Ervine, who moved to London from Ireland in the early stages of the war: 'Although war horrible, glad we are in it to defeat the German brute.'[39] Given this prevailing mood, the determination of the IWFL to prevent demonisation of the German people is all the more laudable. Personal experience was an important factor. Áine Wyse-Power, whose mother Jennie was a leading figure in nationalist circles, returned from Germany one month after the start of war. At a suffrage meeting she told the audience that 'in many respects German women were better off than British and Irish women'. Hanna Sheehy Skeffington, as a graduate in German and one who had travelled extensively in Europe, spoke also, emphasising the 'fine freedom of thought' of German women novelists.[40]

In September 1914 the Hungarian feminist Rosika Schwimmer travelled to America to persuade President Wilson to support a plan for a mediation conference of neutral nations. Emmeline Pethick-Lawrence reached the United States shortly afterwards and the two women, despite belonging to countries at war with each other, then toured America together. In January 1915 a Women's Peace Party was formed at a mass gathering of women in Washington. Included within its policies was a plan for a conference of neutrals. In Europe, women were also considering ways in which to bring together representatives from countries now at war. At a meeting in Amsterdam in February 1915, women from Holland, Belgium, Germany and Britain came together and called for a Congress of Women to gather at The Hague on 28 April. From America, Jane Addams (as a woman from a neutral country) agreed to preside at the Congress and to bring over an American delegation.[41] Despite the action of the British government in closing the North Sea to all shipping, 1,136 women from twelve countries participated in the Congress as voting members. They drew up a proposal for the institution of a process of 'continuous mediation', to be offered by neutral countries and to be continued until all disputes were resolved. During May and June fourteen countries were visited by delegates from the Congress as the women relayed their peace proposal, but their suggestions were ignored. The one positive result from this historic meeting was the decision to set up an International Committee of Women for Permanent Peace. It later became the Women's International League for Peace and Freedom.

The reaction of Irish suffragists to plans for a conference at The Hague was mixed. The Irishwomen's Reform League discussed whether or not to send delegates. Lucy Kingston wrote in her diary that 'hot debates' took place on whether Ireland should be represented, concluding that 'ultra Loyalists' objections' would prevent it. She added: 'Mrs Sheehy Skeffington very good and non-party'.[42] There were also differences between the IWRL and the IWFL to be negotiated, as Louie Bennett objected to the IWFL including 'pro-Germanism, recruiting, etc' in their public meetings. She wanted the suppression of all personal opinions and a concentration on the cause of international peace to be agreed before she would speak at an IWFL meeting. In a private exchange of correspondence, Hanna replied that many in Ireland were pro-German and anti-British and they had to be made to feel that the peace cause would be of benefit to Ireland: 'Peace propaganda in Ireland must be different from England – need to stir up feeling against this particular war by stirring up Irish sentiment. That is why a protest meeting succeeds where a purely peace meeting would not.'[43] Eventually, it was agreed that seven women would travel from Ireland: three from a newly formed Irish Committee, instituted to facilitate the selection of women from across the suffrage groups; three from the IWFL, which retained its separate identity, and one representative from the Northern Committee of the Irish Women's Suffrage Federation. Louie Bennett, Margaret McCoubrey and Hanna Sheehy Skeffington were amongst the delegation. Bennett was the only one to be granted a travel permit by the government. Hanna later jested it was because Bennett was 'discreet' while she 'notoriously was not'.[44] In the end, none of them succeeded in getting further than London, where they besieged the House of Commons and the Home Office without success.

MILITARISM AND REBELLION

For the IWFL, the significance of The Hague lay principally in the fact that Irish suffragists were recognised as a group independent from British anti-war suffragists. They regarded this as a sign that: 'For the first time Ireland has a separate entity and Irish delegates take their place as representatives of their own country. It is the hour of small nationalities.'[45] A protest meeting organised to publicise the government refusal to allow the women to travel revealed the extent to which the IWFL and militant nationalists had developed common political sympathies as a result of their shared anti-British sentiments. This was not straightforward, as illustrated by Margaret Connery's riposte to Patrick Pearse's message of support: 'The present incident will do good if it ranges more of the women definitely with the national forces.' She protested at this 'very masculine inversion' and used the privilege of her position as chair of the meeting to declare: 'The incident ought to have the effect of ranging the national forces on the side of women'. In response, Thomas McDonagh, Director of Training of the Irish Volunteers, accepted the criticism, adding that his work in teaching men the art of fighting would provide a better opportunity than voting to secure the future for both women and men. Margaret Connery admitted her sympathies for the Irish Volunteers, but objected to bloodshed. Louie Bennett, who had been one of the speakers at the meeting, later wrote to Hanna Sheehy Skeffington that those who would justify 'a war for Ireland' had a 'thoroughly superficial form of pacifism'. In her reply, Hanna made a clear distinction between what she termed the Tolstoyan position 'that resistance to all violence is wrong' and pacifists like herself:

> . . . who hold that while war must be ended if civilisation is to reign supreme, nevertheless there may still be times when armed aggression ought to be met with armed defence.

Included within this definition of morally justifiable armed defence was opposition to the British presence in Ireland:

> If I saw a hope of Ireland being free for ever from British rule by a swift uprising, I would consider Irishmen justified resorting to arms in order that we might be free. I should still be radically opposed to war and militarism.[46]

In expressing these views, Hanna occupied common ground with other suffragists, conscious that women's freedom was only one of many freedoms. Many included socialism within their political philosophy. Josephine Eglin's survey of the women's peace movement describes the Women's Peace Crusade demonstrating in support of the Russian Revolution.[47] After 1916, prominent British peace campaigners like Charlotte Despard supported the Irish republicans against Britain.

What caused the most discomfort to those supporting the nationalist struggle in Ireland was the issue of militarism. In England, Helena

Swanwick was one of a number of feminists to write pamphlets explaining the suffragist belief that women's freedom and the defeat of militarism were connected. Elgin has summarised those views:

> ... militarism was the enthronement of physical force as an arbiter of nations, as women, being weaker than men, were in the same position as weak nations oppressed by belligerent ones. As long as the sanctions of brute force continued to dominate the world, men would continue to dominate women.[48]

In an Irish context, Louie Bennett voiced her concern that: 'Militarism in the most subtly dangerous form has its hold upon Ireland.'[49] Frank Sheehy Skeffington was in agreement. His response to McDonagh's speech at The Hague protest meeting was to write his famous 'Open Letter to Thomas McDonagh', in which he supported the objectives of the Irish Volunteers in wanting political freedom for Ireland, while declaring that its underlying militarism 'grows more repellent' and was epitomised by the organisation's denial of membership to women.[50] After making forty public speeches against the First World War, Frank Sheehy Skeffington was arrested and charged with prejudicing recruitment for His Majesty's forces. He won release from a six month sentence by following the suffragette tactic of hunger striking, adding a thirst strike on the sixth day. The Cat and Mouse Act was invoked, but he defied re-arrest by travelling to America, returning in December to an Ireland just months away from armed rebellion against British rule.

The Easter Rising was led by men like Thomas McDonagh and James Connolly, close friends and comrades of members of the IWFL. Hanna was one of the few suffragists to offer her services to the insurgents, carrying supplies and messages between outposts on the second day of the rising. That evening, her husband was brutally murdered by a British army officer after being arrested while he toured the ransacked Dublin streets armed only with a walking stick, trying to prevent the looting of shops. His widow's campaign to force the British government to hold a public enquiry into the murder was supported by suffragists world-wide.

Louie Bennett, distraught by the bloodshed and by the senseless murder of Ireland's best-known pacifist, took over the work of editing the *Irish Citizen*. Suffragists in Australia and America were amongst those who sent donations to keep it in existence, in tribute to its murdered editor. Bennett's involvement with the international peace movement continued and in the wake of the failed uprising, the cause of Ireland as a small nation entered the deliberations of the women's movement. The British branch of the Women's International League in late 1916 declared that the Irish situation was 'the result of tyranny and wrong' and affirmed that it stood for 'feminism, nationalism and internationalism, peace and freedom'. In December 1916, the Irishwomen's International League won acceptance as an independent national organisation, despite the fact that Ireland was still under British imperial rule.[51]

In the later years of the First World War, Irish suffragists would mobilise against the threat of conscription being imposed on Ireland, and in so doing make links with the labour and nationalist movements, but after 1916 all was 'changed utterly' as feminists had to come to terms with changes that included a protracted war against Britain and the rise of a new generation of female activists who argued that women's rights could only be achieved with national independence. With the end of the First World War in 1918 came the granting of suffrage to women over thirty and the election of the first woman to the House of Commons – the Irish republican Constance Markievicz, who took her seat in an Irish institution, Dáil Eireann. While the IWFL and Cumann na mBan campaigned vigorously for her election, the extent of political differences within the Irish suffrage movement was revealed when Anna Haslam announced that she supported the Conservatives and Unionists, and others gave their vote to the Irish Party. Political ideology challenged gender loyalty.

NOTES

1. Paraphrased from an article by Hanna Sheehy Skeffington, 'The Duty of Suffragists', *Irish Citizen*, 15 August, 1914.
2. Letter from Hanna Sheehy Skeffington, refused publication in the press, printed in *Irish Citizen*, 15 August 1914.
3. M. Joynt to Hanna Sheehy Skeffington, 13 August 1914, MS 22,666, Sheehy Skeffington Papers, National Library of Ireland.
4. Ouditt, S. *Fighting Forces, Writing Women: Identity and Ideology in the First World War* (London: Routledge, 1994), p. 133.
5. Letter from Hanna Sheehy Skeffington, refused publication in the press, printed in *Irish Citizen*, 15 August 1914.
6. Pankhurst, S. *The Homefront* (London: Hutchinson, 1987), p. 38.
7. Suffragette Box 1, General Prisons Board, Dublin Castle, National Archives, Dublin.
8. Margaret Cousins to Hanna Sheehy Skeffington, 17 August 1914, MS 22,666.
9. Suffragette Box 1.
10. R. Jacob to Hanna Sheehy Skeffington, 5 October 1914, MS 22,667.
11. Quinlan, C. *Genteel Revolutionaries: Anna and Thomas Haslam and the Irish Women's Movement* (Cork: Cork University Press, 2002) p. 178.
12. *Irish Citizen*, 24 October 1914.

13. Emmeline Pethick-Lawrence to Hanna Sheehy Skeffington, Hotel Sutter, California, 9 March 1915, MS 22,672.
14. Margaret Cousins to Hanna Sheehy Skeffington, 17 August 1914, MS 22,666.
15. Mrs McCracken, Belfast, to Hanna Sheehy Skeffington, 21 October 1914, MS 22,667.
16. *Irish Citizen*, 15 August 1914.
17. Marguerite Palmer to Hanna Sheehy Skeffington, 11 August 1914, MS 22,666.
18. *Irish Citizen*, 23 August 1914.
19. *Irish Citizen*, 24 October 1914.
20. Ryan, L. *Irish Feminism and the Vote, an anthology of the Irish Citizen Newspaper 1912–1920* (Dublin: Folens, 1996) p. 78.
21. *Irish Citizen*, 3 October 1914.
22. Mary Hayden to Hanna Sheehy Skeffington, 27 October 1914, MS 22,667.
23. Ryan, p. 78.
24. Marion Holmes to Hanna Sheehy Skeffington, Braintree, 30 August 1914, MS 22,666; Marion Holmes to Hanna Sheehy Skeffington, n.d., MS 22,667.
25. Hearne, D. 'The Irish Citizen 1914–1916: Nationalism, Feminism and Militarism' in *The Canadian Journal of Irish Studies*, 18, 1 (1992), pp. 1–14.
26. See Ward M. *Unmanageable Revolutionaries: women and Irish nationalism* (London: Pluto Press, 1983, reprinted 1987, 1995).
27. Catherine Marshall, 'Women and War', in M. Kamester and J.Vellcott (eds), *Militarism Versus Feminism: Writings on Women and War by Mary Sargant Florence, Catherine Marshall, C.K. Ogden* (London: Virago, 1987) p. 40.
28. Sheehy Skeffington, H. 'The Duty of Suffragists', *Irish Citizen*, 15 August 1914.
29. Violet Crichton, Croydon, to Hanna Sheehy Skeffington, 21 August 1914, MS 22,666.
30. Mellone, D. 'ISF and Relief Work', *Irish Citizen*, 12 September 1914.
31. Louie Bennett to Hanna Sheehy Skeffington, 1 October 1914, MS 22,667.
32. Marion Holmes to Hanna Sheehy Skeffington, 30 August 1914, MS 22,666.
33. Connery, M.K. 'Irish Militants, the War and Relief Work', *Irish Citizen*, 19 September 1914.
34. Sylvia Pankhurst to Hanna Sheehy Skeffington, 18 March 1915, MS 22,672.
35. *Irish Citizen*, 27 March 1915.
36. Mrs McCracken to Hanna Sheehy Skeffington, 24 March 1914, MS 22,672.
37. Walter Carpenter, Irish Labour Party, Liberty Hall, to Hanna Sheehy Skeffington, 7 November 1914, MS 22,668.
38. Quinlan, *Genteel Revolutionaries*, pp. 179–83.
39. Laura Ervine to Hanna Sheehy Skeffington, 15 September 1914, MS 22,666.
40. *Irish Citizen*, 29 September 1914.
41. For more details of The Hague Congress see Bussey G. and Timms M. (eds) *Pioneers for Peace: Women's International League for Peace and Freedom 1915–1965* (London: Allen and Unwin, 1965, reprinted 1980), pp. 17–24.
42. Swanton, D. L. *Emerging from the Shadow: The Lives of Sarah Anne Lawrenson and Lucy Olive Kingston, based on personal diaries, 1883–1969* (Dublin: Attic Press, 1994), p. 71; Cullen Owens, R. *Louie Bennett* (Cork: Cork University Press, 2001), pp. 33–4.
43. For more details, see Ward, M. *Hanna Sheehy Skeffington: a Life* (Cork: Cork University Press, 1999), pp. 138–9.
44. Ibid., p. 139.
45. Sheehy Skeffington, H. *Irish Citizen*, 17 April 1915.

46. For more on this controversy between Bennett and Sheehy Skeffington, see Ward, M., 'Nationalism, Pacifism, Internationalism: Louie Bennett, Hanna Sheehy Skeffington and the problems of "Defining Feminism"', in Bradley A. and Valiulis M.G. (eds) *Gender and Sexuality in Modern Ireland* (Amherst: University of Massachusetts Press, 1997) pp. 60–84; Cullen Owens, R. 'Women and Pacifism in Ireland 1915–1932', in Valiulis, M. and O'Dowd, M. (eds), *Women & Irish History* (Dublin: Wolfhound Press, 1997), pp. 220–38
47. Eglin, J. 'Women and peace: from the Suffragists to the Greenham women', in Taylor, R. and Young, N. (eds) *Campaigns for Peace: British Peace Movements in the Twentieth Century* (Manchester: Manchester University Press, 1987), pp. 232–3.
48. Ibid., p. 232.
49. *Irish Citizen*, 22 May 1915.
50. *Irish Citizen*, 10 April 1915.
51. Cullen Owens, *Bennett*, pp. 38–40.

CHAPTER NINE

'Untouchability', Vegetarianism and the Suffragist Ideology of Margaret Cousins

CATHERINE CANDY

Through economic independence women will be in a position to enforce their naturally chaste instincts regarding sex questions. One knows of cases which make one think that decent polygamy would be better than indecent licence within the monogamic tie, and that the speedy death of a prostitute would be preferable to the slow murder of a legal wife . . . Legally and conventionally the wife is bodily her husband's slave, to be used as he desires, and there will be no real emancipation of women which does not give her freedom of body as well as of pocket and mind.[1]

INTRODUCTION

As an Irish suffragist, Margaret Cousins is best known for her sequel career at the helm of Indian feminist movements. After she and her husband, poet James Cousins, emigrated to India in 1915 as disciples of the theosophical movement, Margaret Cousins played a critical role in nationalising the Indian women's movement by founding and leading, with Indian women, the two major national Indian women's organisations of the twentieth century, the Women's Indian Association (1917) and the All India Women's Conference (1927).[2]

In an effort to chart the budding of Margaret Cousins' feminist consciousness about sex and power, this essay explores the transimperial logic which underpinned the formation of her Irish suffragist ideology as it was cast in the context of suffragist ideologies circulating around her in London and Dublin. It places the emergence of Cousins' body politics as an Irish mediation of British feminist orientalist thinking. In large part unbeknownst to Cousins until later, such ideologies were constituted to a significant degree by the historical imperial representation of 'oriental' sexuality. It therefore accounts for the occult drive of her Irish suffragist vision in the history of colonial sexual and caste/class politics between Britain and India.[3]

Cousins' orientalist thinking was largely inspired by a long history of late nineteenth century British vegetarianist feminist thinking which was in some part later formalised by the Theosophical Society, which she, together with a remarkable number of Irish writers of the period, would join.[4] Theosophy was based on the idea that all religion and knowledge, whether hidden or not, were part of one ancient wisdom. Magic, science and philosophy were syncretised in a broadly anticolonial challenge to European reason. The Theosophical Society was founded in New York City in 1875 by the Russian Madame Blavatsky. By 1881 its international headquarters had been established in Madras, India (now Chennai). Membership of the Theosophical Society simply required agreement with three main objects: 1. To form the nucleus of a universal brotherhood of humanity, without distinction of race, creed, sex, caste, or colour; 2. The study of ancient and modern religions, philosophies and sciences, and the demonstration of the importance of such study; and 3. The investigation of the unexplained laws of nature and the psychical powers latent in man.[5]

THE POWER OF CHASTITY AND THE FEMINIST USE OF THE OCCULT

Cousins became a spirit medium before she became a theosophist. I argue that her mediumship was a resource against sexual domination. Cousins has been noted in Irish literary studies for her writing about her rejection of sexual intercourse.[6] From about 1901 to 1904, as she diffidently courted James Cousins, Margaret Cousins experienced a profound religious crisis. On her marriage she also experienced a prolonged sexual crisis. The two traumas would soon be resolved together. In her autobiography, published in 1950s Madras, Cousins recalled:

> It was providential that there were so many interests claiming my attention during those first years. I remember that I grew white and thin during our first married year. People thought this was due to my

being a vegetarian. But I knew it was due to the problems of adjustment to the revelation that brought me as to the physical basis of sex. Every child I looked at called to my mind the shocking circumstance that brought about its existence. My new knowledge, though I was lovingly safeguarded from it, made me ashamed of humanity and ashamed for it. I found myself looking on men and women as degraded by this demand of nature. Something in me revolted then, and has ever since protested against, certain of the techniques of nature connected with sex. Nor will I and many men and women of like nature, including my husband, be satisfied, be purified and redeemed, life after life, until the evolution of form has substituted some more artistic way of continuance of the race.[7]

Cousins was anxious to make it clear that she was not alone. There were many men and women of like nature awaiting satisfaction, purification and redemption. It is at the level of shame, degradation, power, control, and art that she seems most obviously to reject 'this demand of nature'. In the course of a lifelong campaign against compulsory motherhood she adopted an alternative utopian evolutionary framework of reincarnation, through aesthetic reproduction, in which her 'Higher Self' would be eventually 'purified and redeemed, life after life' by a 'more artistic way of continuance of the race'.

In 1903 the meaning of Cousins' existence was transformed by her encounter with what she called various 'Time-spirits'. In Dublin of 1906, as she experimented with her gifts as a spirit medium and automatic writer, she was visited for weeks by a male medium called Asianus who, according to her, had lived in Persia, during the third century C.E., under the late Roman empire. Asianus communicated to Cousins her detailed biographical horoscope.[8] He reconfirmed to her that her mission would be best served by avoiding 'the animal passions'. He also reassured her that her love life would be happy although there would be '(temporary) mental trouble' in her life. As her musical career was drowned by the Irish literary renaissance, he told this semi-professional musician that her mark would not be made in the arts; 'not owing to any lack of talent', but because of her deeper commitment to 'justice and equality'. Instead, he predicted that she would soon be writing and lecturing more than she would ever have imagined: 'Yours is an old highly-evolved soul with a special work to do in the world. You have a message to give to the world, a message connected with the mystical teaching of religions', which mission would take her to a far away land.[9] With hindsight one can see that the horoscope validated and confirmed the directions in which she was already moving. She used such readings to make sense of her history and to ordain herself into a spiritually powerful feminist internationalist mission.

Such mediumship granted alternative authority to female intellectuals. Diana Burfield has noted that many female converts to theosophy and spiritualism were intellectually gifted.[10] Cousins' choice of non-motherhood was also typical of theosophists. Theosophical women 'tended to limit domestic commitments'. 'Even the happy marriages seem to have involved some measure of sexual trauma.'[11] Many women remained unmarried, or their husbands died young, after which they developed emotional ties with other women, or could still, like Cousins' fellow Irish suffragist, Charlotte Despard, contact the deceased at arm's length via the planchette (instrument for automatic writing). 'The model for man-woman relationships was that of comrades or "chums". Freedom implied freedom from sex, not sexual freedom.'[12] Theosophists looked forward to the coming age when sex would be transcended.[13] Despard was childless. Annie Besant, president of the Theosophical Society during the Cousinses' time had lost custody of her children owing to the atheism of her pre-theosophical days.[14]

Mediumship also regularly cured the youthful illnessness of Victorian middle class women. Alex Owen has observed how such illness often happened at puberty when girls came to realise painfully all of what being female entailed.[15] It often recurred on the point of initiation to adulthood, when on marriage perhaps young women realised that they had exchanged one unequal power relationship for another. Owen has suggested that mediumship offered more than attention, status or recognition. It also mediated marital conflict and provided a contained theatre for its expression. It both expressed an inner tension with the script of femininity and also provided a method of reconciling that tension.[16] Women mediums preempted the psychoanalysts.

EVOLUTIONARY TIME-SPIRITS AGAINST THE BIBLICAL CURSE OF MOTHERHOOD

In feminist debates about sexual morality in Britain from the 1880s to the First World War, there prevailed a current of thought about the sexually lustful, egotistical beast which lay within us all, but which was closer to the surface in men.[17] This coincided with feminist demands for the abolition of the double standard of chastity which protected the sexual lustfulness of the male as 'natural', while making deviation from chastity inexcusable for women. As discussed in other chapters in this book, women challenged the double standard, with its implication that women were the property of men, by calling for a new sexual morality and political economy in which men would be held to the same standards as women. This in turn involved a major effort to reform the legal system, which had been boosted by Josephine Butler's relatively successful campaigns against the Contagious Diseases Acts in the 1880s.

As Lucy Bland has outlined, feminists sought to reclaim the moral high ground by representing women as the sex which had more self-control.[18] Rather, however, than seeking to abolish marriage outright, because they feared the vulnerability of a life outside of marriage, instead feminists often opted to 'purify and reconstruct' marriage as a site of true liberty for women.[19]

Many turn of the century English feminists such as Frances Swiney and Elizabeth Wilstenholme Elmy, and earlier American feminists such as Charlotte Perkins Gilman, had argued for the transmutation of physical sexuality into psychic love.[20] The same arguments were sharpened by Christabel Pankhurst, who stressed the need to transcend the physical body to enable a development of the spiritual self.[21] Such faith in the superiority of the mind and spirit over the body resisted both the categories of the sexologists, as well as those current ideas of sexual aesthetes who argued that 'love, art, music, all loveliness spring from sexual intercourse'. Swiney believed that since parthogenesis occurred in some animal species it could also occur in humans eventually, elimi-nating the need for sexual intercourse altogether.[22] Although Cousins does not explicitly mention Swiney as an influence, Swiney was one of the most prominent theosophists, and her writings published from about 1905 were much admired by contemporary feminists.[23] In 1915 Cousins elaborated an idea very close to Swiney's in a key article entitled 'The Curse of Eve'. [24]

This article was also Cousins' attempt to reconcile her theosophy with the thinking of her most profound feminist influence, Anna Bonus Kingsford, the English mystical feminist and famous anti-vivisectionist, whose biography Cousins had just reviewed, and whom she cited as the one who had 'prepared her mind' for the cause of feminism.[25] Cousins took her version of 'the Curse of Eve' from Kingsford, who had a vision 'of three veils ['Blood, Idolatry, and the Curse of Eve'] drawn by the corrupt priesthood of the fallen church, shutting out from man the perception of divine truth'.[26] Kingsford too had once been a prominent theosophist until she fell foul of Blavatsky because she privileged Christianity more than the religions of the East.[27] Kingsford had also been a prominent suffragist until 1873 when she retired in disapproval, allegedly, according to her notably overbearing mentor and biographer, because of what she saw in its spirit 'as hostility to men, and to women, as the wives and mothers of men'.[28] But Cousins reconciled herself with Kingsford, writing that: 'She [Kingsford] found the suffrage workers of her time emulating the masculine rather than seeking honour for the feminine, and this alienated her sympathy from the personnel of the movement, though not from the principles.'[29] The piece was published at the height of the war as Cousins delivered sermons in Liverpool for the new feminist Church of the New Ideal, and while she had become exasperated by the lack of 'sex loyalty' she encountered in the battered wives of alcoholic husbands with whom she was doing wartime volunteer work in England.[30]

Like Cousins, Kingsford was pro-marriage, if anti-sex.[31] The curse was when God told Eve: 'In sorrow shalt thy bring forth children; and thy desire shall be to thy husband, and he shall rule over thee.' Cousins translated the biblical story into Blavatskian terms: that 'a primary unit, the Absolute', was necessary first, from which emanated a duality . . . the Divine Hermaphrodite . . . 'male and female created he them'. 'Cosmically then,' she continued, 'Adam portrays life and Eve, form, . . . and in its original state of beauty the form was not subject to death or corruption . . . But when Eve sought its sustenance from Knowledge rather than Spirit, when it was tempted by parts of itself – colour, smell, taste – then occurred "the Fall" through which form became subject to birth and death, instead of being self-existent.'

> A husband is entitled by the law of conjugal rights to force his attentions on his wife just as he wishes, irrespective of her approval or disapproval. Instead of being man's helpmeet she is his white slave, often more so within the marriage bond than outside it . . . The conspiracy of silence, enwrapping all the truth of sex matters, has prevented us from realizing the burden of pain which woman bears . . . It is not to be concluded that motherhood is wrong at the present stage of the world's history. It is in fact most necessary, so that forms may be ready for the gaining of experience by still imperfect souls. But motherhood is not in itself a virtue. Motherhood is to woman what the cross is to the male Jesus, the symbol of death and resurrection . . . The new world ideal must be the attainment of the state of the Blessed Virgin. Such perfect purity and chastity can be won by man and woman alike. It was the condition of Adam and Eve in the Garden of Eden, it was the very nature of

Jesus Christ – who is considered the first fruits of the perfecting humanity . . . Then will the golden Age be reached whether individually or collectively, when the divine Spirit working within has completed the generation of the human being, making it spiritually in the "image of God, male and female".[32]

INNOCENCE AND THE FEMINIST POTENCY
OF VEGETARIANISM

From Kingsford Cousins drew the idea of intuition overcoming intellect, and the evolutionary need for balance and harmony between the sexes.[33] Because of the idea that intellect was, in Kingsford's terms, 'bound to sense-nature', feminine intuition made it women's duty to rescue the world from being run entirely by 'sense-nature'. It required for instance that women be vegetarian. Kingsford saw scientific cruelty to animals as one of the most salient signs of base sensuality and materialism. Kingsford had appeared to Cousins in a dream urging her to complete her animal rights, vegetarianist work.[34]

It was in connection with the vegetarianist movement that the Cousinses had first become internationalists, representing Irish vegetarianists in England, where they were protégés of the physical regenerationists, the Wallaces. It was at vegetarian meetings that Cousins first sounded her voice in public.[35] She became the first secretary of the Irish vegetarian society in 1905, which led to friendship with vegetarian reformers from England and Scotland. She would become the president of the Liverpool vegetarian society in 1914, and she even founded a vegetarian society of New York City during a stay there in 1932.[36]

Cousins emphasised that an animal diet could lead one to 'diseases of the nervous systems, tempers, minds' and to become 'degenerated . . . depraved in body and soul . . . Those who feed on animals become like animals'.[37] A central contradiction abounded in such feminist vegetarianism and animal rights advocacy of the time which was informed by imperial Darwinianist thinking. This was that men who beat women behaved like animals, and women who were beaten by men were also treated like animals.[38] But women could break this cycle by refusing to eat animal flesh, thereby refusing to become like animals, and by refusing to engage in sex (animal-like activity). Woman was the passive (but aggressive) medium through which men would therefore necessarily evolve beyond animal-like status, which, in turn, was the only way to protect women from brutal masculinist abuse. Women, therefore, had the potential to control men. It is precisely for this reason that it was so exciting for women such as Cousins at the turn of the twentieth century to envisage themselves behind the controls of evolution. Vegetarianism was potent.

Although never so precisely articulated, it would appear that there was something of a loosely held compact in Cousins' ethical choices between her revulsion from touching/eating animal flesh and her revulsion from 'certain of the techniques of nature connected with sex'. The roots of the two policies sprang from the same mission. In the end Cousins' friends may not have been quite so far off the mark when they attributed her sexual trauma to her vegetarianist politics. Her celibacy and her vegetarianism emerged at precisely the same hour. It was literally at her wedding banquet where Cousins announced her decision to join her husband in his vegetarianism. She recalled her conversion in Kingsfordian idiom:

> . . . as in a blinding light of unarguable truth . . . It was like a betrothal of spirits. He never doubted that I would live up to my vision of a bloodless, slaughterless dietary, just as I never doubted that he would carry out his promise about sex-relationships. So we were very happy between ourselves, like wise children.[39]

And James Cousins was happy too with his side of the bargain:

> I had not even hoped that my assurance to her of complete freedom in all our relationships would be met by any concession from her side. Her voluntary determination to join me in the purification of our physical lives, in setting ourselves right with the creatures that shared life with us on the planet, was to me an invisible marriage, deeper and more binding than the ritual of conventional respectability through which we had just passed.[40]

Cousins would by 1907 explicitly link the 'vegetarian instinct' with the 'feminist instinct', arguing, in the *English Vegetarian Messenger and Heath Review*, in true Kingsfordian idiom, that a woman:

> instinctively shrinks at first from having to touch raw meat, but through repetition of these unpleasant so-called duties, a veritable veil of blood envelops us by degrees, which obscures the intuitions of our better selves from us, and at length causes us to be content with that against which we at first rightly rebelled . . .[41]

It was the moral corruption of the woman's native innocence which Cousins emphasised more than the actual pain caused to animals. Vegetarianism granted the Cousinses a sense of innocence and right-eousness, a freedom from guilt. They could 'look the animal kingdom innocently in the face'.[42] The link between women and animals as fellow creature victims of systemic masculinist cruelty was in popular currency amongst suffragists. In British suffrage memoirs and plays around 1912, women and animals were depicted as 'cornered like animals', as victims of man's coarse, insensitive brutality. George Bernard Shaw wrote the Cousinses a famous letter saying: 'I have not tasted a fellow creature in twenty-five years.'[43] Charlotte Despard argued that the connection between theosophy and the women's movement was based on allowing the sub-human to speak.[44]

THE ONE LIFE

If it was vegetarianism which first led Cousins to theosophy and then to suffragism, it was theosophy which made her vegetarianism part of her grander feminist political mission. Theosophists worked to make vegetarianism part of the suffragist agenda. Theosophists had an organic habit of uniting activities that might seem at first glance to be unrelated. The whole point of being a theosophist was to make obvious such links that were often taken for granted. Charlotte Despard argued that: 'Vegetarianism was really at the base of a great many things: Food seemed only a humble thing, but if they realised what did and might go through them through the body, then perhaps they would think the question of food was one of the greatest importance.'[45] There was no separation for theosophists between the sacred and the secular. All was part of the idea of 'the One Life'. As Cousins put it: 'Whether the movement be one of dress reform, educational reform, eugenics, labour, politics, or Church reform, it is reinforced by all others. All are part of the great inclusive movement for the emancipation of woman.'[46] Cousins also reminded vegetarianists that: 'The suffrage movements are more closely connected with the Food Reform movement than the enthusiasts of either are usually aware of.'[47]

The occult ideological dismantling of the idea of private and public spheres served suffragists well. For Cousins, vegetarianism was a radically subversive feminist strategy against the state because the domestic economy was the one area in which women held the most private as well as public control. A vegetarian reorganisation of domestic energy could have potentially far-reaching effects on 'the race' and on the state: 'Time wasted on unnecessary cooking could be devoted to self-culture, having a direct result in the physical and mental regeneration of the race.' She argued that a woman is so 'used up' by housekeeping arrangements that 'she has no time to think, no time to worry her mind with intellectual and social problems'.[48] While the simple vegetarian way would liberate women from long hours in the kitchen, this did not mean 'the reign of idleness or the opportunity for all kinds of selfish pleasures', it would instead allow women 'time to think of how their experience in life allows them to cope better than men and as a result there would be more spontaneous demand from all women . . . for service in the state'.[49]

IMMANENTISM AND SUFFRAGISM

Historian of theosophy, Joy Dixon, has traced a utopian element in the British left of the late nineteenth and early twentieth centuries which argued that the moral transformation of the individual was central to social transformation: that the personal, in short, was political. Under the guidance of Annie Besant, theosophists too were issued a mandate to transform the material world as a sacred duty. Increasingly, theosophists made themselves felt on the street as they became more and more engaged in a range of social and political activist movements. Political scientist Mark Bevir has similarly traced a new theology of immanentism which underpinned the new British socialism and new liberalism of the 1890s.[50] Within this immanentist way of thinking the divine was 'not a transcendent being, separate from creation, but was immanent in an evolving material world'.[51] Immanentism became the basis for new kinds of solidarity between women. There was a sense that the time of woman had arrived; hence, the Cousinses' immanentist emphasis on the 'Time-Spirit'. Woman would be the medium which, once in power, would transform the order of the world. To theosophists such as Cousins, proof of the broad swell of 'the Time-Spirit' was the range of radical causes parading before the public eye.

The Theosophical Society was itself a major source of this organic way of thinking. Theosophists had long promoted the idea of an organically united universe. As Dixon has elaborated, the radical collapse of the history of religion and science which theosophists narrated as one knowledge, as the history of 'the one life', radically recast the role of the body in history. The human body was part of a larger social body. This organicist way of thinking meant that the body was already literally, physically, as well as metaphysically, connected to all other bodies. The individual body, as an inherent part of the larger social body politic, was thus granted enormous power to affect the state. While bodies might appear to be physically separate, they were connected in very real ways at the higher astral, mental and spiritual planes. Bodies therefore did not require sexual intercourse for connection or for social reproduction. There were other levels at which bodies could reproduce reality to make real social change.

The belief in 'the One Life' was grounded in claims about a different kind of bodily experience. Leading theosophists such as Charles Leadbeater taught that each individual had access to several bodies. He drew a distinction between the Higher Self (the reincarnating individuality) and its mortal vehicle (the personality). The Higher Self gratified the liberal notion of a worthwhile individualism, while the body that 'man owns' was, as Dixon put it, 'not entirely his own, and not necessarily under his control'.[52] It was vulnerable to both friendly and unfriendly 'elementals', or thought-forms, produced by negative emotions such as jealousy, anger or lust. Sexual thoughts and vibrations could float independently from one body to influence or violate other bodies. Leadbeater predictably recommended abstinence from all drugs and meat as a way to protect the body from such floating impurities. Dixon has noted how this line of theosophy theoretically disrupted the idea of bourgeois subjectivity – the liberal notion of the autonomous self – by tying the individual to the idea of the Higher Self, which stretched across several historical lives, while at the same time stressing the possibilities of self-transformation – the self evolving.

VEGETARIANISM AND IRISH MIDDLE CLASS FEMINIST POWER

It is on the issue of vegetarianism that Cousins was most explicit about her thinking on class. Cousins, like Besant, believed that the professional middle classes would emerge as the new spiritual aristocracy. She argued that aristocratic ladies could not be expected to be the leaders in diet reform because their chief work was the art of play and pleasure-seeking. Also, they had no idea of the time unnecessarily wasted in the production of meat and were too bound by convention. Neither, however, could the impetus for dietetic reform be found in the working classes who had time neither to reason nor to experiment with new dishes. Rather it was middle class women who held the leverage between the upper and lower classes:

The lower classes are always the imitators of the higher. But we middle class women . . . it is because we have the power and the opportunity to set this new fashion that the responsibility rests so heavily on us . . . The middle class women, occupying the balancing point between the other two classes, can, by their thought and actions influence both sides, causing the one to think and demand, the other to follow their lead.[53]

Cousins emphasised how self-sacrifice underlay all other reasons for vegetarianism. As self-sacrifice was always associated with women, owing to women's 'instinct of motherhood' and for caring for the weak, the law of evolution demanded that 'the higher shall live for the lower' according to 'the Christ-principle of self-sacrifice for the good of all'. Cousins' definition of the weak included women and animals. She drew on Besant's metaphor of the state as a family, which facilitated inequality of power by reference to the natural seniority of siblings. Besant drew on Indian kinship structures of the extended family for a metaphor of how such families should be run by love and duties, rather than by western models of mutual contracts and rights. It was the duty of the elders to self-sacrifice for the good of the state, to develop a spirit of noblesse oblige. As the eldest of eleven, such social responsibility must have resonated with Cousins all the more gravely. But such elitism, as Dixon has reminded us, was not always incompatible, historically, with a broadly feminist and socialist approach, and in the interim it could provide a ready modus operandus for middle class feminist engagement with working class women.[54]

THE COLONIAL 'INNOCENCE' OF THE IRISH SUFFRAGIST AND THE LOW-CASTE INDIAN WOMAN

But how radical was this feminist philosophy in terms of the imperial state? The western feminist challenge to practices and beliefs of western embodiment was not necessarily as radically anti-imperial as it looks at first. The Theosophical Society had to find new ways of policing the interpenetration of bodies and found a ready resource in orientalist readings of Indian caste politics and untouchability.[55] Cousins' bodily renunciation was deeply influenced by orientalist valorisations of Indian Brahmanical ideologies of purity and pollution which historically regulated patriarchal structures of caste in Hindu society. Theosophical constructions of the spiritually and morally superior Indian vegetarian body were invested by a casteist elitism which rendered the lower caste Indian body as less evolved, as closer to animals. In Brahmanical diet rules, animal blood was considered a vehicle for base elemental forces; a flesh diet would strengthen the animal passions.[56]

The fact that such a casteist construction of the body was long encouraged by the British administration together with Indian elites to solder caste hierarchy in India would appear to have been lost on Cousins until well into her Indian years. While Cousins would espouse an anti-caste democratist position in India and would later champion various causes of lower caste Indian women and their rights to sexual autonomy, famously for example against Gandhi in the 1930s, she would never quite confront the theoretical bind in which theosophists exalted Brahmanical vegetarianist body politics, even though there was a thriving radically feminist anti-caste movement under her nose in 1920s South India, which had astutely dubbed Besant 'the Irish Brahmani'.[57] In short, abstracted from the elitist, materialist and imperial caste hegemony of contemporary India, and imperial politics more broadly, Irish theosophical thinking on the body became infused with high caste notions of sexual purity and pollution which lent a useful platform to Cousins in Dublin from which to launch a moral critique of the imperial sexual politics of the state. The bodily implications of such an ideological ensemble for lower caste Indian women were never a concern of Cousins while she was in Ireland and Britain. Cousins' feminisation of the Hindu Brahmanical high moral vegetarian ground, whose alleged self-control justifed social control, and which she conceived through an Anglo-Irish orientalist matrix, yet allowed her to disrupt patriarchal conventions of sexual control in her own life and to envision a radical change in the Irish sexual status quo, while deferring change in the Irish (and British and Indian) class structure.[58] Whatever of Cousins' obliviousness to the material effects of ideologies of caste on low caste Indian women in the imperial state during her Irish and British phases, it was such orientalism which would soon after compel her anti-colonial campaigns with middle class Indian feminists.

What Cousins' case underscores is that the leadership of at least the militant wing of the Irish suffrage movement was powerfully and perhaps inevitably mediated by the history of imperial orientalism. It also suggests how Irish feminists used imperial readings of history to reposition the private/physical/body as both a material and spiritual ground from which to challenge the public sexual politics of the imperial state, in ways that empowered at least Irish middle class women in the first instance. Before she left for India it was in part as a mask of Irish feminist innocence that vegetarianism appealed to her. As she made her way in India, she came more and more to see systemic colonial cruelty against women and animals as her explicit target.

NOTES

1. Margaret Cousins, 'The Emancipation of Woman, Part II', *Irish Citizen*, 9 October 1915.
2. Mrinalini Sinha, 'Suffragism and Internationalism: the Enfranchisement of British and Indian women under an Imperial State' in Ian Christopher Fletcher, Laura E. Nym Mayhall, and Philippa Levine *Women's Suffrage in the British Empire: Citizenship, Nation, and Race* (eds) (London: Routledge, 2000), pp. 224–41; Catherine Candy, 'Competing Transnational Representations of the 1930s Indian Franchise Question,' pp. 191–207 in same volume; Candy, 'The Inscrutable Irish-Indian Feminist Management of Anglo-American Hegemony, 1917–1954', *Journal of Colonialism and Colonial History*, 4.2 (2001).
3. The author is deeply indebted to the pioneering work of Dixon, J. from whom the general analytic frame of the essay is borrowed: Dixon J. *Divine Feminine* (Baltimore: Johns Hopkins University Press, 2001) and 'Ancient Wisdom, Modern Motherhood' in Antoinette Burton (ed.), *Gender, Sexuality and Colonial Modernities* (London and New York: Routledge, 1999).
4. For histories of Theosophy see Campbell, B.F. *Ancient Wisdom Revived: A History of the Theosophical Movement* (Berkeley: University of California Press, 1980); Washington, P. *Madame Blavatsky's Baboon* (New York: Schocken Books, 1993); for links between feminism and spiritualism see Oppenheim, J. *The Other World: Spiritualism and Psychical Research in England, 1850–1914* (Cambridge, Massachussetts: Cambridge University Press, 1985); Braude, A. *Radical Spirits: Spiritualism and Women's Rights in Nineteenth Century America* (Boston: Beacon Press, 1989); Owen, A. *The Darkened Room: Women, Power and Spiritualism in late Victorian England* (London: Virago, 1989); Burfield, D. 'Theosophy and Feminism: Some Explorations in Nineteenth Century Biography', in Pat Holden (ed.), *Women's Religious Experience* (London: Croom Helm, 1983), pp. 28–45; Despard, C. *Theosophy and the Woman's Movement* (London: Theosophical Society, 1913); Basham, D. *The Trial of Woman: Feminism and the Occult Sciences in Victorian Literature and Society* (Macmillan: Basingstoke, 1992).
5. Anderson, N.F. 'Annie Besant as Champion of Women's Rights', *The American Theosophist* (Autumn, 1994), pp. 3–5; Visvanathan, S. and Nandy, A. 'Modern Medicine and its Non-Modern Critics: A Study in Discourse', in Frederique Apffel Marglin and Stephen A. Marglin (eds), *Dominating Knowledge: Development, Culture, and Resistance* (New York: Oxford University Press, 1990); Lowman Wessinger, C. *Annie Besant and Progressive Messianism* (Lewiston: The Edwin Mellon Press, 1988).
6. Angela Bourke *et al.* (eds), *Field Day Anthology of Irish Writing IV and V,* (Cork: Cork University Press, 2002), pp. 983–90.
7. Cousins, J.H. and Cousins, M.E. *We Two Together: A Duography* (Madras: Ganesh, 1950), p. 108.
8. 'The Delineation of a Horoscope by Automatic Writing', *Modern Astrologer* volume 2, (March, 1906), pp. 116–22.

9. 'The Delineation of a Horoscope by Automatic Writing', *Modern Astrologer* volume 2, (March, 1906), pp. 116–22.

10. Burfield, D. 'Theosophy and Feminism: Some Explorations in Nineteenth Century Biography', in Pat Holden (ed.), *Women's Religious Experience* (London: Croom Helm, 1983), pp. 28–45.

11. Cousins' Irish contemporary writer, suffragist and medium, Geraldine Cummins (1890– 1969) was married to poet Austin Clarke for just ten days, which of course may reveal as much about Clarke as it does about theosophists. Geraldine Cummins, 'Psychic', *Cork Examiner* April, 20 1984.

12. Burfield, 'Theosophy and Feminism: Some Explorations in Nineteenth Century Biography', p. 52.

13. Jeffreys, S. *The Spinster and Her Enemies: Feminism and Sexuality 1880–1930* (London: Pandora, 1985), p. 44.

14. Besant made a u-turn between 1877 and 1894 from a firm stance against celibacy: 'until nature evolves a neuter sex celibacy will ever be a mark of imperfection,' cited in Fryer, P. *The British Controllers* (London: Secker and Warburg, 1965), p. 155. She recanted this position in 1894: 'Now the sexual instinct that man has in common with the brute is one of the most fruitful sources of human misery . . . It follows that theosophists should sound the note of self-restraint within marriage, and the restriction of the marital resolution to the perpetuation of the race.' Besant, A. *Theosophy and the Law of Population* (London: Free Thought Publishing, 1901), p. 6, cited in Jeffreys, *The Spinster and Her Enemies,* pp. 44–5.

15. Owen, *The Darkened Room*, p. 209.

16. Ibid.

17. Bland, L. *Banishing the Beast: English Feminism and Sexual Morality 1885–1914* (London: Penguin, 1995), p. xiii; Jeffreys, *The Spinster and Her Enemies;* Margaret Jackson, *The Real Facts of Life: Feminism and the Politics of Sexuality, 1850–1940* (London: Taylor and Francis, 1994); Kingsley Kent, S. *Sex and Suffrage in Britain, 1860–1914* (Princeton, NJ: Princeton University Press, 1987); Mort, F. *Dangerous Sexualities: Medico-Moral Politics in England since 1830* (London: Routledge and Kegan Paul, 1987); Showalter, E. *Sexual Anarchy: Gender and Culture at the Fin de Siecle* (London: Bloomsbury, 1991); Walkowitz, J. *City of Dreadful Delight: Narratives of Sexual Danger in Late Victorian London* (London: Virago, 1992).

18. Bland, *Banishing the Beast*, pp. 304–5.

19. Ibid.

20. See Hausman, B. 'Sex Before Gender: Charlotte Perkins Gilman and the Evolutionary Paradigm of Utopia' *Feminist Studies*, 24, 3 (1998), pp. 489–511.

21. Oram, A. 'Sex is an Accident' in Lucy Bland and Laura Doan (eds), *Sexology in Culture: Labelling Bodies and Desires* (Chicago: University of Chicago, 1998), p. 217.

22. Swiney, F. *The Awakening of Women, or Woman's Part in Evolution* (London: William Reeves, 1905); *Woman and Natural Law* (London: C.W. Daniel, 1912); Robb, G. 'Eugenics, Spirituality, and Sex Differentiation in Edwardian England: The Case of Frances Swiney', *Journal of Women's History*, 10, 3 (1998), pp. 97–117; Robb, G. 'The Way of All Flesh: Eugenics, Degeneration , and the Gospel of Free Love', *Journal of the History of Sexuality* (1996), pp. 589–603; For an American comparison see Tedesco, M. 'A Feminist Challenge to Darwinism: Antoinette L.B. Blackwell on the Relations of the Sexes in Nature and Society' in Diane L. Fowlkes and Charotte S. McClure (eds), *Feminist Visions: Toward a Transformation of the Liberal Arts Curriculum* (Alabama: The University of Alabama Press, 1984).

23. This idea of Swiney was also advocated by the Uranians, a group with whom Cousins would not appear to have had social contact, although she was probably familiar with their organ, *Urania*; Oram, A. 'Feminism, Androgyny and Love Between Women in *Urania* 1916–1940', *Media History*, 7, 1, (2001).
24. Cousins, M.E. 'The Curse of Eve', *Adyar Bulletin*, 8, 4 (April, 1915), pp. 142–56.
25. Ibid., p. 129.
26. Cousins and Cousins, *We Two Together*, p. 104.
27. Maitland, E. *Anna Bonus Kingsford: Her Life, Letters, Diary and Work* Vol II, (London: George Redway, 1896), p. 20.
28. 'Kingsford resigned when Koot Hoomi's writings [a Tibetan adept] were found to bear an awkward similarity to an American spiritualist named Kiddle, which she saw as plagiarism.' Dixon, *Divine Feminine*, p. 30; 238n.54.
29. Maitland, E. *Anna Bonus Kingsford: Her Life, Letters, Diary and Work* Vol. I (London: George Redway, 1896), p. 20 and pp. 454–5.
30. Cousins, M.E. 'The Citizen's Bookshelf: Life of Anna Kingsford M.D.', *Irish Citizen*, 30 May 1914.
31. Cousins, M.E. 'Sparks from the Anvil of War', *Irish Citizen*, 12 September 1914.
32. Cousins, M.E. 'The Curse of Eve', *Adyar Bulletin*, 8, 4 (April, 1915), pp. 142–56.
33. Burfield, 'Theosophy and Feminism', pp. 40–1; Cousins, M.E. 'Discovery of the Femaculine', *Irish Citizen*, November/December, 1913.
34. Cousins and Cousins, *We Two Together*, p. 118.
35. Cousins and Cousins, *We Two Together*, p. 133.
36. Cousins and Cousins, *We Two Together*, p. 106, p. 232, p. 550.
37. Cousins, M.E. 'Woman's Place in the Vegetarian Movement', *The Vegetarian Messenger and Health Review*, Volume 4, 1907, p. 296.
38. See for example Bauer, C. and Ritt, L. '"A Husband is a Beating Animal": Frances Power Cobbe Confronts the Wife-Abuse Problem in Mid-Victorian England', *International Journal of Women's Studies*, 6. 2 (1983), pp. 99–118; Leneman, L. 'The Awakened Instinct: vegetarianism and the women's suffrage movement in Britain', *Women's History Review*, Volume 6, 2, (1997), pp. 268–80; Bland, *Banishing The Beast*, p. 306, for more on sexual/ animal connections see Jennifer Ham and Matthew Senior (eds), *Animal Acts: Configuring the Human in Western History* (London: Routledge, 1997).
39. Cousins and Cousins, *We Two Together*, p. 90.
40. Ibid., p. 83.
41. Cousins, M.E. 'Woman's Place in the Vegetarian Movement', p. 296.
42. Cousins and Cousins, *We Two Together*, p. 91.
43. Cousins and Cousins, *We Two Together*, p. 133.
44. Despard, C. *Theosophy and the Women's Movement* (London: Theosophical Publishing Society, 1913), p. 44.
45. Cousins and Cousins, *We Two Together*, p. 227.
46. Cousins, M.E. 'The Emancipation of Women' *Irish Citizen*, 2 October 1915.
47. Cousins, 'Woman's Place in the Vegetarian Movement', pp. 294–9.
48. Ibid.
49. Ibid., and see Leneman, 'The Awakened Instinct', p. 276.
50. Bevir, M. 'The West Turns Eastward: Madame Blavatsky and the Transformation of the Occult tradition', *Journal of the American Academy of Religion*, 62, 3 (1994), pp. 747–67.
51. Dixon, *Divine Feminine*, p. 122.
52. Dixon, *Divine Feminine*, p. 127.

53. Cousins, 'Woman's Place in the Vegetarian Movement', pp. 295–6.
54. Dixon, *Divine Feminine*, pp. 147–8.
55. Dixon, *Divine Feminine*, chapter 5.
56. Ibid., p. 133.
57. Pandhian, M.S.S. 'Beyond Colonial Crumbs: Cambridge School, Identity Politics and Dravidian Movement(s)', Working Paper No. 125, (Adyar, Madras: Madras Institute of Development Studies, 1994), p. 42. Of course there were already counter-caste movements in operation for centuries in South Asia and beyond, such as the formation of Buddhism in the fifth century B.C.E., Sufism in the fourteenth century C.E., and various nineteenth century *bhakti* devotional movements. The challenge to upper caste hegemony had taken a more self-consciously radical political turn in the early twentieth century particularly in South India and Western India, with Periyar's Self-Respect movement and the Justice Party, and Phule in Maharashtra, but Cousins seems not to have been aware of such movements either in Ireland or in India. See also Dixon, J. 'Of Many Mahatmas: Besant, Gandhi, and Indian Nationalism', in Harold Coward (ed.), *Indian Critiques of Gandhi* (Ithaca: State University of New York Press, 2003).
58. For similar contradictions in another Anglo-Irish feminist see Hamilton, S. 'Making History with Frances Power Cobbe: Victorian Feminism, Domestic Violence, and the Language of Imperialism', *Journal of Victorian Studies* (Spring, 2001), pp. 437–60.

CHAPTER TEN

Rosamond Jacob: nationalism and suffrage

LEEANN LANE

INTRODUCTION

Throughout the first two decades of the early twentieth century Rosamond Jacob was an intermittent member of a unique circle of women based in Dublin. From 1908 Jacob made frequent visits to the capital, presenting such forays as an escape from the confines of the small Waterford Quaker community in which she was brought up. Interaction with Dublin feminists, nationalists of various hues and cultural activists allowed Jacob's nascent political and feminist awareness to mature. Jacob's involvement in Dublin and Waterford political and cultural activities in the period testify to the links between the cultural revival, nationalist politics and the feminist programme. In the recent past, historians and literary critics have placed a new focus on under-standing the multiplicity of intersections that informed the discourse of the Irish cultural renaissance. P.J. Mathews' recent work, *Revival*, examines the 'commonality of purpose' between such 'self-help' groups as the Gaelic League, the Irish Agricultural Organisation Society, Inghinidhe na hÉireann and Sinn Féin.[1] It is artificial to examine the campaign for suffrage and the wider women's rights-based initiatives as a distinct movement divorced from the dominant discourse of revival in the early twentieth century.[2] Women such as Jacob did not neatly compartmentalise the various campaigns in which they participated; the actual lived experience indicates the holistic approach many activists took in considering Irish political, cultural and feminist advancement in the period. Tension is a very different concept to division; tensions can be resolved or circumvented, division implies a much more unqualified breach and ignores complexity. Instead of absolute division between apparently binary oppositions, notably suffrage and nationalism, this essay will argue that various stratagems were utilised by women such as Jacob to resolve the incompatibilities and strains which participation in more than one form of political activism made manifest. As Louise Ryan states in her study of the *Irish Citizen* newspaper: 'The situation is not a simple clear cut case of two opposing ideologies.'[3] Moving in the same small circles, female activists and women involved in the nationalist campaign were forced to establish a modus vivendi; the necessities of day-to-day interaction worked in many instances to transcend or shelve dissension. This essay will also highlight a new or hitherto under-explored form of Irish female activism of the period. Jacob acted as a reporter; educating herself in the issues of nationalism and suffrage through reading and attendance at meetings, she in turn domesticated contemporary political topics for friends and family through debate and discussion and in the process brought the aims and values of the suffrage campaign into such diverse forums as the Gaelic League.

Jacob's daily diary testifies to intersections rather than divisions in feminist and nationalist politics. Her account of political and cultural life in Dublin in the early twentieth century and an examination of her novel, *Callaghan*, set between 1913 and 1915, illuminates the hitherto under-examined interactions and intersections between the first wave feminist movement in Ireland and the wider cultural and political environment in which Irish female activists lived and participated. Ryan has rightly noted how the cultural revival was a vital 'backdrop to Irish feminism'.[4] *Callaghan* is laced with references to the GAA and the Gaelic League. Andy Callaghan's love of the Irish landscape is described in terms that echo many of the theosophically-based nature writings of George Russell (AE), one of the key literary figures of the period.[5] Looking at the fir trees and wild wasteland surrounding his house, he concluded that he 'seemed to be in the presence of a consciousness . . . loving and welcoming him like a transcendent mother'.[6] *Callaghan*, this chapter contends, together with the evidence of Jacob's diary, acts as a map of social, cultural and political activism in Ireland in the period before the Easter Rising. Danae O'Regan cites republicanism as the major theme in *Callaghan*. While she discusses Frances Morrin's suffrage activities and offers an interesting analysis of Jacob's refusal to present a one-dimensional and uncritical portrayal of republicanism, O'Regan fails to fully transcend a purely nationalist reading of the text.[7] As a map of pre-1916 activism, *Callaghan* signals junctions and connections; the marriage between republican activist Andy Callaghan and suffrage campaigner Frances Morrin can be read as a paradigm for

Jacob's view of the centrality and importance of feminist ideals within the nationalist campaign. This is not to suggest that the suffrage–nationalism 'marriage' was uncomplicated for Jacob but rather to argue that her focus was connection rather than disconnection.

'ACTIVISM BY STEALTH'

The focus on division in the historiography of Irish female politicisation may be consequent on the type of literature examined in a consideration of the suffrage campaign. Attention has focused on polemical and journalistic speeches or retrospective autobiographical accounts rather than on the more immediate narratives of which Jacob's diary offers an example.[8] Accordingly, sustained concentration has been placed on the political conflicts which divided the suffrage campaign: the division between the militant suffragettes in the IWFL and the constitutional suffragists of the IWSLGA and that between suffrage women and those who felt that the suffrage movement was an English cause and therefore antagonistic to the national struggle for independence.[9] Work on unionist women has similarly placed the emphasis on division within the women's movement; as the third Home Rule Bill was debated, unionist suffragists were torn between opposing the bill or fighting for the inclusion of women in any settlement that would be made.[10] Of course, as Ryan has argued, a close reading of the *Irish Citizen* shows how the paper acted as a forum for suffrage women of all political persuasions to negotiate and discuss political difference.[11] Indeed, Ward notes how women on both sides of the nationalist versus suffrage divide often respected and even developed a liking for each other.[12] While Jacob faced similar tensions to those experienced by feminists in a nationalist Ireland that declared a moratorium on all social, economic and political aspirations until independence had been achieved, her diary testifies to the manner in which the female activists were centrally local within the revival ethos of the early twentieth century. Ryan notes how the campaign for the vote was a unifying symbol masking political division among nationalists, liberals, socialists and unionists.[13] This paper argues that cultural activities did more than that. The movements and activities of the cultural revival provided a common meeting ground for feminists of different political persuasions. What is noteworthy is how the female activists of Jacob's circle were able to express divergent viewpoints and still maintain and negotiate relationships within a female grouping that offered support networks and friendships independent of political persuasion. Often it was in the activities of the revival movements such as the Gaelic League that female activists were able to re-establish and re-affirm relationships damaged by political controversy. In March 1913, for example, Hanna Sheehy Skeffington persuaded Jacob to march with the suffragists in the St Patrick's Day Language Procession, stressing that it was not necessary to be part of any society. Later that night at the Gaelic League céilidhe, she was introduced to the suffragist Helen Laird.[14] Jacob's visits to Dublin typically comprised visits to the Abbey theatre, and Gaelic League activities; in keeping with the revival's focus on the spirit world she attended séances and took a passing interest in theosophy.[15] She became interested in the question of buying Irish goods and the revival of a national costume.[16] Jacob's nationalism was multi-focused in keeping with the prevailing revival discourse of early twentieth-century Irish society. For Jacob, cultural and political expressions of nationality were not easily divisible; rather they intersected and combined, working as they did towards the one goal – a distinct Irish society and polity and crucially one in which women were equal citizens. It was the latter priority that explains the description of Frances Morrin in *Callaghan* as someone who was 'a suffragist ever since she was old enough to know what a vote was, but the fact had generally remained quiet and unobtrusive in the background of her mind'.[17]

Jacob's diary records her growing sense that women were elided from the historical picture. In September 1907 she paid a visit to the nationalist monument on the Grand Parade in Cork. While she found the list of names on the monument 'very instructive', she registered her disapproval of the absence of 1848 women and the manner in which Anne Devlin's name appeared at the bottom of all the 1803 men, 'the only woman there at all'.[18] Critical of a society that accorded women the weaker sex and ascribed meek and passive characteristics to them, Jacob's early involvement in cultural activism was fraught with frustration. Aside from irritation with the bureaucracy and lack of dynamism in the local Gaelic League branch, she was increasingly perturbed by the lack of female representation at committee level, despite the fact that the women attended meetings more frequently than the men. Natural justice should, she believed, ensure that both sexes be represented on the committee and amongst the officers.[19] Jacob opposed the way in which women used their socially ordained role as mothers to argue for the franchise. Her belief in the concept of equal rights was clear in her account of a talk at the Quaker meeting-house in Waterford on 26 November 1913 by Dr Mary Strangman:

> Edith Bell was saying how you had to blush for the doings of militants . . . she thought someone said suffragists were against marriage, so I said that was the queerest thing said yet, in face of all the motherhood rot in the suffrage journals . . . & that women always seem to think it necessary to blush for what any woman does, but men never take the crimes of other men on the shoulders of their sex that way.[20]

This sense of standing apart as a female cultural and political activist in her local community was a theme of much of Jacob's diary at this period.

Given Jacob's innate consciousness of the lack of sexual equality in society, her involvement in the suffrage campaign was inevitable. From 1905 she lost no opportunity to air her views in favour of the vote for women and to question others as to their stance, bringing the topic into such forums as the Gaelic League.[21] The commonality of intellectual space and discourse generated between the suffrage cause and the revival needs to be noted. What stood out for Jacob as a 'fine night' at the League was one in which the local language activist, Mr Brett, spent an hour discussing 'home life in ancient Ireland, & how the woman bossed everything in the home . . . '[22] What is evident is the manner in which Jacob's activism manifested itself in an educative approach. Many of the Gaelic Leaguers in Waterford believed that 'a woman's right place is in the kitchen'; Jacob worked through debate and through the example of her own politically conscious life to dissuade them of this viewpoint.[23] Throughout 1909–14 Jacob's active work on behalf of the suffrage cause appeared to be confined to collecting signatures and distributing copies of *Bean na hÉireann*, advertising the publication through such forums as the Gaelic League.[24] Yet her refusal to hide her views and her willingness to debate on the issue of female suffrage was a form of activism by stealth; her discussions gradually normalised the issue of the vote for women for many within her social circle. She noted on 13 November 1909 'a heated Suffragette argument after tea' and commented how Mr Orr 'would give women votes the way he wd throw a bone to an importunate dog, and that is a good way for him to have got I think. He wouldn't have gone so far 3 years ago'.[25] The importance of this form of activism is reflected in *Callaghan* as Miss Doran, secretary to the IWFL, attempts to encourage members in the provinces: 'They educate their friends and acquaintances and prepare the ground.'[26]

Family commitments, in particular to her mother, prevented Jacob from taking a more active role in the suffrage campaign. Jacob, as a single woman, was throughout her life considered responsible for the care of older family members, women who did not have children still being expected to adopt a caring role.[27] The main reason, however, for Jacob's failure to take a more active and decisive role in the cause was her growing republicanism. Although she intermittently attended IWFL meetings from early 1912, Jacob was opposed to what she perceived as the links between the militant campaign in Ireland and the WSPU. In 1907, to be a suffragette was for Jacob the height of 'revolutionary opinions'. She described the language activist, Mr Upton, as 'something of a suffragette, so I don't see how he could have more revolutionary opinions'.[28] Increasingly, however, Jacob came to see the republican cause as one that had to take precedence over suffragism. Jacob's anti-Englishness contributed to her unwillingness to join the IWFL.[29] In 1912, when an English suffragette threw a hatchet in the carriage in which the English Prime Minister, Asquith, and Irish Parliamentary Party leader, Redmond, were travelling, Jacob dismissed the hyperbole of the press but made very clear her hostile attitude to the involvement of English suffragists in the Irish campaign.[30] Jacob was obliged to explain at a Waterford suffrage meeting in 1914 why she didn't join the MWFL, as earlier she had 'to explain at length why I didn't join the IWFL'.[31] She explained to Mrs Hayden that she did not join the Munster Women's Franchise League 'partly because I was a Separatist & partly because they did nothing but import English speakers'.[32] Unlike many of her fellow suffragists, notably Hanna Sheehy Skeffington, Jacob believed that there could be no freedom for women in political rights granted by a foreign parliament.[33] For Jacob, political freedom was the ultimate achievement without which language revival or the attainment of female suffrage was of little or no value. 'Wales', she wrote, 'is a melancholy example of the state to which the Gaelic League without the help of politics, would bring Ireland. Nationality without a language is better than language without nationality.'[34] The ideal was a person 'who can combine a passion for the language with thorough good Fenian sentiments', as did her fictional Andy Callaghan. Jacob dismissed James Stephens' *The Crock of Gold*, published in 1912, for the way he 'carefully ignores politics & nationality & everything of that sort'. Despite the plethora of suffrage organisations that existed by the early 1910s Jacob noted the central lacuna and wrote a letter to the *Irish Citizen* in March 1913 'on the desirability of a Nationalist women's franchise society'.[35] This letter indicates her prioritising of the national cause over suffrage but also indicates that this was an uneasy choice for her; the ideal was a forum where she could commit herself fully as a woman and as a nationalist. Gender equality was crucial to the full implementation of the nationalist campaign. Jacob did not, therefore, eschew suffrage for nationalism but sought to establish a synergy of commitment at various intersecting levels.

Jacob's early activism in the campaign for Irish independence was in the anti-welcome campaign, the response of Irish nationalists to the royal visit of 1911. Jacob was to the forefront in collecting signatures for the 'disloyal protest'. The unwillingness of some women to sign the protest rankled heavily with her and she attributed their actions to their lack of status in a patriarchal society: 'I went along Ballytruckle . . . but found everyone either impenetrably stupid or averse to do anything without asking their husbands.'[36] Anxious to start a branch of Cumann na mBan in Waterford on hearing how the Dublin branch was 'booming', Jacob noted how a serious obstacle to achievement was the inert nature of the local women.[37] In August 1914 a local branch was established but from the outset it was beset by a lack of members.[38] The high point of the First Aid meetings organised under its auspices was on 9 September 1914 when seventeen attended, a figure that was to diminish steadily in the following weeks.[39] The branch suffered from a lack of focus; no sustained objectives were established at any point. On 12 January 1915 a diminished meeting 'tried to think of something a small branch with no money could do. We thought of getting a dozen or two *Volunteers* every week & selling them to people'.[40]

Shortly after the dissolution of the Waterford branch of Cumann na mBan on 19 January 1915, Jacob went to Dublin for the first time in nearly eight months. Encouraged by Hanna Sheehy Skeffington she sold copies of the *Irish Citizen* during the anti-recruiting meetings on 7 March 1915 and later in the week on Grafton Street.[41] It is important to note how Jacob tried to maintain commitment to the issue of female suffrage although she felt that she could not formally join a suffrage society. Despite both Francis and Hanna's condemnation of her proposed nationalist suffrage society as 'useless', she continued to enjoy their company and was willing to listen to different political views.[42] With the Sheehy Skeffingtons she attended the suffrage meeting in O'Connell Street on 19 March at which Sylvia Pankhurst was due to speak.[43] Despite her lack of official affiliation to a suffrage organisation, Jacob continued to attend suffrage activities in Waterford. On 13 February 1914 she attended a 'sort of suffragist at home', targeted at 'non-members, to get them interested'.[44] This testifies to the manner in which division could be circumvented. It was not always nationalism versus suffragism; the situation was more complex and fluid than it has often been represented.

Back in Waterford by April 1915, Jacob's correspondence and news from visitors kept her in touch with escalating political events. Although Jacob was prepared to put her nationalist sentiments ahead of an official commitment to feminism, she was critical of the auxiliary role of women in such nationalist organisations as Cumann na mBan. This is noteworthy, since historians tend to delineate a clear-cut division between women such as Sheehy Skeffington, who refused to consider that female rights would organically follow independence, and women like Mary McSwiney, who were content to fulfil a subordinate female role in the interests of the greater good of the national campaign.[45] At the end of April 1915 Eilis Ní Chárthaigh, a travelling Cumann na mBan organiser, visited Waterford; Jacob's censure of her attitude to the status of the organisation testifies to her own refusal to accept uncritically all aspects of the nationalist programme and power structures.

> She . . . seemed . . . to look on Cumann na mBan too much as an auxiliary to the Volunteers, but it would be strange if she did not, finding all the provincial branches almost entirely dependent on the kindness and encourgement of the local Volunteers. Miss Brodar agreed with me in blaming the women's uselessness on their upbringing, and in thinking that C. na mB. should be more independent of the I. V. I think she must be something like a suffragist.[46]

Jacob was highly critical of the concept of female only organisations, as highlighted in her account of the IWFL meeting on 18 March 1913 at which she made clear her diametrically opposed views to those of Margaret Cousins.

> She . . . talked a lot of nonsense about how women had better keep out of organisations started & mostly controlled by men, how they can't work freely in them or find proper scope, but shd stick to organisations of their own . . . Then the discussion was opened to everyone. I started it by disagreeing . . . saying women should take their equal share in these organisations started & at present run by men, like the Gaelic League, and run them equally with the men, instead of keeping out . . . Mrs Cousins answered me, sticking to what she said, & was followed by Mrs Connery, both saying that women ought to have separate Gaelic Leagues & other societies (which is just what men wd like, & wd simply mean their falling in the position of a 'Ladies Auxiliary', & the men hogging all the power & lime light for themselves).[47]

CALLAGHAN: AN IRISH SUFFRAGE NOVEL

The literature of the English suffrage campaign has received a degree of attention.[48] With the foundation of the Women Writers Suffrage League as an auxiliary of the National Union of Women's Suffrage Societies in 1908, female writers were a striking part of the campaign.[49] Joannou notes how the figure of the suffragette is embedded in the mainstream culture of twentieth-century Britain, citing the example of Mary Poppins as an 'immediately recognisable icon' of resolute English womanhood.[50] The Irish suffrage campaign was very rarely represented in fiction; for most Irish women writers their relationship to the political creeds of unionism or nationalism was more important than feminism. Certainly Gerardine Meaney's analysis of the subversive potential of female political writing has to be acknowledged; late nineteenth-century nationalist women writing in defence of the nation could claim the right of women to participate in the political life of a newly independent Irish State.[51] Jacob herself reflected the view that female participation in the national cause was simultaneously feminist activism in the statement by Bridie Quinlan in *Callaghan*: 'Do you think women are going to kill themselves collecting money and burying guns and learning first aid for you, and then let themselves be barred out of parliament. Nice fools they'd be.'[52] *Callaghan* offers one of the unique fictional accounts of the Irish suffrage campaign and therefore, notwithstanding its limited aesthetic value, is an important text.[53]

Despite, as indicated above, limited official activism, Jacob continued to educate herself in the ideologies and beliefs of the feminist campaign and, very importantly, her close observation of the different political, cultural and feminist campaigns that variously intersected and converged throughout the first two decades of the twentieth century provided the raw material for *Callaghan*. In many respects Jacob can be seen in the role of unofficial journalist of the period; that this role constituted a form of activism should be recognised. The first stage comprised transcribing and analysing the events, issues and tensions of the period in diary form. These diary entries, and thereby Jacob's own lived experience of the period, can be viewed as a form of journalistic fieldwork for *Callaghan*.

In many respects *Callaghan* fits the paradigm of English suffrage literature. *Callaghan* ascribes to the type of dialogic texts produced by English writers involved in the suffrage campaign. Norquay describes the latter as 'full of discussion and debate; the novels packed with reported speech, the poetry full of declamation ... the clash and clamour

of many voices is inescapable'.[54] *Callaghan* situates itself within a series
of interlocking dialogues, notably the debate between suffrage and
nationalist demands. The novel subscribes to the form of English
suffrage fiction but it presents a different context given its Irish focus.
The tension between form and context may explain its lack of commercial success. Unlike English suffrage fiction, there was no readership
for a novel set in Ireland attempting to negotiate a space for feminism
within a nationalist novel; anti-colonial cultural nationalism has been
described as 'traditionally inhospitable to gender politics'.[55] *Callaghan*
offers a unique example of an attempt to incorporate issues of gender
within the parameters of a polemical text premised on the principles of
cultural and political nationalism. O'Regan suggests that Jacob's
unwillingness to present an uncritical portrayal of republicanism, in
particular her readiness to critically analyse the escalation of republican
violence exemplified in the violent proclivities of Andy Callaghan, may
explain why it took her ten years to find a publisher for her next novel,
The Troubled House.[56] However, Jacob's refusal to adhere to the principles
of 'successful popular indoctrination' by relying on repetitive nationalist
imagery and plot demanded of political fiction may also be a reason to
explain why *Callaghan* was such a publishing flop and the consequent
difficulties she had in bringing out her later work.[57] In many respects
Callaghan was the fictional equivalent of *Bean na hEireann* with its dual
focused slogan: 'Freedom for our Nation and the complete removal of all
disabilities to our sex'.[58]

Frances Morrin challenges representations and expectations of early
twentieth-century femininity. A single woman at the beginning of the
novel, she lives with her married brother and his family in rural Ireland.
Frances is criticised by other members of the community for her refusal
to adhere to the role expected of women in society. Notably, she shocks
the rector's wife by her attendance at a Sunday hurling match.[59] Frances
objects to the way in which she and her sister-in-law are referred to in
the neighbourhood as Dr Morrin's sister and Dr Morrin's wife, never by
their own names. Like Jacob, Frances becomes enmeshed in the suffrage
campaign as she moves between rural Kilmartin and Dublin. However,
unlike Jacob, Frances is willing to become an active member of the
IWFL.[60] No attention has been paid to how this tension between
women in the suffrage campaign and nationalist women manifested
itself in literature beyond the level of polemical debates conducted in
papers such as *Bean na hEireann* and the *Irish Citizen*. *Callaghan* shows
Jacob attempting to reconcile the inward tensions given her commitment to female equality and her support for the national campaign. In

her refusal to prioritise suffrage over the national cause, Jacob is represented in the novel by Una. This debate, arguably modelled on the
debate between McSwiney and Sheehy Skeffington, is one of the chief
instances of Jacob's reliance on the dialogic approach of English suffrage
novels.[61] Frances attends her first suffrage meeting in the company of
Una to hear Mrs Wall, newly released from prison, speak on the life and
work of Josephine Butler, the leader of the Ladies National Association
for the Repeal of the Contagious Diseases Acts. Jacob rehearses many of
the arguments used by female activists in their demand for the vote,
utilising the form of question and answer at the end of Mrs Wall's
speech. The moral argument in favour of women's suffrage is highlighted, as is the commonly held recognition that the vote was not a
panacea for all manifestations of gender equality. Enfranchised women
would, however, Mrs Wall argued, be in a position to tackle the
economic causes of prostitution.[62] To this point Jacob's suffrage text
subscribed to the English model. However, the crucial issue of campaigning for the vote from an English parliament causes her text to
diverge and become peculiarly Irish. Una decries Mrs Wall as speaking 'as
an Englishwoman throughout'. She offers her reasons for not joining the
IWFL, the following discourse rehearsing the arguments for and against
the suffrage campaign in Ireland from the perspective of nationalism:

> I'm a prejudiced, narrowminded Separatist, and I don't want a vote
> for the British Parliament, and I couldn't make friends with British
> suffrage societies or belong to any political organisation that
> recognises this country as part of the United Kingdom, and mixes
> itself up in British politics, the way all Irish suffrage societies do ...
>   Well, I'm an extreme Nationalist myself, said Miss MacDermott,
> but that doesn't prevent me working as a suffragist too. I want a
> vote for whatever Parliament is governing me.

Una believes that earlier campaigns directed at the British parliament, such
as the Catholic Emancipation campaign of the 1820s, merely acknowledged the right of the British to rule the Irish and introduced the disabling
concept of parliamentarianism; she proudly accepts the title Sinn Féiner,
indicating her commitment to Arthur Griffith's concept of withdrawal
from Westminster. Yet, Una was willing to sell suffrage papers with Frances
on Grafton Street and attend in her company a suffrage At Home.[63]
Frances spends eight months in Dublin, filling her time very much as Jacob
did with the exception of her role in an official suffrage organisation.

Frances' tasks indicate the multi-focused nature of female activism in the period. She worked:

> as assistant secretary to a suffrage society and unofficial helper to other revolutionary organisations . . . to cook soup by the gallon for locked-out workers and their children . . . to do propaganda work among poor women without losing her temper, to heckle speakers at public meetings, and to make speeches herself. She had come to be on intimate terms with almost every suffragist in Dublin . . . and she had made a creditable name for herself among them. They spoke of her as a thoroughly dependable woman, who could be trusted always to fill a gap and never to make one, who never lost control of herself, and who was pleasant to everyone.

Although the work was mundane, Frances enjoyed the excitement of transcending the prescribed role of women in society and living by contrast 'an independent life, full of incident and interest'.[64]

Although attracted to the republican activist, Andy Callaghan, Frances is repeatedly brought into conflict with him over his attitude to women. On the level of aesthetics he disapproves of women smoking as it yellows their hands. He believes that the O'Meagher family who built his house died out when the last son was killed during the Cromwellian period, despite surviving daughters: it 'was evident that the daughters did not matter'.[65] On the engagement of Frances and Andy, Jacob utilises one of the 'reiterant plot forms' identified by Joannau as a feature of English suffrage literature – 'conflicting desire to be loved and the desire to be active and independent'. 'When presented with a choice between the claims of her male admirer and the claims of political commitment, the suffragette usually opts for love . . . But sometimes she is able to dispense with an unsympathetic man's services . . . or else to convert a seemingly intractable opponent of women's suffrage to the suffragette cause . . .'[66] Callaghan is opposed to Frances returning to her suffrage work following their engagement; he had difficulty in 'trying to assimilate the idea that a woman might have public duties which seemed to her so important as a man's . . . It was too difficult'.[67]

Earlier, Callaghan had prevented Frances protesting against Redmond's refusal to consider the issue of female suffrage. Crucially, he used his superior strength to constrain her. Callaghan's fear of violence being directed against Frances by Redmond's supporters was no barrier to his belief that he had the right to restrain her; Jacob highlights the fundamental nature of male power over women in a scene with heavy connotations of sexual assault. Arguably, this scene was designed to make a wider point about the manner in which male power and superior strength was utilised as a weapon against the suffragettes; the controversial issue of forcible feeding must have been in Jacob's mind in constructing this scene. The physical brutality meted out to suffragettes was a feature of such English suffrage novels as Elizabeth Robins' *The Convert* and like Jacob's scene such violence 'takes on the quality of a rape'.[68]

> . . . Callaghan . . . stood up and caught her abruptly in his arms, holding her with his left arm round her waist, and, with his right hand on the back of her head, pressing her face against his breast, to keep her from screaming in her sudden terror, until she could neither speak nor breathe.'Be quiet!' he said roughly, as Frances made a desperate attempt to free herself and did her best to cry out.

Frances, against herself, is physically attracted to Callaghan at this point. He is conscious of her 'soft form' as he restrains her; afterwards he falls 'limply' to a chair. Almost in post-coital mode, he lights his pipe in a 'half-conscious craving for consolation'. Again, Jacob utilised many of the devices of English suffrage fiction to make points about the nature of patriarchal power: 'She could not feel just then that it mattered much what his motives had been; what mattered was that he had thwarted her by means of physical force, and that she could not defend herself or retaliate.' Callaghan, the physical match for any man, cannot understand 'the sense of utter helplessness that he had aroused in Frances'. Before Frances could go to bed she had to wash her hands and face 'severely and hang her dress out the window to "purify" it'. Frances is only able to restore her sense of equanimity and re-establish a relationship with Callaghan when she gains an insight into his physical vulnerability when, following a car accident, he lay 'helpless and senseless in the hands of others'.[69]

Opposed to Frances' independent political protest in the cause of suffrage as unbefitting to her sex and her duties to him as her future husband, Callaghan has less issue with her involvement in a dangerous arms smuggling incident in which he rushes a police barrier and kills an officer. Attempting to dissuade her, the struggle manifests itself as a half-hearted verbal argument rather than the physical assault prompted by her feminist politics.[70] For Jacob, male objection to female political involvement is masked behind notions of respectability and inherent gender characteristics; in reality the issue was a concern with female independence from the constraints of patriarchy. Callaghan had no sustained objection to Frances' activism when it was under his tutelage and in the service of a campaign which underscored the gender hierarchy, as the division between the Irish Volunteers and Cumann na mBan so abhorred by Jacob reflected.

Received notions of masculinity and femininity are exposed in *Callaghan*. Andy is opposed to Frances' activism but he believes that she could only despise him as a man if he did not take the risks necessary in defence of his political principles. He intends to break up a recruiting meeting despite the certain jail sentence if apprehended. Notably, whatever Frances' objections are, she is aware that she cannot restrain him by force as he did her.[71] When the two get married at the close of the novel, Jacob appears once again to depend on a reiterant suffrage plot form. When Frances announces her engagement, her brother's response is typical; her suffrage activities will, as a matter of course, come to an end. Again, issues of power, both physical and otherwise, are to the fore as he remarks, albeit teasingly: 'You'll have someone to keep you in jolly good order now, Fanny.' Yet Jacob did not portray Callaghan as completely anti-suffrage; he admired Frances' commitment and the 'regal air' she was prone to adopt in defence of her principles. His fundamental problem was his inability to 'assimilate the idea that a woman might have public duties which seemed to her so important as a man's'.[72] In this, Jacob testifies to the manner in which entrenched patriarchal attitudes would be far more difficult to eradicate than the opposition to the vote itself. And in many respect this scenario plays true in her novel; the gender hierarchy is re-established with the closing marriage and nationalism is prioritised over suffragism. While the latter reflects Jacob's own inability to formally join the suffrage cause, the re-establishment of gender power structures is more problematic and arguably reflects the manner in which Jacob's novel mirrors the forms of English suffrage literature; Frances opts for love rather than continued activism. Although she insists on paying half the registry office fee, there is a sense that Callaghan's priorities subsume hers. As they attend their wedding breakfast, Callaghan's house is raided; the issues of nationalism are to the fore then at the close of the novel. Earlier Frances had realised that 'nothing else in the world counted for half as much with her' as Callaghan.[73] She vehemently denies Dr Morrin's assertion that her feminist activism will cease on marriage. Yet when she and Callaghan appear in Jacob's next novel, *The Troubled House*, she occupies the domestic role of wife and mother. She is described, not as a feminist, in this novel, but as a pacifist.[74] While Frances' brother informs Callaghan that he cannot continue to engage in reckless politically motivated actions after his marriage, it is clear that this is just rhetoric; Callaghan in *The Troubled House* is still fully implicated in the intrigue and danger of the national struggle.

CONCLUSION

The elision of feminist politics from Frances' life post-marriage to Callaghan can be read on a number of levels. Arguably, Jacob herself prioritised nationalism over suffrage but the situation is not as simple as that. The structuring element of *Callaghan,* like so many English suffrage novels, is romance ending in marriage; in these novels the issue of choice is crucial. Norquay cites *A Fair Suffragette* as an example of a choice amiable to the dominant ideologies of the day, notably the importance of marriage as one of the key institutions on which the future of the English race is predicated. In this novel by Mollow, the heroine accepts to continue her activism in a limited sphere, but crucially giving up the campaign for the vote. She submits to patriarchal authority. 'For a writer to place the cause in opposition to marriage meant playing upon such anxieties, whereas a reconciliation of personal and political commitments was infinitely more reassuring.'[75] Arguably, the format of English suffrage literature was an unsuitable model for an Irish author who wished to negotiate intersection between the demands of feminism and nationalism. To reaffirm the social order through marriage as demanded in much English suffrage fiction meant, in the fictional Irish context Jacob created in *Callaghan,* prioritising male nationalist demands over female suffrage claims. In her own life, Jacob attempted to negotiate a more subtle balance between the twin causes that shaped her activism in the early twentieth century. Unlike *The Troubled House, Callaghan* does not manifest any of the features of a modernist text. In this novel, as in her diary, Jacob was interested in describing and discussing the political issues which galvanised her, a form of dissident activism because not so easily identifiable as the foot soldier struggling with the policeman. For modernist women writers who eschewed the political activism, by contrast 'it was essential to present not what had happened to them, but what it was like *to be* them'.[76]

NOTES

1. P.J. Mathews, *Revival. The Abbey Theatre, Sinn Féin, The Gaelic League and the Co-operative Movement* (Cork: Cork University Press, 2003). See also essays on the revival in *Irish University Review*, 33.1, 2003.
2. Cliona Murphy rightly places the IWFL within the context of the Irish cultural revival at the turn of the century. Cliona Murphy, *The Women's Suffrage Movement and Irish Society in the Early Twentieth Century* (New York: Harvester, 1989), p. 90.
3. Louise Ryan, *Irish Feminism and the Vote. An Anthology of the Irish Citizen Newspaper 1912–1920* (Dublin: Folens: 1996), p. 143.
4. Louise Ryan, 'Traditions and Double Moral Standards: the Irish suffragists critique of nationalism', *Women's History Review* vol. 4, no. 4 (1995), pp. 487–504, p. 491.
5. See Nicolas Allen, *George Russell (Æ) and the New Ireland, 1905–30* (Dublin: Four Courts, 1993); Leeann Lane, '"It is in the Cottages and Farmers' Houses that the Nation is Born": Æ's *Irish Homestead* and the Cultural Revival', *Irish University Review*, 33, 1 (Spring– Summer, 2003).
6. F. Winthrop, *Callaghan* (Dublin: Martin Lester, n.d [1920]), p. 128.
7. Danae O'Regan, 'Representations and attitudes of republican women in the novels of Annie M.P. Smithson (1873–1948) and Rosamond Jacob (1888–1960) in Louise Ryan and Margaret Ward (eds), *Irish Women and Nationalism. Soldiers, New Women and Wicked Hags* (Dublin: Irish Academic Press, 2004), p. 82, p. 86, p. 95.
8. Much excellent work, for example, has been done on the *Irish Citizen*. See Ryan, *Irish Feminism and the Vote*. See also Margaret Ward (ed.), *In Their Own Voice: Women and Irish Nationalism* (Dublin: Attic, 1995).
9. See Rosemary Cullen Owens, *Smashing Times: A History of the Irish Women's Suffrage Movement 1899–1922* (Dublin: Attic Press, 1984); Margaret Ward, *Unmanageable Revolutionaries, Women and Irish Nationalism* (London: Pluto Press, 1995); Maria Luddy, *Hanna Sheehy Skeffing*ton (Dundalk: Historical Association of Ireland, 1995); Myrtle Hill, *Women in Ireland: A Century of Change* (Belfast: Blackstaff, 2003).
10. See Diane Urquhart (ed.), *The Minutes of the Ulster Unionist Women's Unionist Council and Executive Committee 1911–1940* (Dublin: Irish Manuscripts Commission, 2001); Diane Urquhart, *Women in Ulster Politics, 1890–1940: A History Not Yet Told* (Dublin: Irish Academic Press, 2000).
11. Ryan, *Irish Feminism and the Vote*, p. 147.
12. Margaret Ward, *Hanna Sheehy Skeffington A Life* (Cork: Attic Press, 1997), p. 58. Ward cites the friendship of Sheehy Skeffington and Constance Markievicz as a case in point.
13. Ryan, *Irish Feminism and the Vote*, p. 154.
14. Rosamond Jacob diary (hereafter RJD), 15 March 1913, NLI, Ms 32,582(24).
15. See, for example, 7 February 1909 when she recorded her attendance at the private séance held by T.H. and Roger Webb at the Standard Hotel every Sunday. RJD, 7 February 1909, Ms 32,582(17); 17 August 1912, Ms 32,582(23).
16. In Dublin in early 1911 she went to Kellett's in Great George's Street and 'got a pattern of cream hopsack, intending to get myself a national costume'. Fashion historians have noted how 'craft revival in the late nineteenth century frequently was linked with national or ethnic identity' and thereby worked to bring to mind historic pasts and ideas of independence. Janice Helland, 'Embroidered spectacle: Celtic Revival as aristocratic display', in Betsey Taylor Fitzpatrick and James H. Murphy (eds), *The Irish Revival Reappraised* (Dublin: Four Courts, 2004), p. 96.

17. Winthrop, *Callaghan*, p. 69.
18. RJD, 15 September 1907, Ms 32,582(15).
19. RJD, 16 October 1905, Ms 32,582(10).
20. RJD, 26 November 1913, Ms 32,582(25).
21. RJD, 28 November 1906, Ms 32,582(13).
22. RJD, 4 December 1907, Ms 32,582(15).
23. RJD, 20 November 1907, Ms 32,582(15).
24. RJD, 21 May 1909, 18 July 1909, Ms 32,582(18).
25. RJD, 13 November 1909, Ms 32,582(18).
26. Winthrop, *Callaghan*, p. 73.
27. RJD, 6 June 1913, Ms 32,582(25); 5 August 1912, Ms 32,582(23).
28. RJD, 9 March 1907, Ms 32,582(14).
29. At this point in her life Jacob's anti-Englishness was quite unrefined and instinctual, arguably a reflection of her youth and lack of fully developed political principles. Andy Callaghan reflects Jacob's anti-Englishness: 'his objection to Englishmen amounted to a mania'. Winthrop, *Callaghan*, p. 43.
30. RJD, 25 July 1912, Ms 32,582(23).
31. RJD, 13 February 1914, 15 December 1913, Ms 32,582(26).
32. RJD, 17 October 1913, Ms 32,582(25).
33. See Hanna Sheehy Skeffington, 'Sinn Féin and Irishwomen' in Maria Luddy (ed.), *Women in Ireland 1800–1918. A Documentary History* (Cork: Cork University Press, 1995), pp. 301–3.
34. RJD, 13 January 1910, Ms 32,582(19).
35. RJD, 19 March 1913, Ms 32,582(24). By 1910 there were eighteen suffrage societies in Ireland, which made provision for various political and religious beliefs. Rosemary Cullen Owens, *Louie Bennett* (Cork: Cork University Press, 2000), p. 13.
36. RJD, 13 March 1911, Ms 32,582(21).
37. RJD, 13 May 1914, Ms 32,582(26).
38. RJD, 17 August 1914, Ms 32,582(27).
39. RJD, 9 September 1914, 16 September 1914, Ms 32,582(27).
40. RJD, 12 January 1915, Ms 32,582(28).
41. RJD, 7 March 1915, 9 March 1915, 12 March 1915, Ms 32,582(28).
42. RJD, 19 March 1913, Ms 32,582(24).
43. RJD, 17 March 1915, Ms 32,582(28). In the event Sylvia Pankhurst did not attend due to the Liberal Government's decision to allow women to do work designated male to facilitate enlistment.
44. RJD, 13 February 1914, Ms 32,582(26).
45. See, for example, Ward, *Unmanageable Revolutionaries*.
46. RJD, 23 April 1915, Ms 32,582(28).
47. RJD, 18 March 1913, Ms 32,582(24).
48. Glenda Norquay, *Voices & Votes. A Literary Anthology of the Women's Suffrage Campaign* (Manchester: Manchester University Press, 1995), pp. 2–3.
49. Elaine Showalter, *A Literature Of Their Own* (London: Virago, 1999), p. 220.
50. Maroula Joannou, 'Suffragette fiction and the fictions of suffrage', in Maroula Joannou and June Purvis (eds), *The Women's Suffrage Movement. New Feminist Perspectives* (Manchester: Manchester University Press, 1998), p. 101.
51. Gerardine Meaney, 'Women and Writing, 1700–1960', in Angela Bourke et al. (eds), *The Field Day Anthology of Irish Writing*, vol. v (Cork: Cork University Press, 2002), p. 766, p. 769.
52. Winthrop, *Callaghan*, p. 224.

53. See Wendy Mulford, 'Socialist-feminist criticism: a case study, women's suffrage and literature, 1906–1914', in Peter Widdowson (ed.), *Re-Reading English* (London: Methuen, 1982) on the value of moving attention from 'aesthetic and moral questions of the value of the text, to a broader analysis of literary production in its period' in the context of feminist and socialist historical investigation.

54. Norquay, *Voices and Votes*, p. 9.

55. Antoinette Quinn (ed.), 'Ireland/Herland: Women and Literary Nationalism, 1845–1916' in Angela Bourke et al. (eds), *The Field Day Anthology of Irish Writing*, vol. v (Cork: Cork University Press, 2002), p. 896.

56. O'Regan, 'Representations and attitudes of republican women', p. 85, p. 87.

57. Quinn, 'Ireland/Herland', p. 896. On 29 May 1922 Jacob noted how only 330 copies had been sold in total and only 70 in the past year. RJD, Ms 32,582(41).

58. Quinn, 'Ireland/Herland', p. 898.

59. F. Winthrop, *Callaghan* (Dublin: Martin Lester Ltd., n.d.), p. 29, p. 11, pp. 16–17.

60. Winthrop, *Callaghan*, pp. 69–70.

61. For McSwiney's position see Bourke, *The Field Day Anthology of Irish Writing*, vol. 5, pp. 102–3.

62. Winthrop, *Callaghan*, pp. 72–3.

63. Winthrop, *Callaghan*, pp. 73–4.

64. Ibid., pp. 119–20.

65. Ibid., p. 3, p. 50.

66. Joannou, 'Suffragette fiction and the fictions of suffrage', pp. 111–12.

67. Winthrop, *Callaghan*, p. 174.

68. Showalter, *A Literature Of Their Own*, p. 222.

69. Winthrop, *Callaghan*, pp. 137–9, p. 143.

70. Ibid., p. 190.

71. Ibid., p. 200.

72. Ibid., p. 156, p. 170, p. 171, p. 174.

73. Winthrop, *Callaghan*, p. 145.

74. R. Jacob, *The Troubled House: A Novel of Dublin in the 'Twenties* (Dublin: Browne and Nolan Ltd, 1938), p. 91.

75. Norquay, *Voices and Votes*, pp. 31–2.

76. Gillian Hanscombe and Virginia L. Smyers, *Writing For Their Lives: The Modernist Women 1910–1940* (London: The Women's Press, 1987), p. 9.

CHAPTER ELEVEN

Labour and Suffrage: Spinning Threads in Belfast

DENISE KLEINRICHERT

INTRODUCTION

Working women in the north of Ireland found little hope in the political climate in the nineteenth and early twentieth centuries. The impact of industrialisation failed to stimulate a demand for the vote for the women employed in the textile mills of Belfast. Despite the large presence of women recruited into the mills and factories, they were not considered to have any political importance. Their influence could have been a public force in providing support for a number of political causes, including party candidatures, trade union organisation and socialist and nationalist agendas. The suffragist movement in Ireland, primarily middle class, did not fully embrace women labourers' experiences, nor address how the issues of wages and working conditions could be factored into the demand for the vote. Further, a socialist agenda for trade union organisation of women in the mills, despite its attempt to encourage suffrage efforts, sought political support by adopting a militant approach. This may have frightened women workers who were dependent on their employers for their wages and for their homes.

The Belfast socialist movement's isolation from the suffrage movements in Dublin and Britain also hindered its ability to address women workers' concerns about wages and working conditions. In part, this was due to the fact that the Second International failed to define the role of socialists in the British colonies. Moreover, the question regarding how women ought to be involved in socialist politics concerned not class and the vote, but also the wider issue of what 'limited franchise' meant for a working class concerned to ensure that its male workers would also be enfranchised.[1] Not every male citizen was entitled to the vote; they were required to qualify for the privilege based on their ownership or relationship to occupying property of value. This further hampered politicising women workers, most of whom did not own property. The history of women's suffrage efforts in the north of Ireland has been thoroughly discussed in Myrtle Hill's chapter in this book and provides the background to the demarcation between middle class and working class women. Further, Hill discusses much of the twin approaches of philanthropic and religious influences on northern suffrage.[2] Despite the work of a small core of suffragists in Belfast, much of the suffragist effort for working women emanated from Dublin and focused on gaining the vote for women on the same basis as the extension of the vote for men. Although some suffragists advocated votes for all individuals of a certain age, regardless of gender or property ownership, the movement did not hold a consensus on this issue. My intent is to focus on the twin approaches of organisation for suffrage and the organisation of trade unions among the working women of Belfast's textile mills.

WORKING WOMEN AND ORGANISED VOICES

The mechanisation of spinning yarn from flax had transformed the private sphere of the rural cottage industry of women. This heralded the beginning of collective work endeavours outside the home for women, and an opportunity for political involvement in the public sphere. Burgeoning linen demands created an urban working class as the industrialisation of Belfast took shape in the 1830–40s. By the 1850–60s, the development of mechanised weaving looms furthered a labour-intensive demand for female workers in factory settings designed to incorporate the production of linen within large, concentrated sites. The increased demand for looms and linen mill machinery also necessitated the development of an engineering industry. The export of textiles and the expansion of British trade resulted in increased shipbuilding. In 1858, Belfast's major 'big yard,' Harland and Wolff, was developed.[3] This created collective work processes for men, and allowed trade union organisation to develop, with influences from British models for unskilled male workers. The working class male factory workers and shipbuilders, who did not have access to vote in Parliamentary elections, began to collectively organise by trade in order to improve wages and working conditions in the industry. However, mill women were excluded from the nine organised trade unions in the linen industry[4] and, without enfranchisement, women did not have a public voice to present grievances about their wages or working conditions. However, they did belong to this emerging 'working class', stratified and segregated from access to the vote 'by notions of power and property within the productive process'.[5] Nonetheless, discussions of the particular concerns of women and labour were absent from the forefront of labour dialogue at the time, as evidenced in Louise Ryan's analysis of the Dublin-based suffragist newspaper, *Irish Citizen*, and June Hannam's account of the journalistic coverage of socialism and the Independent Labour Party in the early twentieth century.[6] In addition, the historiography of the period rarely mentions working women. For example, they are not mentioned in Claire Fitzpatrick's account of the labour movement concerns in Belfast.[7]

For women, the notion of class politics is historically interwoven with the suffrage movement. John Belchem identifies 'the complex historical process by which voters, having become conscious of their economic situation, came to recognise a common interest with those similarly placed and a common hostility to those with opposing economic interests'[8] after the Second Reform Act of 1867. As working class women were not necessarily regarded as having interests in common with male workers, no automatic class alliance in pursuit of women's right to the vote was likely to develop. Instead, politicising women took the complementary, then radical, form of establishing a women's organisation within the labour movement. However, this task was problematic, given the type of work and industry in which women in Belfast were situated. The historical records reflect that initially 'women were concentrated in occupations which were the most difficult to organise: outwork, small workshop and domestic employment, often part-time or seasonal'.[9] As women moved into the low-wage industrial market, this way of thinking continued to define the mind-set of male trade union organisations. The prevalent view of trade union organisers 'upheld the principle of the male family wage, sufficient earnings to keep wife and children out of the labour market'.[10] Having stepped outside their 'separate spheres', women were considered to be competing for jobs with men.

By 1890, the Belfast Trades Council, in conjunction with the London-based Women's Trade Union League, acknowledged that the horrendous working conditions and low wages of female linen workers demanded organisation into a trade union. This initiative, a gendered separatist approach, initially recruited women into three trade organisations designated for corresponding linen production processes. Unfortunately, the number of women remaining in these organisations declined within a short period of time.[11] Thus, the affiliated Textile

Operatives' Society of Ireland was formed in 1893. This second initiative by the Belfast Trades Council's secretary of the organising committee, William Walker, was sought to alleviate the male council members' concerns regarding the growing numbers of unorganised women workers in the mills. In fact, male workers of equal skill were earning 40% more each week.[12] Walker became the Textile Operatives Society of Ireland's secretary, a position he held from 1894–5, before turning over the role to Mary Galway. The realisation that the initial 750 women members fell to 250 members within a year (partly attributed to a lack of identification of women workers with male organisers and their part-time male secretary) led to recruitment of a female secretary. This role entailed more than bookkeeping, maintaining members' names, and attributing dues and fines. It included holding society meetings, starting new branches, recruiting for new members, and mobilising members regarding grievances. By 1897, despite the paternalism of the Belfast Trades Council towards women workers, Mary Galway became president of the Textile Operatives.[13] The efforts to organise working women into trade unions seemed to prove difficult, which appears to have been a factor in later attempts to develop their interest in suffrage activism.

The increased demand for skilled and unskilled labour stimulated the population growth of Belfast from 19,000 in 1800 to 349,000 in 1901, and 50,000 – 60,000 women linen workers[14] faced working lives outside the home. Despite early attempts to recruit women, the labour organisation of women did not become a significant concern until after the First World War. Further, the issue of suffrage and its relationship to labour was an even more difficult enterprise, due to the social perspectives of women's roles. While Belfast's industrial development was unmatched by Dublin, Glasgow, Manchester, or Liverpool by the end of the nineteenth century,[15] industrial expansion created large wage and political disparities between male and female workers. The large mills readily employed unskilled women, due to their acceptance of lower wages. This climate was ripe for the development of an organised voice for working women – through both enfranchisement and labour organisation.

Women, at lower wages, outnumbered male workers by a ratio of three to one[16] within the mills, predominantly filling the unskilled and lower skilled functions in the preparing, spinning, and reeling processes. Many women lived in nearby housing provided by the mill owners. Therefore, although the mill women worked outside the home, they were still confined to the private sphere of the mill with little to account for a move from domestic to public spaces. Further, girls often started work at eleven years of age (some as young as eight years prior to the Factory and

Workshop Act of 1901) because they had small, nimble fingers; schoolgirls worked three days a week and attended school three days (they were called 'half-timers'). A full day for all mill women and girls would extend until at least 6:00 p.m. The work week stretched to fifty-five and a half hours.[17] The ventilation was extremely limited, and the air temperatures rose to high levels due to the combination of climate, crowded working conditions, and mechanised equipment.[18]

Unskilled working women of this period were oppressed and exploited in the mills. Voteless, they lacked a political voice; they could not hold public office and were not represented in traditional trade unions. The only public 'voice' mill women possessed was the strike. For example, in 1906 some 15,000 flax spinners went on strike for higher wages. Mill owners retaliated by laying off other workers and closing some thirty factories to all workers.[19] The owners of the mills staunchly defended their means of production as efficient, modelled on the successes of the English factories, which provided much-needed family income.

Beginning in 1907, skilled women workers in Belfast joined the all-male Flax Roughers' Trade Union, to Galway's initial dismay, and subsequently the Textile Operatives admitted male workers who were not covered by other union memberships.[20] These mixed unions served to further politicise working women's efforts towards wage grievances. There has been little sustained analysis of Galway's role in organising and politicising skilled women workers; however, Theresa Moriarty has illuminated the multi-faceted role of Galway in her efforts for Belfast working women. Galway began to speak publicly about votes for women in 1908 when, as Moriarty paraphrases, 'women should have the same political rights as men, and they should be admitted to parliament'.[21] She spoke publicly at women's suffrage meetings in Belfast in 1910.[22] Galway's efforts for working women reflected a strong advocacy for women's enfranchisement due to their public roles in the workplace and their desire for the well-being of their communities.

The 'Suffragists' Catechism', as outlined in the *Irish Citizen* in, 1913[23] echoed Galway's concerns regarding equal voting rights. The Suffragists' Catechism noted that working women were often criticised for not staying in the domestic sphere and 'minding their homes instead'.[24] The 'Catechism' illuminated the concerns of working women, arguing that: 'There are large numbers of women at work in the world, in factories, shops and offices, earning their own bread as independent beings.'[25] The concerns of the household, the private sphere of women, were affected by women's wages, and therefore 'politics are vital'.[26]

Although much of the historical literature points to rumours of Galway's apparent compromise with employer considerations, further analysis seems to reflect a political tension borne out of the twin agendas of trade union organisation for women and suffrage as a mechanism to liberate working women. Nevertheless, Galway eventually became the most prominent woman trade unionist in Ireland when she joined the parliamentary committee of the Irish Trades Union Council (ITUC).[27] She was one of the first trade union women to speak publicly about suffrage in the context of trade organisation for skilled women workers.

The estimated 11,000 skilled working women spinners in Belfast in 1911 were largely unorganised; only roughly 3,000 had affiliated with Galway's Textile Operatives' Society of Ireland. The TOSI represented the skilled, higher end of the industry, and largely Protestant unionist workers. Some historians have reported that Galway had essentially neglected the social and domestic plight of many of the unskilled Catholic women linen workers, although Moriarty's research has shown that Galway was Catholic. Many of the women TOSI members felt that any pay rise obtained by Galway through negotiation with the mill owners was subsequently followed by an increase in the trade operative's dues.[28]

A wave of demonstrations and strikes of some 15,000 unorganised women across Scotland and England during the summer of 1911 had brought working women's issues, such as low rates of pay, to the forefront in Britain. As a result, working women in the Belfast linen industry instigated a strike for two weeks, beginning 4 October 1911, which led to notoriety for syndicalist James Connolly. The women textile mill workers sought out Connolly to assist them in their grievances on the eve of the spinners' strike in the linen mills. The strike had started in one mill when a compulsory production speed-up was instituted. Further, employers levied fines on the mill women for violation of posted rules against singing, laughing, talking, or 'adjusting hair' during work hours. Mill owners feared the songs stimulated solidarity among the women and thus considered the activity threatening. In a bid to stop the singing, fines were levied against the instigators among the mill women.[29] Connolly advised them to enter the mill as a group, singing. If one was reprimanded for laughing, all the women should leave at once. The striking women were largely unorganised, unskilled, and predominantly Catholic. When they had approached Galway for assistance with the strike, they were reportedly rebuffed.[30] The strike spread to several other mills. The strike coverage in the Belfast-based nationalist *Irish News* newspaper, employer reactions, and the opposition by the skilled working women's Textile Operatives Society under Galway emphasised the futility of a continued strike.

The strike was the only public action mill women felt they could use to publicise their plight. It appealed to them because it was a tangible element by means of which they hoped to gain some control over their lives, rather than looking to the vote and placing control in others to make decisions for them.

In Dublin, suffragists were divided over the question of working class votes. Some of the most prominent, middle-class women were concerned only with votes for propertied women, while a smaller number advocated inclusion of working women as a socialist ideal.[31] The *Irish Citizen* provides a backdrop to the social and historical context and oftentimes divergent complexities of working class women, including those mill workers in Belfast. Louise Ryan provides a comprehensive analysis, with excerpts which illuminate the difficulties suffragists and working women faced in reconciling their misconception of social forces and political voices. Marion Duggan, writing in the *Irish Citizen* on 20 February 1915 on the subject of labour and suffrage, advocated the use of trade unions to work towards suffrage efforts.[32] Up to this point, there was little public discourse about the vote for working women in Belfast.

Galway seemed concerned with Connolly's appeal to all mill women, regardless of skill, religious background, age, or marital status, to join the Irish Textile Workers' Union, a section of his union, the Irish Transport and General Workers' Union. The tradition of segregation of workers' organisations by gender was classically British (and accepted by James Larkin, in Dublin), but it was in ideological conflict with Connolly's socialist espousal of one industry, one union for all. Galway's perspective of union organisation of women and enfranchisement, and her apparent reluctance to work with his colleague, Winifred Carney, seems counterproductive to the cause of alleviation of the plight of working mill women. Connolly based his appeals on the shipyard workers' efforts at organisation, and their commercial connection to the import of raw materials such as flax and the export of linen, all associated with the production processes of the textile mills. Many of the mill women were relatives of the men working the low docks, who were affiliated with the ITGWU.

Under the socialist efforts of their trade union organisation of working women, Carney and others working with Connolly focused on suffrage efforts among the women factory workers. Women suffragist speakers from Dublin were brought to Belfast to speak to mill women. However, those speakers were not working women but middle class women with a single focus on suffrage. In a series of public meetings designed to educate Belfast's working women about the role of the vote in their lives, these Dublin suffragists seemed to convey an air of condescension. In other words, class differences, coupled with the geographic distinctions, led to allegations of 'elitism' from a trade union woman, Helena Moloney.[33] The Dublin suffragists argued that, without the vote, working women would be destined to continue in exploitative work environments for unskilled, gendered roles in the linen and textile factories. The mill workers felt both intimidated and dissociated from the purpose of the vote in their own lives in Belfast, seeking practical, immediate impact on their lives through collective public demonstrations and work strikes.

Despite open-air meetings and Irish cultural dances to attract women mill workers, Connolly was unable to attract unskilled women into a labour union espousing radical means such as strikes. Perhaps a strategy based on the suffrage issue for working women in Belfast and using the vote to address women's needs might have been more successful.[34] The suffrage and trade union organisation efforts among Belfast working women were a difficult proposition from a number of perspectives. Firstly, although trade union propaganda was designed to stimulate working women into fighting for their own needs and fifteen public meetings were organised over the 1911–12 period, 87 per cent of these were conducted outside Belfast, despite its working class population. In the following year, some thirty-three meetings were held in Ireland and, once again, the overwhelming numbers of meetings, 85 per cent, were conducted outside of Belfast.[35] Secondly, the young age at which girls were recruited into the factories, with their naiveté and lack of experience working outside the home, presented a great obstacle to developing an understanding of the outside world. In addition, their families' need for their additional income precluded many from taking a militant stance, either for suffrage or for trade union membership. Historically, numerous cases of employer retaliation against union membership among women and girls had been noted, as Galway testified:

> It is easy to understand why so many hundreds of women and girls, knowing that their weekly wage is all that stands between them and starvation, are terrified to do anything that might deprive them, even for one week, of that wage.[36]

A history of poverty, starvation, and emigration served as a legacy among the mill workers of Belfast. By 1911, 56 per cent of Belfast Catholic women over the age of twelve had a stated occupation, as opposed to 43 per cent of the Presbyterian women in the city.[37] Further, 37.3 per cent of all linen workers were Catholic women. The eldest daughters and other family members served as 'wee mummies' while their sisters and mothers worked, creating an atmosphere of quiet acquiescence:

> When you were eight, you were old enough to work. If you got married you kept working. Your man didn't get enough for a family. You worked till your baby came and went back as soon as you could, and then you counted the years till your child could be a half-timer.[38]

Women's lack of politicisation, either for the vote or for trade unions, was accentuated by sectarian differences. This served to differentiate women and to 'preclude an independent working class movement' between the Protestant and Catholic, skilled and unskilled, in the shipyards and textile mills.[39]

Connolly's activism on behalf of workers, despite his interest in representation for women in suffrage and socialist trade union efforts, seems to have failed to fully support an advancement of working women through political mechanisms, even as his two daughters, Ina and Nora, and labour colleagues, Marie Johnson and Winifred Carney, served as active suffragists in Belfast with support from Dublin influences.

WOMEN ACTIVISTS IN BELFAST

Women's public roles were much more profound than has been previously regarded by historians. Carney's and Galway's contributions to suffrage and trade union organisation reflect their deep-seated convictions that political mechanisms were the response to 'the terrible exploitation of women's labour in factories, mines and mills'.[40] Carney did not approach women's labour organisation from a separatist perspective, as Galway initially did. Nor did she embrace suffrage separately – rather, she looked to a socialist ideal of women and men's endeavours in partnership for a common working class. Carney's upbringing was one of a Catholic lower middle-class family, the youngest of six children of a Protestant father who eventually abandoned them. She was a former junior teacher at a staunchly nationalist Christian Brothers' Catholic School. She grew up in a family that provided exposure to intellectual stimulation, 'rambling and adventure', and rebellious Irish nationalist writings. Serious and reserved, she was uninterested in marriage and was seeking more than a secretarial role in an office. She had the makings of an organiser and activist with the desire to gear her life towards working women's political rights.

In 1911 Carney co-founded the Irish Textile Workers' Union with Delia Larkin, sister of the labour organiser, James Larkin. On 1 September 1912, aged twenty four, Carney accepted the more comprehensive position of secretary to the ITGWU in Belfast, working under the direction of James Connolly. This was her opportunity to see her efforts for unionisation put to professional use in working for Belfast working women. For example, mill women lacked medical coverage for their illnesses until the National Health Insurance plan for workers was instituted in July 1912. The ITGWU established an insurance pro-gramme. Carney readily organised the tasks to disseminate information and provide assistance to women in securing the requisite forms for their individual insurance needs.[41] She was also instrumental, along with Marie Johnson and Nellie Gordon, in attempts to not only organise the women mill workers into the ITGWU,[42] but to seek support for enfranchisement of working women. Marie Johnson was married to socialist labour leader and *Forward* editor Tom Johnson, who also advocated the vote for all women.

Carney's acceptance of the role of full-time secretary and organiser to the ITWU in Belfast, following labour activist and suffragist Marie Johnson's part-time honorary commitment, provided a visible role for both labour and suffrage causes. Carney wrote an article, 'The Sweated Women Workers of Belfast', in the *Irish Citizen*, 28 December 1912. While she placed emphasis on the low wages and poverty of the mill women, the role of working women in Belfast society, and their integral position in the linen industry, she also demanded that all spinners receive a minimum wage. Further, she demanded that the government provide a female inspector for the factories. Importantly, she noted that these demands were made under the collective endeavour of the ITWU trade union because working women lacked 'political power to enforce their economic necessities, [because] the sweated woman workers of Belfast are virtually powerless to secure the legislative changes which they demand'.[43] This role of activist would eventually transform her from a silent radical into 'the typist with the Webley', who joined the insurgents in the GPO during the 1916 Uprising. She edited and typed Connolly's numerous articles, writings and speeches, not only on behalf of the ITGWU but also his political treatises. Her greater role is evident in the composition of some of these writings. One such open letter, addressed 'To the Linen Slaves of Belfast', was issued over the names of Carney and Gordon with his name added as 'Organiser'.

The *Irish Citizen* included occasional articles, including one on 19 July 1913 which argued for the importance of the vote for working women, particularly highlighting their plight despite the existence of the Labour Party: 'The labour members do not represent women, they represent men. And yet people can be found who say that votes have nothing to do with wages!'[44] As Marion Duggan stated in her 20 February 1915 letter to the *Irish Citizen*, the twin effort of the vote and trade union organisation for women was of such importance that despite male trade union lack of support for working women, 'Votes without Industrial Organisation are of little use to workers as workers.'[45]

Although, by her own choice she had a limited public speaking role, Carney was an avid writer and contributor to labour treatises and meticulous in her organisational skills. She garnered trust from her colleagues, and continued her involvement in the mill worker recruitment meetings in Belfast.[46] These meetings provided a combined effort towards trade union organisation and enfranchisement of the mill women. One such meeting, 'Strikes as a Revolutionary Weapon', featured Countess Constance Markievicz who spoke about the Dublin Lockout of August 1913. Although Markievicz, an upper class feminist, espoused Connolly's socialist ideals, Belfast mill women failed to identify with her, but they were impressed by her well-dressed presence and forthright speech.[47] Despite the lack of connection they felt for Markievicz, Carney instigated fundraising in Belfast to secure financial support for the locked-out workers of some four hundred firms in Dublin. She also sought housing for many of the locked-out Dublin working women who had come to Belfast in search of alternate work.[48] Further, Carney honed her organisational efforts in the establishment of the Fianna boys and girls (the militant nationalist youth movement) and reported her experiences in the 1 November 1913 issue of the *Irish Worker*.[49]

By 1914 Carney had become interested in both suffrage, as espoused by the *Irish Citizen*, and in nationalism, an opportunity provided by the formation of Cumann na mBan that year.[50] But her nationalist militancy acted as a disincentive for unionist women to work with nationalist women on suffrage or labour issues. Carney and Gordon joined the first Cumann na mBan branch in Belfast. The suffragist and labour efforts of Nora and Ina Connolly also became less important as they formed the only female branch of the Fianna. Military drilling for both men and women was initiated as nationalist hopes rose.[51] It is important to recall, however, that this movement was developing while international pacifism also strengthened in the wake of the Great War, as demonstrated in much of the later editorial perspectives of the *Irish Citizen*, and personified by women such as Dublin suffragist and labour activist Louie Bennett and Belfast's L.A.M. Priestly, a unionist and member of the Irish Women's Suffrage Society.[52]

Just months before Carney joined Connolly in membership of the Irish Citizen Army in Dublin, she issued his encouraging words regarding women's roles in 'A Happy New Year' address, which appeared on 1 January 1916 in the *Workers' Republic*:

> Division of labour has been pushed to an extent hitherto undreamed of. Women have been harnessed to the wheels of production in places and at operations hitherto performed solely by men – and so harnessed with none of the rights with which men safeguarded their positions – and the whole industrial population has been made accustomed to browbeating and driving from those set in authority.[53]

Carney's responsibilities to the union and the continuation of its enterprise remained, despite a fire that damaged the ITGWU Belfast premises sometime in January 1916. However, she believed that constitutional politics would not achieve a workers' republic and she further sought to align herself with the wave of republicanism centred in Dublin, rather than focus on women's right to vote. She viewed Connolly's Irish Citizen Army as the militant embodiment of the working class, regardless of gender and political affinity, and more significant than a continued effort on the sole issue of the vote.

The suffrage impetus was not firmly embedded within Ireland by 1916. Nationalistic endeavours took precedence and large-scale suffrage efforts waned in Belfast as Carney, a number of other female and male labour activists from the ITGWU, and the Textile Operatives Union soon discovered, despite suffrage meetings and a paper that was freely distributed in the city centre.

After the Rising, and the execution of Connolly and the other leaders, Carney was imprisoned for several months. The *Irish Citizen* contained editorials and articles on the prominent roles women held in public discourse and activism. The articles contained tributes to men as well, such as Connolly, who exhibited 'the wisdom of true statesmanship . . . he recognised that the cause of Woman and Labour was twin . . . '[54] The list of those included as revolutionaries who fought and were imprisoned for their efforts, yet were friends to suffragists for the cause of Ireland, included both men and women of Dublin. Noticeably absent is the name of socialist trade union organiser, Winnie Carney, of Belfast. Socialist historical works, both past and contemporary, have focused singularly on Connolly and his efforts, oftentimes disregarding the role of many women socialist activists for suffrage and women's labour, and thus presenting a distorted picture of the events.

At the time of her internment, the British government's preoccupation with Carney's Belfast-based trade union work and affiliation with James Connolly was evident. Laurence Ginnell, Dublin-based MP, appealed to have her charged (she was an unsentenced prisoner) or released in October 1916. The issue was brought before the Secretary of State for the Home Department, Mr Samuel, who was questioned by Ginnell as to whether 'that of being a trades unionist' was her crime. Samuel's response was that she was interned 'upon the recommendation of a competent military authority on the ground that she is of hostile associations and reasonably suspected of having favoured, promoted or assisted an armed insurrection against His Majesty . . . I am informed that both she and Miss Helena Moloney are trade union officials, but I need hardly say that the fact that she was a trade unionist had nothing to do with her internment'.[55] However, a mention of the plight of two trade union women who were active in the suffrage movement, interned without trial, Moloney (of Dublin) and 'Kearney' (Belfast's activist, Carney, is misspelled) appeared in two editorials in the *Irish Citizen*, first in September and then in December 1916:

> It is strange that these two women have been singled out for this treatment. Is it possible that why these women are detained is that they are both women who are connected with the Trades' Union Movement in Ireland? From answers given in Parliament about wages paid to women workers in Belfast it would appear that Miss Kearney's (sic) presence there is badly required to organise the women workers.[56]

Three of the five women held at Aylesbury after the Rising were socialists and directly involved in suffrage and trade union organisation efforts in Belfast. Carney remained interned, with Moloney, until their quiet, unnoticed release at Christmas 1916.

By late 1917 the *Irish Citizen* contained encouraging commentary regarding working women. Louie Bennett, now organiser of the Irish Women Workers' Union, was acting editor and sought to make the paper a voice piece for trade union women. The indications of greater trade union organisation among working women was attributed to a growing confidence and a 'realisation that their fate is in their own hands'.[57] Bennett analysed this in an article in January 1918, indicating that this confidence had increased the membership, activity, and awareness of working women. Nationalism had reached its practical level, but importantly 'women will find the best means of serving Ireland through the power of the trade union' and the 'broader directions' that suffrage would offer as a new feminism based on economic justice.[58]

1918 AND THE VOTE

In February 1918, the British Parliament granted the vote to women over thirty years of age, although all men over twenty-one were eligible. This age discrepancy was to ensure that the electorate would not be female dominated. The 1918 Representation of the People Act was extended further in November to include a one-clause act that permitted women to be members of Parliament for the first time. I would argue that, if the working women of Belfast had been more solidly approached by labour organisers and socialist leaders, women mill workers could have posed a formidable presence in this election. The Labour Party in Ireland did not choose a woman candidate (although Louie Bennett was rumoured to have been approached), largely because the party represented conservative male heads of households who were affiliated with the industrial trade unions for men. This was similar to the British experience, where only four women were recruited by Labour, two of whom were suffragists, and 'all the work had fallen on to the inexperienced candidate'.[59] Sinn Féin chose Carney, who was elected as the Belfast delegate to the National Convention of Cumann na Ban in the autumn of 1917, as a token candidate to campaign against a staunch, conservative Ulster Unionist Labour candidate in predominately Protestant unionist East Belfast (the Victoria Ward). The selection was without solid Sinn Féin support. Sinn Féin's decision reflected Carney's militant nationalist activism, not her suffrage and labour activism. Despite this, she stood as an avowed socialist who advocated an independent Ireland and a Workers' Republic, contrary to conservative Protestant and Catholic views in the North.[60] Given the large new voting block of unorganised conservative Belfast women mill workers, this seems to have been a misstep that significantly hindered her efforts at gaining votes among working women.

The local media, which included the Catholic and conservative nationalist paper, *Irish News*, purposely neglected Carney's candidacy, in an 'unwinnable constituency'.[61] The speeches of the other two candidates in attendance at a public meeting were widely reported and quoted. The *Irish News* only reported on one of her election meetings throughout the campaign. The *Irish Citizen* provided only a brief couple of paragraphs to the two Irish women candidates, Carney and Constance Markievicz, in their December 1918 edition. This is despite the Irish Women's Franchise League provision of support to Carney through the organisation of a meeting in which Dublin suffragist Margaret Connery addressed the audience.[62] Sinn Féin also brought in Dr Kathleen Lynn from Dublin. Carney did receive some assistance from Belfast Cumann na mBan women, but these supporters understood little of the complexities of this election.[63] During the campaign she spoke directly to the mill women regarding their newly given right to vote, with the suggestion that women could vote more productively than men had in the past. This appears to have been insufficient to move their vote; the unskilled mill women largely lived outside the ward Carney was seeking to represent. Recent historians, in their analysis of the 1918 election in Belfast, fail to mention Carney, yet provide the background of the other two male candidates and of their public debates.[64]

Despite women now forming a substantial part of the electorate, Sinn Féin was the sole Irish party to stand female candidates in the general election. In assessing the chances of Markievicz and Carney, the *Irish Citizen* concluded:

> But both seats chosen are bound to be hotly contested and it is probable that not more than one woman candidate will be elected for the whole of Ireland. Great Britain has at least thirteen women candidates of varying parties: it looks as if Irishmen (even Republicans) needed teaching in this matter.[65]

In the final vote tally, Carney received just 395 votes. The victor, who then failed to achieve any measures of any great importance while in Parliament, received nearly 10,000 votes. Margaret Connery was angered by the result, as she wrote to Hanna Sheehy Skeffington: 'The very nerve of Sinn Féin sets my teeth on edge. The one woman they have thrown as a sop to the women of the country has her interest neglected.'[66]

Carney attributed her defeat to the lack of support from her own party, Sinn Féin, rather than on her gender or her socialist politics:

I had neither personation agents, committee rooms, canvassers or vehicles, and as these are the chief agents in an election, it was amazing to me to find that 395 people went to the ballot on their own initiative, without any persuasion. The organisation in Belfast could have been much, much better.[67]

Claire Eustance provides a trenchant analysis of the way in which women's suffrage efforts and access to a public voice on an elected political platform were thwarted, even after the vote was extended to include women's candidature in the 1918 election, concluding that, despite appearances, women suffragists were misled in their 'assumptions that male support for women's suffrage was straightforward and unproblematic'.[68]

CONCLUSION

In the late nineteenth and early twentieth century, working women in Belfast lived in an era and social context where female workers in the mills were regarded as 'girls'. The issues surrounding identity politics were gendered in terms of labour and social roles. The suffrage movement seemed foreign to the mill women, locked in their struggle for survival, despite the fact that suffragists were not wholly unaware of the reality of working class life. Margaret Connery's article in the 4 January 1913 issue of the *Irish Citizen* was full of indignation on their behalf: 'The woman of the labouring class to-day, whether as industrial worker or as wife and mother, is the most exploited and overdriven slave on the face of the earth.'[69] However, the working women's suffrage movement lacked the cohesive strength of a committed political party dedicated to the woman worker/labour issue. The political force necessary had no mechanism without women's vote – no spinner's wheel – to articulate the specific interests of working women.

These factors eventually overshadowed Carney's candidature in the 1918 elections, and were to have a decisive and negative impact on the future for working class women in the North. Carney avoided electoral politics after that unsuccessful attempt, although she continued to work as a labour activist against the backdrop of continued wage disparities between women and men in industrial Belfast. Her work for the ITGWU and the labour movement was groundbreaking as she sought to improve the position of working class women while insisting on their right to be included within the general trade union movement. She did not support separate, gender-based unions. As she did not seek public acknowledgement for her labour and suffrage efforts, many historians and biographers of women suffragists and labour organisers have overlooked her role in the advocacy of suffrage and labour rights for Belfast mill women. Carney did not leave a body of written work of her own accord, nor did she receive press coverage of her silent, but relentless endeavours to better the lives of working women. Carney's biography and Nellie Gordon's autobiography have had little public distribution. Historian Helga Woggon, in discussing why so little has been known of Carney, does not attribute this to either her socialism or her gender, noting instead that perhaps she did not 'readily fit in with the dominant conceptions of either the Connolly renaissance or the passion for the working class autobiography [of the late 1960s and into the 1970s]'.[70]

Carney married George McBride, a Belfast trade union colleague and former British soldier from a Protestant working class family. She was marginalised further within the nationalist movement as a result. In reflecting on their fifteen year marriage, McBride spoke fondly of the days spent working in partnership with her in the cause of labour. He never remarried after her premature death but spent the next forty five years thinking about her, noting her integral presence in Irish labour and feminist interests. In my interview with Woggon, she relayed her personal discussions with McBride, when he 'spoke about her as if she'd just left the room'.[71]

It would be over twenty years after Carney's death in 1943 before a mass effort for working class civil rights would be instigated by women in Northern Ireland.[72] The historical record reflects much about the activism of various women towards achieving a public voice for women, but the particular voice of working women in Belfast took much longer to gain strength, despite the extension of the vote in 1918. A number of factors can be cited in explanation; most importantly, the record has neglected to weigh the silent, persistent radicalism of the working women themselves, proscribed to a 'private' room inside the confines of the industrial workplace, rather than the 'public' room of the political space.

NOTES

1. June Hannam, 'New Histories of the Labour Movement,' in Ann-Marie Gallagher, Cathy Lubelski, and Louise Ryan (eds), *Re-presenting the Past: Women and History* (Edinburgh: Pearson Education Ltd., 2001), p. 164.

2. Myrtle Hill, 'Ulster: Debates, Demands and Divisions: The Battle For (and Against) the Vote,' chapter in this book.
3. Austen Morgan, *Labour and Partition: The Belfast Working Class 1905–23* (London: Pluto Press, 1991), p. 5; Ged Martin, 'The Origins of Partition,' in Malcolm Anderson and Eberhard Bort (eds), *The Irish Border: History, Politics, Culture* (Liverpool: Liverpool University Press, 1999).
4. Therese Moriarty, 'Mary Galway (1864–1928)', in Mary Cullen and Maria Luddy (eds), *Female Activists: Irish Women and Change 1900–1960* (Dublin: Woodfield Press, 2001), p. 12.
5. John Belchem, *Class, Party and the Political System in Britain 1867–1914* (Oxford: Basil Blackwell Ltd., 1990) p. 2.
6. See Louise Ryan, *Irish Feminism and the Vote: An Anthology of the* Irish Citizen *Newspaper 1912–1920* (Dublin: Folens Press, 1996) and the co-edited work of A. Gallagher, C. Lubelska, and L. Ryan, *Re-presenting the Past: Women and History*.
7. Claire Fitzpatrick, 'Nationalising the Ideal: Labour and Nationalism in Ireland, 1909–1923', in Eugenio F. Biagini (ed.), *Citizenship and Community: Liberals, Radicals and Collective Identities in the British Isles, 1865–1931* (Cambridge: Cambridge University Press, 1996).
8. Belchem, p. 3.
9. Ibid., p. 79
10. Ibid., p. 80.
11. Moriarty, p. 14.
12. Ibid., p. 15.
13. Morgan, pp. 62–3; Moriarty, p. 14.
14. Moriarty, p. 11.
15. Morgan, p. 6.
16. Moriarty, p. 16.
17. Helga Woggon, 'Ellen Grimley (Nellie Gordon)', *Irish Labour History Society: Studies in Irish Labour History* 6 (Dublin: Services, Industrial, Professional & Technical Union, 2000), p. 18; Peter Collins, *The Making of Irish Linen* (Belfast: Friars Bush Press, 1994), pp. 18–20; Betty Messenger, 'Folklore of the Northern Irish Linen Industry, 1900–1935', PhD dissertation, Department of Folklore, Indiana University, Bloomington, Indiana (1975), p. 53.
18. Mary Galway, 'Trades Unions and Women's Employment,' *Irish Citizen* (Dublin: 11 December 1915).
19. Moriarty, p. 21.
20. Ibid., p. 24.
21. Ibid., p. 24.
22 Ryan (1996), p. 33.
23. Ibid., p. 34.
24. Moriarty, p. 25.
25. Ryan (1996), p. 34.
26. Ibid., p. 34.
27. Morgan, p. 151.
28. Sheila Lewenhak, *Women and Trade Unions: An Outline History of Women in the British Trade Union Movement* (New York: St. Martin's Press, 1977), pp. 130–1; Messenger, p. 311; Morgan, pp. 151–2.
29. Messenger, pp. 7–8.
30. Lewenhak, p. 136; Messenger, p. 311; Morgan, pp. 152–3.
31. Ryan (1996), p. 111

32. Ibid.
33. Ibid., p. 113.
34. Morgan, pp. 151–3.
35. Richard English, 'Socialist Intellectuals and the 1916–23 Irish Revolution,' pp. 15–16, The Nature of the Irish Revolution 1913–23 Symposium, Queen's University Belfast, September 1999.
36. Mary Galway, *Irish Citizen*, 11 December 1915.
37. Mary Daly, *Women and Work in Ireland* (Dublin: The Economic and Social History Society of Ireland, 1997), p. 4.
38. Jonathon Hamill, 'Childcare Arrangements Within the Belfast Linen Community, 1890–1930,' in Bernadete Whelan (ed.), *Women and Paid Work in Ireland, 1500–1930*, quote of elderly mill hand, (Dublin: Four Courts Press, 2000), p. 122.
39. Andrew Boyd, *The Rise of the Irish Trade Unions* (Dublin: Anvil Books, 1985), p. 79.
40. Harry Pollitt (ed), *Women and Communism* (London: Lawrence and Wishart, 1950), p. 27
41. Helga Woggon, 'Silent Radical – Winifred Carney, 1887–1943: A Reconstruction of Her Biography', *Irish Labour History Society: Studies in Irish Labour History* 6 (Dublin: Services, Industrial, Professional & Technical Union, 2000), p. 13.
42. Kit and Cyril Ó Céirín, *Women of Ireland* (Galway: Tír Eolis, 1996), p. 38; Frank Glenholmes, 'Winifred Carney', *Belfast Graves*, Vol. 2 (Belfast: Belfast Graves Association, c. 1985); Woggon, *Silent Radical*, pp. 10–13.
43. Ryan (1996), p. 119–20.
44. Ibid., p. 127.
45. Ibid., p. 131.
46. Connolly, 'To the Linen Slaves of Belfast'; Morgan, p. 155; W.K. Anderson, *James Connolly and the Irish Left* (Dublin: Irish Academic Press, 1994), pp. 16–24; Woggon, *Silent Radical*; Woggon, *Ellen Grimley (Nellie Gordon)*, pp. 11, 13, 19.
47. Jacqueline Van Voris, *Constance de Markievicz: In the Cause of Ireland* (Amherst: University of Massachusetts Press, 1967), p. 126.
48. Woggon, *Silent Radical*, p. 14.
49. Van Voris, p. 124 ft; Woggon, *Silent Radical*, p. 14.
50. Liz Curtis, *The Cause of Ireland, From the United Irishmen to Partition* (Belfast: Beyond the Pale Publications, 1994), pp. 236–7; Woggon, *Silent Radical*, p. 15.
51. Margaret Ward, 'Ulster Was Different? Women, Feminism, and Nationalism in the North of Ireland', in Yvonne Galligan, Eilís Ward and Rick Wilford (eds), *Contesting Politics – Women In Ireland, North and South* (Oxford: Westview Press, 1999), pp. 230–1; Diane Urquhart, *Women in Ulster Politics* (Dublin: Irish Academic Press, 2000), p. 111.
52. Dana Hearne, 'The Development of Irish Feminist Thought: A Critical Historical Analysis of the *Irish Citizen*, 1912–1920', PhD dissertation, Social & Political Thought (York University, North York, Ontario: June 1992), p. 356; Ryan (1996), p. 79, 115. See also the chapter by Margaret Ward in this volume.
53. James Connolly, 'A Happy New Year', (1 January 1916), in Aindrias Ó Cathasaigh (ed), *The Lost Writings of James Connolly* (London: Pluto Press, 1997), p. 191.
54. Editorial, 'Suffrage Casualties', September 1916, in Ryan (1996), p. 171.
55. Minutes of Daily Debates, House of Commons, 27–31 October 1916, HO 144/1457/314179, Kew Public Record Office, London.
56. 'Is Trade Unionism Illegal?', *Irish Citizen* (December 1916).
57. Ryan (1996), p. 134.

58. Ibid., pp. 135–6.
59. Joanna Alberti, *Beyond Suffrage: Feminists in War and Peace, 1914–28* (New York: St Martin's Press, 1989), p. 80.
60. Ó Céirín, pp. 38–9; Woggon, *Silent Radical* pp. 18–19.
61. Ward, *Hanna Sheehy Skeffington: A Life*, p. 226.
62. Ibid.
63. Morgan, pp. 220–2; Ward, *Contesting Politics*, p. 234; Curtis, pp. 304–6; Ward, *Unmanageable Revolutionaries, women and Irish Nationalism* (London: Pluto Press, 1983), p. 135.
64. Morgan, pp. 220–1; Woggon, *Silent Radical*, p. 19.
65. 'Women Candidates', *Irish Citizen*, (December 1916).
66. Excerpt from Sheehy Skeffington Papers as referenced by Ward, *Hanna Sheehy Skeffington: A Life*, p. 226.
67. Diane Urquhart, *Women in Ulster Politics* (Dublin: Irish Academic Press, 2000), p. 114.
68. Eustance, p. 113.
69. Ryan (1996), p. 125.
70. Woggon, *Ellen Grimley (Nellie Gordon)*, p.10.
71. Helga Woggon, phone interview with author, 19 November 2001.
72. Ward, *Contesting Politics*, p. 237.

CHAPTER TWELVE

Ulster: debates, demands and divisions: The battle for (and against) the vote

MYRTLE HILL

INTRODUCTION

In the North, as in the rest of Ireland, the campaign for the women's vote was waged on several different fronts, attracting passionate supporters and equally ardent opponents. However, as recent scholars have acknowledged: 'It is not possible to understand the suffrage campaign without reference to local government politics, patterns of employment, culture and the presence and activities of other organisations.'[1] This seems particularly true of the north-eastern corner of the island, dominated by long-standing and deeply entrenched political/religious divisions which impacted on all aspects of life.[2] The Ulster experience of suffrage has tended to be encompassed within all-Irish narratives, though Diane Urquhart has produced an account that is both detailed and comprehensive, while Margaret Ward's analyses provide considerable insight into the distinctive nature of the nationalist/feminist debate in this region.[3] This chapter aims to contribute to the historiography by placing the Northern Irish suffrage experience in the context of local female agency as it evolved during the course of the late nineteenth and early twentieth centuries, thus providing a context for the differing positions taken up in the period immediately preceding the outbreak of war.

WORKING IN 'WOMANLY WAYS':[4] THE EMERGENCE OF SUFFRAGISM IN THE NORTH

A focus on the early period of suffrage activity in the North is particularly useful in facilitating an analysis of the discourse pre-dating the Home Rule crisis that came to dominate both the contemporary political arena and subsequent historical enquiry. This approach serves to uncover significant continuities and links between suffrage and other concerns prioritised by female activists. As Sandra Stanley Holton has stressed, suffrage activity was not marginal but inter-related with other aspects of 'the politics of ordinary everyday life' in the 'tangle' of different power structures that determine the 'complexity of multiple identities'.[5] It has also been clear that for many of those involved in suffragism, 'ordinary life' centred on charitable and philanthropic endeavours, mostly, though not always, motivated by a religiously-determined sense of the social and moral duty of the privileged to those less fortunate. This argument is particularly pertinent to the north of Ireland where by the mid-nineteenth century evangelicalism, which particularly impacted on women by opening up a range of new opportunities outside the domestic arena, had become a dominant force in the major Protestant religious denominations.[6] An examination of the early suffrage pioneers in the north of Ireland indicates the importance of this context.

Although precise details of the early membership of the Northern Ireland Women's Suffrage Society (NIWSS) formed in 1871 are not available, Elizabeth Crawford identifies two prominent men (a Unionist MP and the moderator of the Irish Presbyterian Church) in addition to Margaret Byers and the secretary, Isabella Tod.[7] It is likely that the role of the men, though important, was largely supportive, with most of the day-to-day activities carried out by female members. Even without their involvement in the struggle for the extension of the franchise to women, Byers and Tod have earned a place in Irish feminist history, particularly in the field of female education, where their pioneering activities brought about lasting change.[8] Tod's life in particular was one of continuous public activism devoted to the furtherance of female citizenship: in 1871 she was responsible for the Belfast branch of the Ladies' National Association, and she made important contributions to the debates on married women's property. In addition, both she and Byers contributed to the 'rescue' work of Belfast Midnight Mission and were centrally involved in the temperance campaign, Tod pointing out that it was church-based mission work that brought the latter issue to her attention, convincing her that alcohol was 'the main cause of poverty, and in a yet larger measure ... of domestic discord and misery'.[9] Indeed, the strong sense of duty that motivated both women was underpinned by deep religious conviction, with Byers remarking that 'women can do anything under God'.[10]

While they were the most articulate female champions of social and moral reform, Tod and Byers represented a larger constituency of ardent campaigners; the élite middle-class Presbyterian congregations to which they belonged – Elmwood and Fisherwick respectively – were amongst the most influential in Belfast in terms of philanthropic activities.[11] Writing in the 1890s, Tod drew attention to the link between women's church-based engagement and the demand for the vote, noting that the difficulties of reforming work gradually 'stimulated a desire for powers to remove such [wrongs] as were alterable by legislation'.[12] With government increasingly intervening in areas of social reform, it could also be argued that it was 'conspicuously necessary for women to meddle with politics'.[13] Margaret Barrow echoes this point in her exploration of the rationale for the evolving link between temperance and suffrage advocates in Britain,[14] and Karen Hunt agrees that it was through this kind of informal politics that many women 'found ways to conceive of themselves as political actors'.[15] While not suggesting that all suffragists can be neatly categorised, or that voluntary civic action always led to political mobilisation,[16] the relatively small numbers involved enables us to identify these recurring themes in the lives of activists. Thus, for example, when Fisherwick Presbyterian Working Women's Association was formed in 1884 to 'inspire and instruct women of the church to engage in women's work for women both at home and abroad', seven of its most active members also served on the thirteen-strong committee of the NIWSS.[17] The emphasis which Tod and Byers placed on education as the means of ensuring progress for women was also inseparable from their Christian principles; as founder and principal of Victoria College in Belfast, the most successful academic institution for girls in Ireland, Byers endeavoured to 'reach the very heart of girls ... uniting them in high aims and kindling within them the spiritual life'.[18] The early formation of a branch of the NIWSS in the college, where Tod was a frequent visiting speaker and prolific contributor to the in-house magazine, suggests the ability of both women to exert influence over several generations of young middle-class Protestant girls, and reinforces the sense of a strong and vibrant local sub-culture which, operating through tightly-knit networks centred on family and church, was disproportionately significant in terms of its social influence.

In terms of strategies, the NIWSS organised a tour during the early months of 1873. Setting out from Belfast, Tod, accompanied by a representative from the London society, brought the call for female suffrage to Carrickfergus, Coleraine, Armagh, Dungannon, and Derry – where, despite their initial noisy reception, a local branch was formed.[19] While this established a pattern of generating publicity that would be followed by the next generation of suffragists, lobbying was the main approach employed in the endeavour to influence the political debate. In common with contemporaries from other parts of Britain and Ireland, the concern of these early activists was to win the vote for women on the same grounds as men – on the basis of a property qualification; a claim seen as entirely logical:

> If men who are possessed of property have a right to vote at the election of those who make laws that affect such property, will any one attempt to say that it is not an interference with the rights of property to deprive women who are likewise possessed of property, of a vote in the election of such men?[20]

A resolution passed by the Belfast committee in 1875 clarified that their target was the Parliamentary franchise, with the suggestion that local power would follow on the heels of such an achievement. By the mid 1880s, however, the focus had shifted, and the NIWSS's subsequent lobbying for the local franchise met with early success, a bill of 1887 granting the rate-paying women of Belfast the right to vote in municipal elections.[21] Participation in local government proved a significant step forward for those wishing to influence policy; the aims of the Belfast Women's Ratepayers' Association (of which Isabella Tod was secretary) – 'to promote temperance, sanitary reform and the observance of peace and order on the streets'[22] – reflect the central focus on progressive social and moral reform, and again reiterate the links between the concerns of philanthropy and local governance.

The wider political context in which suffrage was to be granted was also of course significant, with important implications for future citizenship, and the tensions between gender and national aspirations were to become perhaps the most critical factor for politicised women in late nineteenth, early twentieth century Ireland. The first indication of this came in the second half of the 1880s with Gladstone's 'conversion' to the principle of Home Rule for Ireland. The crisis that this political u-turn caused within liberalism impacted with particular severity on the province of Ulster where Irish Presbyterians were heavily concentrated.[23]

Social, economic, political and religious reasons were cited for the (almost) unified Presbyterian opposition to the proposal to separate Ireland from British rule. As a committed Unionist, Isabella Tod was the first really prominent suffragist whose total rejection of Home Rule caused controversy within the wider women's movement; her 'shock' at this turn of events clearly discernible as she envisaged, under Catholic rule, 'the stoppage of the whole of the work of social reform for which we had laboured so hard'.[24] Heloise Brown argues that Tod's Unionist political identity was in many ways complex and contradictory, particularly given her liberal critique of imperialist expansion.[25] But as she goes on to suggest, moderate reformism such as that proposed by Tod attracted little political support in late nineteenth-century Ulster. Tod was well aware that many of her former colleagues in the suffrage campaign might 'draw back' at her speaking out in support of the privileged Unionist position,[26] and indeed, old friendships, like that with Josephine Butler who had once described her 'as one of the ablest, and certainly the most eloquent, of our women workers',[27] came to an abrupt end.[28] And while the death of Tod in 1896 was undoubtedly a blow to the northern suffrage movement to which she had given such strong leadership, it was already clear that for a majority of politicised women for whom the constitutional link with Britain was important, political priorities had shifted.

'STRENUOUS PROPAGANDA WORK':[29] THE EARLY TWENTIETH CENTURY CAMPAIGN

As documented elsewhere in this volume, the early twentieth century saw an intensification of the suffrage struggle, and the reconfiguration of groupings in the North paralleled those in Britain and the rest of Ireland. The NIWSS underwent a couple of shifts, but by 1908 had become the Irish Women's Suffrage Society (IWSS), with branches in Belfast, Derry, Whitehead and Bangor. Lisburn Suffrage Society was formed in 1909, and its founder, Lilian Metge, together with Miss L.A. Walkington, were instrumental in establishing the Irish Women's Suffrage Federation (IWSF) in 1911, the northern committee of which accounted for 70% of the overall Irish membership by 1913.[30] Within a year the joint membership of the northern branches of the IWSF and the IWSS, which remained independent of the federation, accounted for about one third of the Irish total.[31] In terms of size therefore, the north-east was certainly significant, and the records make clear that the local campaign was well integrated into the wider suffrage movement, in Ireland, Britain and internationally.

As in the earlier period, a small number of committed individuals took the lead in organising events, generating publicity and sustaining interest in any area. A brief survey of those whose names occur with most frequency in the pages of the *Irish Citizen* confirms that involvement in philanthropic activities continued to be a common feature of the suffragist's social background. However, though they were still broadly definable as middle-class, the term increasingly embraced a wider range of experience, with the professional status of women themselves becoming more notable. Mary Edith Cope, a prolific contributor to debates on suffrage, was an Englishwoman who brought her passion for suffrage to Armagh when she married John Garland Cope, a member of the local landed gentry.[32] Dora Mellone, another Englishwoman who became secretary of Warrenpoint and Newry Suffrage Society, was the daughter of an Anglican minister,[33] while solicitor's wife Elizabeth A.M. McCracken was an established author, L.A.M. Priestly.[34] Born in Glasgow, Margaret McCoubrey worked for a living from the age of twelve; however, sources on her lifestyle in Belfast, where she moved following her marriage to a trade unionist in 1905, suggest a fairly prosperous lifestyle.[35] Margaret Robinson of Whitehead Suffrage Society, daughter of a mill manager, ran a small private school,[36] while Mabel Small (Belfast Suffrage Society) was a teacher. Also based in Belfast, Elizabeth Bell, the first female doctor to qualify in Ireland in 1893, managed a private practice, while education pioneer L.A. Walkington was the first Irishwoman to take an LLD degree. Mellone and Bell were particularly involved in temperance campaigning, though the latter also worked with the Women's National Health Association. Walkington's main charitable interest was in the Workshops for the Blind, and she also served on the board of the Charity Organisation Society set up in 1906.[37] While lacking detailed information on all suffragists, numerous articles in the *Irish Citizen* reflect the movement's ongoing concern with issues of social and moral control, particularly temperance and white slavery, with talks on the latter reported to have given 'a fresh spiritual impetus' to the movement in 1912.[38]

Religious influence also remained important in its own right. Dora Mellone claimed that 'the religious spirit was the heart of the women's movement',[39] while Mrs Priestly McCracken argued that their campaign represented 'a great spiritual awakening, a real religious revival among the best and noblest-thinking women of the times, who perceive that religion and morals, the home, the child, the nation, and the race, are in a perilous state as long as women's subjection and enslavement continue'.[40] Clearly, despite the constraints on female behaviour imposed by religious tradition, the responsibilities of their religious commitment could lead women to a more public and activist 'faith-inspired service'.[41] The formation of a branch of the Church League for Women's Suffrage (CLWS) in Belfast in 1912 provided an additional forum for those suffrage campaigners of a religious nature to demonstrate their support.[42] The League was relatively small (the membership of eighteen increasing to forty by 1914),[43] and its membership overlapped with that of other groups.[44] However, given the more common and pronounced rejection of the female campaign by religious institutions, the desire expressed by a few Belfast clergymen, 'to be in the front rank of the woman's movement', is worthy of note.[45] Significantly, those ministers most directly involved, both in this organisation and as speakers and supporters at suffrage meetings, were also those deeply committed to the temperance campaign and local missions, both of which were heavily dependent on women's contributions, and where cooperation was thus mutually beneficial.[46] Cliona Murphy points out that the attitudes of women and clergy to suffrage were 'complicated and unpredictable'.[47] Nonetheless, during a period when evangelicalism in the North was at its most influential, it is worth considering that the connection between the public expression of inner faith and political activism, while by no means the only stimulus, has perhaps been underestimated as a motivating force in the story of Ulster suffrage.[48]

In this later period, others were clearly inspired by left-wing political rather than religious zeal; socialist Margaret McCoubrey and labour activist Marie Johnston, for example, ensured that working conditions for women and the importance of their contribution to the economy were recurring topics at street corner meetings. Elizabeth Bell's professional work and her immersion in voluntary activities amongst women and children deepened her concern with poverty and its associated health problems, and she thus advocated more married women in the workplace.[49] Moreover, although by no means all trade unionists supported the suffrage campaign, a small minority recognised the necessity of engaging with the female labour force of the industrial North, where the burgeoning linen industry ensured a high level of female employment.[50] For example, at a 1910 rally organised by the Trades Council in Belfast's Ulster Hall, Mary Galway, General Secretary of the Textile Operatives Society of Ireland, 'urged the women in the audience to agitate until they got the franchise and representation in

Parliament',[51] arguing that 'those who obeyed the laws of the land should have some part in framing them'.[52] Similarly concerned, Winifred Carney of the Irish Textile Workers' Union appealed to the suffrage movement for help 'in our endeavour to encourage these long neglected sweated sisters of ours to organise for their own advancement'.[53] However, as Margaret Ward points out, differing priorities and the growing links between the trade union and nationalist movements mitigated against the development of sustained cooperation.[54]

'SUFFRAGISTS OPEN FIRE':[55] MILITANCY IN THE NORTH

It was already clear, therefore, that differing motivations and priorities lay beneath the common objective of female suffrage, and both individuals and societies continued to employ a wide range of strategies in pursuit of that goal. Drawing room meetings facilitated small-group planning, while public lectures with well-known speakers on a host of topics were complemented by regional tours, poster parades, picnics and sixpenny teas. Diane Urquhart notes that the main strength of the IWSS, despite the interest generated by provincial tours, was in Belfast, while the IWSF had a broader geographical base.[56] The Belfast branch of the IWSS was the most vociferous and proactive of the Ulster societies. Two key members, Elizabeth Bell and Margaret Robinson, had served prison sentences for stone-throwing activities in London in 1911 and, feeling increasingly frustrated by lack of progress, this group was gradually convinced of the merits of militancy. Stones were thrown in November 1912, attacks on pillar boxes were reported in February 1913 and a rural post office was also targeted in the same month. A magistrate received a bomb threat in Belfast police courts in May and more windows were broken during the Unionist 'marching season' in July.[57] The strategy of holding boisterous outdoor meetings in urban working-class areas also ensured the greater visibility of these activists; the arrival in town of a group of assertive women, replete with banners and posters, decorating the pavements with chalked slogans, and engaging in heated public debate certainly attracted attention. The *Belfast Evening Telegraph* reported in January 1913 that when 'Suffragists Open[ed] fire in Derry', with the 'invasion' from Belfast of Mrs McCoubrey and Dublin (Mrs Palmer), 'things . . . warm[ed] up in the Maiden City'. They commented: 'That the ladies should come and commence a vigorous campaign in their midst at this crucial period was the last thing Derry folk wished for,' though the militancy on this occasion appears to have been confined to the media rhetoric.[58] Margaret McCoubrey's daughter provides a particularly vivid illustration of her mother's activities when she entertained visitors from the Women's Social and Political Union, during the period when English suffragettes extended their militancy into Ulster. Revealing the more humorous side of their activities, and the links between suffrage and 'everyday' life, this extract is worth quoting at length:

> In Donegall Place in Belfast there was a very fashionable cake shop and tea room called the Carlton. Their trademark was a cardboard cake box in black and white stripes, it was excellent for carrying cakes and also a good camouflage for carrying firelighters. When one of these visitors stayed with us we always had cake for tea. My mother and two other members of the committee were put under police surveillance. The two other ladies took delight in embarrassing their detectives, they would go in to town to one of the large stores and make a beeline for the underwear/corset department or go to get hold of a young assistant and say that they thought that there was a man following them and she would very likely get them out by the back door. If my father and mother were going to the theatre or the opera house my father booked two seats in one row and one in the row behind for the detective.[59]

The upsurge in militant activities from the Spring of 1913 led to heated debates on the 'morality' of such a strategy within the movement, and conflicting accounts as to its impact on popular opinion. Margaret Montgomery of Belfast felt that 'militancy obscures the real issue, and gives an excellent excuse for people to have nothing to do with them',[60] while in contrast Mrs Baker appealed to non-militants to 'do their share' of the propaganda work that generated public interest.[61] Mrs Priestly McCracken claimed historical precedence for militancy: 'Let it once and for all be understood that women in adopting such methods are only following a sort of natural law in the political world, a law they neither initiated or approved – men have done both, as the whole history of reform proves.'[62] McCoubrey, in a typically robust rallying cry, urged her colleagues to respond to the debate, 'not by deploring and disclaiming all connection with militancy, but by glorifying in the spirit of the women's revolution'.[63] But while militancy undoubtedly brought suffrage to the forefront of public attention, it also alienated more conservative individuals and societies, many of whom switched their allegiance to the

IWSF which maintained its policy of using only constitutional methods.[64] The Belfast society's change of direction – and division within the Ulster movement – was confirmed in September 1913 when, with only one dissenting vote, it pledged itself to militancy.[65]

'ACUTE EPIDEMIC SUFFRAGITIS':[66] PUBLIC PERSPECTIVES

The response of the wider public to suffrage activities changed over time and in relation to the strategies employed. In the summer of 1912 Dora Mellone despaired that the chief obstacle to progress was the 'indifference' of 'very many women',[67] and indeed, while representatives of the conservative and conventional voiced their opinions in the media, the majority of people viewed the campaign as peripheral, either to everyday life or the political agenda. The lack of an organised anti-suffrage movement was also perhaps the result of such 'comparative ignorance',[68] though a 1910 photograph taken in Strabane, County Tyrone provides a rare image of an anti-suffrage demonstration with a group of men masked as women and in female clothing, wielding suffrage posters.[69] Suffrage aspirations were also a source of mockery in the hallowed halls of academia, to which women had only so recently gained admission. A satirical piece in *Queen's College Bulletin* described the symptoms of 'Acute Epidemic Suffragitis':

> An acute specific fever characterised by its virulence, and by the fact that it is confined to the female sex . . . SIGNS AND SYMPTOMS – Patients show a tendency to 'recurring utterances . . . In one recorded outbreak of epidemic suffragitis among an "educated" class of young women, the sufferers herded together in a certain recently-erected building, and invited some 300 men to come and be inoculated.[70]

Nor were events held within the institution treated with the decorum one might expect. When Dorothy Evans from the WSPU attended a meeting at Queen's in December 1913, it was reported that what turned out to be 'a very rowdy event' attracted some forty suffragettes who were outnumbered by 'over two hundred of the sterner sex' and there was 'a wild scene of pandemonium – detonators boomed, squibs fizzled and crackers exploded, often in dangerous proximity to those on the platform'.[71] Jeers and jostles could, however, all too quickly turn to noisy heckling and rough physical abuse.[72] The extract from McCoubrey quoted above suggests that the police could be circumspect (on at least one occasion she received prior warning of an impending raid), and there are other examples of them providing escorts for suffragists under attack from the crowd, and exercising good humour when monitoring events.[73] They could also, however, threaten arrest or intervene to bring a meeting to an end, a response more common after 1913 when the increasingly militant suffrage campaign became embroiled in the wider political debate on the future of Ireland.[74] And while the activities of the militants generated media attention, it was unequivocally hostile: suffragettes were described as 'wild women', 'mad women' and 'fanatics', with much reference to their 'insane wickedness' and 'criminal folly'.[75] The *Northern Whig* recommended the revival of medieval stocks, with the attendant mobs to be given permission to stone these 'unnatural' specimens of womanhood.[76] As Louise Ryan has pointed out, this type of discourse has been responsible for defining – and demeaning – the public activities of unconventional women throughout history.[77]

'THE PRESENT CRITICAL JUNCTURE':[78] SUFFRAGE AND THE HOME RULE DEBATE

With the introduction of the Third Home Rule Bill in 1912, the threat (or promise) of new constitutional arrangements appeared imminent, and the arming of both nationalist and unionist volunteer forces in defence of their respective positions considerably heightened local tensions. The heated debates over the future shape of government in Ireland inevitably impacted on those demanding rights of citizenship within its jurisdiction. As mainstream political parties continued to reject proposals to include female suffrage in their negotiations, many nationalist and unionist women, whether or not they supported the campaign for the vote, turned their energies to this pressing issue. As Margaret Ward has noted, 'the movement for national self-determination that existed in Ireland at the turn of the century was as important for women as for men' and many joined Cumann na mBan or one of a range of cultural, literary and popular movements.[79] On the other side of the political divide the Ulster Women's Unionist Council, formed in 1911, became a magnet for unionist women of all classes. Although membership numbers are difficult to verify, the claim that the UWUC became 'the largest female political organisation in Ireland' is likely to be upheld.[80] While more research is needed to identify individuals, it is likely that many women from Ulster Presbyterian backgrounds made the move from their local suffrage to their local unionist association. Not all did so, of course; amongst a small minority of those with unionist sympathies who continued to prioritise the suffrage cause were Mrs Cope, Elizabeth Bell and Mary Baker of Belfast WSS who asserted that: 'As suffragists we are to have a single aim until we have the vote – party politics and party concerns are not for us.'[81]

Although the Ulster Unionist Party was emphatic that the battle against Home Rule took priority over any other political issue, there was a brief flurry of excitement amongst suffragists in September 1913 when the press published a letter from a senior unionist official indicating that plans being drawn up for a provisional government in the north-east would include granting the franchise to women. This unexpected 'pledge' drew a range of differing responses from local women. Members of the UWUC chose to 'ignore the suffrage part of the letter',[82] but some suffragists, such as Mrs Priestly McCracken, expressed 'jubilation' at the 'marriage of unionism and women's suffrage'.[83] The Northern Committee of the IWSF claimed to have been highly instrumental in influencing unionist opinion, asserting that they had been aware of this shift in opinion as far back as January 1912 – a claim that did not win many friends in the wider movement.[84] Others found it more difficult to accept the apparent change of heart, Mrs E. Chambers arguing that 'for suffragists to go to Sir Edward Carson for votes is to follow a will o' the wisp'.[85] At a meeting of Belfast WSS in January 1914, Mrs McCarthy congratulated the UUC on 'the recognition of equal political rights for men and women', but visiting speaker Louie Bennett was more cautious about the potential for unionist–suffrage cooperation, stating that while 'she would be the last to undervalue the concession of the UUC . . . the women unionists of Ulster . . . were staying away from the suffrage movement'.[86] In addition, of course, the very idea of part of Ireland 'opting out' of Home Rule was anathema to all opponents of British imperialism, including most members of the IWFL who perceived their future in terms of an independent island. At this critical state of British–Irish constitutional negotiations, the WSPU entered the local political arena, establishing a Belfast branch in October 1913. With the nationalist Irish Parliamentary Party refusing to include female suffrage in its Home Rule plans, the English-based suffrage organisation aimed to intensify the pressure on the Unionist Party to honour its pledge. However, in thus accepting the principle of self-governance for Ulster, such a move could not fail to exacerbate the underlying political divisions amongst Irish feminists.

'WE COME NOT TO BRING PEACE BUT A SWORD':[87] SUFFRAGETTES DECLARE WAR

Suspicions of Unionist intent proved justified in the spring of 1914 when Unionist leader Sir Edward Carson asserted that he had never agreed with the suffrage movement. Declaring 'war' on news of this 'betrayal', WSPU organisers Madge Muir and Dorothy Evans were able to utilise 'many of the more ardent and active' of the local suffragists in a greatly intensified campaign of militancy.[88] Amongst the enthusiasts joining the WSPU were Marie Johnson, Elizabeth Bell, Margaret McCoubrey, Margaret Robinson, Mabel Small, Lilian Metge, Mrs Elfreda Baker and Mrs McCracken. As Margaret Ward suggests, their motivations are difficult to disentangle; while some had sympathy with the proposed unionist 'solution' to the political deadlock,[89] others remained firmly focused on suffrage, believing that only 'a frankly militant society' could progress their cause.[90] Baker was later to deny that the English-based initiative had broken up the movement in Ulster, arguing that, in 'stirring things up', they were providing much-needed stimulus,[91] and this seems to be true for a minority of the most articulate Belfast women. Indeed, by April 1914, the defection of its most active members to the WSPU led to the collapse of the IWSS, with the IWSF publicly announcing its opposition to WSPU actions.[92] Splits between moderate and radical elements are common to all left-wing organisations, but in the case of early twentieth century Ulster, antipathy between the various groupings was intensified by the wider political context.

During the summer of 1914 the battle for the female vote in Ulster was waged with a combination of pragmatism and passion. The unionism which dominated both the politics and economy of the north east was the primary target – in all of its manifestations. Senior political figures were boldly and publicly confronted,[93] suffragettes were found infiltrating UVF displays and arson destroyed five unionist-owned buildings. Attacks on Protestant religious establishments and on recreational facilities such as Belfast Bowling and Lawn Tennis Pavilion, the stand at Newtownards racecourse and the greens at Knock Golf Club represented the feminist challenge to both the hierarchical and patriarchal symbols of the ruling élite.[94] Properties rather than people were the targets of violence, and Elizabeth Bell later asserted that she always made sure properties were empty before setting fire to them,[95] but the public response to such 'revolution' was, unsurprisingly, hostile, perhaps at least partly because of the passing of the Malicious Injuries

(Ireland) Act, which meant that payment for damage to private property resulting from such attacks was taken from the public rates.[96]

Thirteen suffragettes were arrested in Ulster between March and August 1914, and the subsequent court cases, with dramatic outbursts from the dock – both verbal and physical – created considerable excitement both within and outside the courtroom.[97] Evans and Muir were particularly loud in their denunciation of the authority of the court; Lilian Metge protested at its actions by breaking the courtroom windows, while schoolteacher Mabel Small hurled bricks at the windows of the Unionist Party headquarters.[98] Women also made tactical interventions in more conventional female arenas. Reflecting their awareness of the 'power of the purse', some called for a boycott of financial contributions to public charities,[99] and in Belfast Cathedral a number of suffragettes interrupted a Sunday service. Left hands upraised, they stood to chant their 'protest against cruelty by the imprisonment of our suffrage sisters'. After about two minutes they sat down and the service resumed.[100] At its finish, these 'eight to ten well-dressed women' went to the nearby police barracks to present their names and addresses. With those suffragettes not already in prison subjected to police questioning following every incident,[101] the intensification of the militant campaign, which distinguished this period from the earlier stage of suffrage activity in Ulster, also resulted in more frequent physical attacks on suffragettes themselves. When Mabel Small, Dorothy Evans and Mrs Baker mounted a protest against Sir Edward Carson at Belfast Docks in late May 1914, for example, a crowd of mill girls set upon Small, 'dragged the hat from her head, pulled her hair, and disarranged her clothing, portions of which were practically torn to tatters'. Rescued by the RIC and the harbour police, she was taken to the nearby Mater Hospital in a state of collapse. Two of her colleagues were also assaulted, one receiving a cut on the head.[102] Lilian Metge's home was attacked by a crowd after the burning of Lisburn Cathedral,[103] and a suffrage heckler at a unionist meeting was pelted with stones.[104] Indeed, hostility against the activists was such that on two separate occasions women tourists visiting the North had to be given police protection against locals who suspected them of being suffragettes.[105]

CONFLICTING IDENTITIES: SUFFRAGISTS, NATIONALISTS AND UNIONISTS

Ulster suffragettes frequently drew attention to the parallels between their campaign and that of the Ulster Volunteers who were taking up arms in defence of their political loyalties. As Baker pointed out, Ulster men, like suffragettes, were saying: 'We are allowed no share in the making of the law, and therefore, as a matter of moral duty, we refuse to obey the law.'[106] They thus demanded similar treatment. A suffrage note left at the scene of one incident urged the authorities who regarded *their* activities as incitement to violence to investigate *The Irish Volunteer*, the organ of the militant nationalists, and the *Covenanter*, the organ of the militant unionists, the latter a 'most militant production; incitement to armed rebellion'.[107] While they were drawing these parallels, however, suffragettes were simultaneously scathing of the 'want of position' of unionist women within a movement in which 'men were happy to use the women'.[108] But the claim that they 'toadied' to the Ulster Volunteers demonstrates a failure to acknowledge the different prioritising and innate identities of unionist women themselves.[109] Similar objections were made to women's 'slavish' adherence to Irish nationalism but, as Heloise Brown points out, while feminist scholars have progressed our understanding of the tensions between feminism and nationalism, 'little work has been done on the construction of a female Unionist identity'.[110] While this perhaps strikes a discordant note in post-colonial discourse, it is nonetheless an important aspect of the 'diverse, multi-faceted and dynamic' nature of Northern Irish women's relationship to the state.

Mrs F.H. Whitaker, secretary of West Belfast branch of the UWUC, which had a membership of over 6,000, explained that for her: 'Home Rule was essentially a women's question. It affected their lives, their homes, and their families, and for that reason they affirmed their declaration to assist the men in opposing and defeating home rule.'[111] With 'the sanctity and happiness of home life', faced with 'peril', and their religious as well as political identity under threat, women's duty to reject 'a priest-governed Ireland' was clear. The appeal to domesticity, maternalist values *and* faith ensured the UWUC a strong populist base, but in addition, there was 'work in the political sphere for women as well as men', with many opportunities for active participation in the constitutional debates raging across Britain and Ireland.[112] Amongst such women, the actions of the WSPU caused 'much indignation in Belfast, and all over Ulster . . . and [Evans'] action, in professing to speak for Unionist women [was] emphatically resented and repudiated'.[113]

Clearly, aspects of identity previously subsumed under the wider umbrella of gender were more powerfully held and more passionately articulated at a time of crisis, although it is also possible that earlier claims to non-partisanship were overstated, with assumptions of commonality at least sometimes based on location and perceptions rather than reality. For example, many suffrage meetings in the north-east appear to have been regularly attended by Protestant clergy who opposed Home Rule, while the routine playing of the national anthem at Whitehead and Bangor Suffrage Societies reflected their allegiance to the British crown.[114] Similarly, the acrimony reflected in *Irish Citizen* debates around the involvement of English suffragettes in Ireland indicates how wider British–Irish relations were deeply problematic within the movement. Margaret Ward notes that it was possible for those suffragists for whom 'militancy was the deciding factor' in supporting or rejecting the WSPU to find themselves on the 'wrong side' in terms of their nationalist or unionist aspirations.[115] For others, loyalty to national self-determination was an ideal held strongly enough to warrant opposition to the WSPU solely on the grounds that 'it is not Irish'.[116] Regarding the British government as 'alien', they insisted that 'the most successful Irish Suffrage Societies are those which have no affiliation with English organisations, but which are entirely native to Irish soil'.[117] Moreover, that several of the most active local women were English born added to the perception that they were 'motivated by British-inspired concerns'.[118] While it is certainly possible to see the WSPU's Irish activities as another example of unwelcome British intervention on the island of Ireland, it is nonetheless the case that some supporters of suffrage in the North were culturally and politically closer to London than Dublin and that, in any event, Westminster was seen as the key forum for political debate.[119] The three-way links between the north and south of Ireland and across the Irish Sea, which had been so important in the early days of the campaign, broke down amidst mutual accusations and suspicion against a backdrop of impending civil war and the clash of conflicting loyalties. As Louise Ryan point out, as in other countries engaging in anti-colonial struggles, 'issues around tradition, colonialism, history and identity posed very serious questions for [Irish] suffragists'.[120]

CONCLUSION

The withdrawal of the WSPU from Ulster at the outbreak of war did not bring suffrage activity in the North to an end, although the IWSF also shifted its focus to war work. In an endeavour to keep the suffrage issue to the fore, Margaret McCoubrey established a branch of the IWFL in Belfast where she was supported by a small group of local die-hards. But Dora Mellone's unwillingness to 'participate in anything that appeared to favour national independence' reflected a more general northern suspicion of the IWFL's political stance,[121] and the Ulster Suffrage Centre, as it was called, struggled to impact on the wider public arena. Requests to meet with both unionist and nationalist leaders were rejected; Craig's assertion that he had 'neither the time nor inclination'[122] to interest himself in women's suffrage typified the general attitude, and the activities of the centre petered out by mid-1915.

The small group of women who fought for the vote in twentieth-century Ulster did not entirely give up on their challenge to gendered discrimination; several of the most active went on to follow other routes to citizenship which reflected their individual talents and interests. Marie Johnson, married to labour leader and future senator Thomas Johnson, continued her involvement with working-class issues in the South. Margaret McCoubrey turned her attention to the Co-operative Guild, while Elizabeth Bell, following service in Malta during the war, worked on Belfast Corporation's Child Welfare Scheme and at Belfast Mother and Babies Hospital. Those involved in the Church League campaigned for an expansion of women's role in religious institutions, and with the links between Britain and the North greatly strengthened by the experience of war, opportunities for women to actively support the unionist cause increased significantly. Longer-term continuity is more clearly seen in the areas of temperance and social reform, but further research on individual suffragists is needed to tease out the trajectories of their experiences, and the diversity of aims and aspirations that motivated them.

In this chapter I hope to have conveyed some of the diversity and vibrancy of the Ulster suffrage movement as it evolved against the dramatic background of the Home Rule crisis and in the context of wider imperial history. However, in trying to recover a sense of our collective past, what such historical research actually brings to light is the fragility of unity in the 'women's movement'. Whether in early or late twentieth-century Ireland, the common causes on which women could come together often faltered in the face of other aspects of multiple, sometimes overlapping, but often conflicting identities. Nonetheless, this should not undermine the importance of recovering, exploring and disseminating the long and difficult history of the battle for gender equity. The hope that a narrative of sustained solidarity may yet emerge rests on learning the lessons of the past.

NOTES

1. Claire Eustance, Laura Ugolini and Joan Ryan, 'Introduction: Writing Suffrage Histories – the "British" Experience', in Claire Eustance, Laura Ugolini and Joan Ryan, *A Suffrage Reader: Charting Directions in British Suffrage History* (London and New York: Leicester University Press, 2000), pp. 1–19, p. 8.

2. See, for example, T. Hennessey, *A History of Northern Ireland 1920–1996*, (Dublin: Gill and Macmillan, 1997).

3. Diane Urquhart, '"An Articulate and Definite Cry for Political Freedom": the Ulster suffrage movement', *Women's History Review*, 11, 2 (2002), pp. 273–92; Margaret Ward's study of leading suffragist Hanna Sheehy Skeffington sheds much light on the internal dynamics of this period of the women's movement in Ireland: Margaret Ward, *Hanna Sheehy Skeffington: A Life* (Cork: Cork University Press/Attic Press, 1997); see also Margaret Ward, 'Ulster was different', in Yvonne Galligan, Eilis Ward and Rick Wilford (eds), *Contesting Politics: Women in Ireland, North and South* (Oxford: Westview Press, 1999), pp. 219–39, and 'Conflicting Interests: The British and Irish Suffrage Movements', *Feminist Review*, 50, (Summer, 1995), pp. 127–47.

4. A description of Margaret Byers during the 1911 prize-giving ceremony at Victoria College, quoted in Alison Jordan, *Margaret Byers, pioneer of women's education and founder of Victoria College, Belfast* (Belfast: Institute of Irish Studies, n.d.) p. 64.

5. Sandra Stanley Holton, 'The Suffragist and the "Average Women"', *Women's History Review*, 1 (1992), pp. 9–24; see also the discussion in Karen Hunt, 'Women as Citizens: Changing the Polity', in Deborah Simonton (ed.), *The Routledge History of Women in Europe since 1700* (Abingdon and New York: Routledge Press, 2006), pp. 216–58, pp. 218–19.

6. See David Hempton and Myrtle Hill, *Evangelical Protestantism in Ulster Society, 1740–1890* (London: Routledge, 1992).

7. Elizabeth Crawford, *The Women's Suffrage Movement in Britain and Ireland: A Regional Survey* (Abingdon and New York: Routledge, 2006), p. 254.

8. Their most important achievement in this area was in ensuring that legislation relating to both secondary intermediate and university education was extended to include female as well as male students. See Jordan, *Margaret Byers*; Maria Luddy, 'Isabella M.S. Tod', in Mary Cullen and Maria Luddy (eds), *Women, Power and Consciousness in 19th Century Ireland* (Dublin: Attic Press, 1995), pp. 197–230.

9. Quoted in Luddy, 'Isabella Tod', p. 209.

10. *Women's Penny Paper* (London: November, 1889), reprinted in *Victoria College Magazine*, referred to by Gillian McClelland.

11. Gillian McClelland, 'Evangelical Philanthropy and Social Control or Emancipatory Feminism? A Case Study of Fisherwick Presbyterian Working Women's Association, 1870–1918', unpublished PhD thesis, Queen's University Belfast, (2000); James Dewar, *A History of Elmwood Presbyterian Church* (Belfast, 1900).

12. My thanks to Gillian McClelland for drawing my attention to this article in *Victoria College Magazine*, 1893.

13. Isabella Tod, *Victoria College Magazine*, (July, 1895), quoted in McClelland, 'Evangelical Philanthropy', p. 292.

14. Margaret Barrow, 'Temperance and Women's Suffrage', in Eustace et al (eds), *A Suffrage Reader, pp. 69–89*.

15. Karen Hunt, 'Women as Citizens: Changing the Polity', p. 249.
16. For an interesting discussion of links between voluntary and state activism, see Seth Koven and Sonya Michel, 'Womanly Duties: Materialist Politics and the Origins of Welfare States in France, Great Britain and the United States, 1880–1920', in Fiona Montgomery and Christine Collette (eds), *The European Women's History Reader* (London and New York: Routledge, 2002), pp. 225–55.
17. In addition to Margaret Byers, these were Margaret McNeill, Mrs Sarah Thompson, Mrs Jane Lindsay, Mrs S.K. Mulligan, Miss Hardy and Miss A.P. Blackwood; all were committee members of charitable and philanthropic organisations, 'Evangelical Philanthropy and Social Control', p. 286.
18. *Victoria College Magazine*, July 1888.
19. Crawford, *The Women's Suffrage Movement*, p. 254.
20. *The Witness*, 20 March 1874.
21. *The Northern Whig*, 23 July 1887.
22. Crawford, *The Women's Suffrage Movement*, p. 258.
23. Noel Armour, 'Isabella Tod and Liberal Unionism in Ulster, 1886–96', in Alan Hayes and Diane Urquhart (eds), *Irish Women's History* (Dublin: Irish Academic Press, 2004), pp. 72–87; for a longer-term view of Ulster Presbyterianism, see also Hempton and Hill, *Evangelical Protestantism*.
24. Heloise Brown, 'An Alternative Imperialism: Isabella Tod, Internationalist and "Good Liberal Unionist"', *Gender & History*, 10, 3 (November 1998) pp. 358–80, p. 365.
25. Ibid., p. 376.
26. *The Northern Whig*, 21 March 1886.
27. Josephine Butler, 1910, quoted in Luddy, 'Isabella Tod', p. 214.
28. Brown, 'Isabella Tod', p. 369.
29. McCoubrey, *Irish Citizen*, 17 May 1913.
30. For details of the chronology of Ulster Suffrage Societies see Diane Urquhart, *Women in Ulster Politics 1890–1940* (Dublin: Irish Academic Press, 2000), Appendix A, p. 205.
31. Urquhart, *Women in Ulster Politics*, p. 12.
32. Cope established Armagh Suffrage Society in the spring of 1912 and later became a vice-president of the Irish Women's Suffrage Federation. See Mary McVeigh, 'Votes for Women: The Armagh Campaign', *History Armagh*, 1, 2, (Autumn, 2005), pp. 21–4.
33. Crawford, *The Women's Suffrage Movement*, p. 272.
34. Kate Newman, *Dictionary of Ulster Biography* (Belfast: Institute of Irish Studies, 1993) p. 152.
35. Elizabeth Hutchinson, 'Reminiscence', unpublished typescript in the possession of the author.
36. Taped interview with Margaret Robinson, Public Record Office of Northern Ireland (hereafter PRONI), TP35.
37. Jordan, *Who Cared?* pp. 235, 266.
38. *Irish Citizen*, 26 October 1912.
39. Ibid., 13 December 1913.
40. *Irish Citizen*, 28 June 1913; Mrs Knox, President of the Whitehead branch of the IWSF, suggested her own prioritising when she claimed that she 'did not approach the question of women's suffrage in any spirit of frivolity, for next to the question of missions, it was one of the greatest causes of the present day', *Belfast Evening Telegraph*, 4 February 1914.

41. Pat Starkey, 'Faith and Practice in Women's Lives', in Siminton, *Women in Europe*, pp. 177–215.
42. *Irish Citizen*, 17 May 1913.
43. Ibid., 28 February 1914.
44. For example, L.A. Walkington, Lisburn Suffrage Society, was secretary of the Belfast branch of the Church League for Women's Suffrage.
45. *Irish Citizen*, 13 December 1913.
46. For example, following an open-air suffrage meeting in Carlisle Circus, Belfast, the Reverend John Pollock of St Enoch's Presbyterian Church took the platform and voiced his support for women's suffrage, adding that he 'knew women had been and would be the friends of Temperance'. The suffragists responded: 'One good turn deserves another, so we left our Temperance friends in possession of "our audience"!' *Irish Citizen*, 13 July 1912.
47. Cliona Murphy, 'The Religious Context of the Women's Suffrage Campaign in Ireland', *Women's History Review*, 6, 4 (1997), pp. 549–65.
48. Hempton and Hill, *Evangelical Protestantism*; see also J.N. Ian Dickson, 'Evangelical Religion and Victorian Women: The Belfast Female Mission, 1859–1903', *Journal of Ecclesiastical History*, 55, 4 (October 2004), pp. 700–25.
49. *Irish Citizen*, 22 March 1913.
50. John Lynch points out that 70% of the linen industry's employees were female, and that as early as 1889 it was reported that there was 'much competition for female labour, and some complaints of its scarcity', *A Tale of Three Cities: comparative studies in working-class life* (London: MacMillan Press, 1998), p. 8.
51. *Belfast Newsletter*, 2 September 1910.
52. ITUC Annual Report 1912, quoted in Theresa Moriarty, 'Mary Galway (1864–1928)', in Mary Cullen and Maria Luddy (eds), *Female Activists: Irish Women and Change 1900–1960* (Dublin: The Woodfield Press, 2001), pp. 9–36, p. 24.
53. Suffrage Correspondence, PRONI, T3259/1/1; Winifred Carney to *Irish Citizen*, 25 November 1912.
54. Margaret Ward, 'Ulster was Different', pp. 230–3; see also Denise Kleinrichert, 'Labour and Suffrage: Spinning Threads in Belfast' in this volume.
55. *Belfast Evening Telegraph*, 23 January 1913.
56. Urquhart, *Women in Ulster Politics*, pp. 13–14.
57. *Irish Citizen*, November 1912; *Irish Citizen*, July 1912; *The Ulster Echo*, 13 May 1913; *Irish Citizen*, 12 July 1913.
58. *Belfast Evening Telegraph*, 23 January 1913.
59. Hutchinson, 'Reminiscence'.
60. *Irish Citizen*, 29 March 1913.
61. *Irish Citizen*, 15 March 1913.
62. *Irish Citizen*, 3 April 1913
63. *Irish Citizen*, 12 April 1913
64. Bushmills Society 'deeply regretted the policy of the militant suffragettes in attacking property'; letter from Mrs Heron in Holywood, leaving the BWSS to join non-militant local Holywood Branch, 29 April 1912, PRONI T3259/1/6. On 16 April 1913, the Derry Branch of the IWSS resolved to 'sever the connection with the Belfast militants and become affiliated to the IWSF, Letter from Robina Gamble, Londonderry, to Mrs Robinson, 16 April 1913, PRONI, T/3259/1/7.
65. *Irish Citizen*, 13 September 1913.
66. *Queen's College Belfast Bulletin*, January 1914.

67. *Irish Citizen*, 15 June 1912.
68. *Irish Citizen*, May 1913.
69. Myrtle Hill and Vivienne Pollock, *Image and Experience: Photographs of Irishwomen c1880–1920* (Belfast: Blackstaff Press, 1993), p. 166.
70. *Queen's College Belfast Bulletin*, January 1914.
71. *Queen's College Bulletin*, December 1913.
72. See, for example, *Irish Citizen*, 9 August 1913, p. 95, where the IWSS reported that they had to close a meeting in Belfast after constant heckling.
73. Hutchinson, 'Reminiscence'; *Irish Citizen*, 9 August 1913, where it was noted that the police were 'very helpful', providing an escort for beleaguered suffragists.
74. See, for example, *Irish Citizen*, 28 June 1913, where Mrs Baker reported that the police insisted she was causing an obstruction when conducting a protest against the Cat and Mouse Act in Belfast, and she was warned of imminent arrest.
75. See, for example, *Belfast Evening Telegraph*, 20 February 1913; *Belfast Newsletter*, 4 June 1914; *Belfast Evening Telegraph*, 27 March 1914.
76. *Irish Citizen*, 24 August 1912.
77. Louise Ryan, '"Furies" and "Die-Hards": Women and Irish Republicanism in the Early Twentieth Century', *Gender History* Vol. 11, No. 2 (July, 1999), pp. 256–75.
78. *Belfast Evening Telegraph*, 7 March 1914.
79. Ward, 'Conflicting Interests', p. 129.
80. Thanks to Sam Fitzimmons, who drew attention to apparent discrepancies in the reported membership figures in a paper presented at the postgraduate workshop, 'Women, Culture and Public Life in Twentieth Century Ireland', at Queen's University Belfast, 11 April 2006.
81. *Irish Citizen*, 8 February 1913.
82. Papers of the Ulster Women's Unionist Association, PRONI, D/1098.
83. *Irish Citizen*, 20 September 1913.
84. *Irish Citizen*, 27 September 1913, the debate on this claim covered several issues.
85. *Irish Citizen*, 20 September 1913.
86. *Belfast Evening Telegraph*, 27 January 1914.
87. Note found amongst suffrage literature following an arson attempt on Lisburn Castle, quoted in *Belfast Newsletter*, 3 April 1914.
88. Suffrage Correspondence, PRONI, T3529/2/7.
89. Ward, 'Conflicting Interests', p. 139.
90. Mrs H.M. Baker, *Irish Citizen*, 27 September 1913.
91. *Irish Citizen*, 14 June 1914.
92. Letter from Northern Committee of IWSF to Sir James Craig. In response, Craig, 'on behalf of the Loyalists of Ulster', expressed gratitude that the federation was 'in no way identified with those who attempt to hinder our leader, Sir Edward Carson, in the efforts he is making to defeat Home Rule', *Belfast Newsletter*, 28 May 1914.
93. For example, two women rushed up to Sir Edward Carson while he was waiting for a train at Greenisland and accused him of 'betraying the women of Ulster', *Belfast Newsletter*, 16 April 1914.
94. For details of the 1914 militant campaign in Ulster see Urquhart, *Women in Ulster Politics*, Appendix B, pp. 206–9.
95. Margaret Robinson interview, PRONI, TP35.
96. For example, County Antrim paid a total of £92,000 in damages for properties destroyed by suffragettes and consequently a three penny levy in the pound was applied to the county's rates, Urquhart, *Women in Ulster Politics*, p. 36.

97. See, for example, *The Northern Whig*, 6 April 1914, reporting on the 'unprecedented' scenes at court; see also Dorothy Evans and Madge Muir, Court Papers, PRONI, BELF/1/1/2/45/8.

98. *Belfast Newsletter*, 11 April 1914.

99. *Irish Citizen*, 12 July 1913.

100. The women apparently said: 'We call upon the Church of Christ to waken from its lethargy, to take a stand with these women who are fighting for a purer life in the state, to dry out against the torture of those who suffer for conscience sake. It is better to be a faithful soldier in Christ's army to be despised of men than to be held in high esteem by the worldly. Rise up ye daughters that are at ease; be troubled, ye careless ones,' *Belfast Evening Telegraph*, 6 April 1914.

101. Hutchinson, 'Reminiscence'; Margaret Robinson interview, PRONI, Tp35.

102. *Belfast Newsletter*, 1 June 1914.

103. Rosemary Cullen-Owens, *A Social History of Women in Ireland 1870–1970* (Dublin: Gill & MacMillan, 2005) pp. 101–2.

104. *Irish Citizen*, 14 June 1914.

105. Suspicions against a group of women in Ballymena centred on their carrying handbags; they were in fact sales representatives, *Belfast Newsletter* 8 June 1914; the wife and daughter of Major Manning, a friend of Carson's, were confronted by a large and hostile crowd while on a shopping trip, *Belfast Newsletter* 9 June 1914.

106. *Irish Citizen*, 13 September 1913.

107. Court Papers, PRONI, Belf 1/1/2/45/8.

108. *Irish Citizen*, 15 February 1913.

109. *Irish Citizen*, 11 April 1914.

110. Brown, 'Isabella Tod', p. 359.

111. *Belfast Evening Telegraph*, 18 January 1913.

112. The participation and politicisation of women within unionism is fully discussed in Urquhart, *Women in Ulster Politics*, pp. 46–84; see also Nancy Kinghan, *United We Stood, the story of the Ulster Women's Unionist Council 1911–1974* (Belfast: Appletree Press, 1975).

113. *Belfast Evening Telegraph*, 7 March 1914, p. 7.

114. Urquhart, *Women in Ulster Politics*, p. 12; *The Ulster Echo*, 18 April 1913.

115. Ward, 'Conflicting Interests', p. 138.

116. *Irish Citizen*, 20 September 1913.

117. *Irish Citizen*, 20 September 1913.

118. Ward, 'Conflicting Interests', p. 145; Dora Mellone, Mrs Cope and Mabel Small were all English-born Ulster suffragists.

119. Ward, *Hanna Sheehy Skeffington*, p. 60.

120. Louise Ryan, 'Traditions and Double Moral Standards: the Irish suffragists' critique of nationalism', *Women's History Review*, 4, 4 (1995), pp. 487–503.

121. Ward, 'Conflicting Interests', p. 142.

122. *Irish Citizen*, 12 September 1914.

CHAPTER THIRTEEN

After the Vote: Women, citizenship and the campaign for gender equality in the Irish Free State (1922–1943)

CAITRIONA BEAUMONT

INTRODUCTION

The passing of the 1918 Representation of the People Act marked an important victory for the Irish suffrage movement. Under the terms of this legislation, Irish women who were over thirty, ratepayers or the wives of ratepayers were eligible to vote in national elections for the first time and to take seats in the Westminster Parliament. In the December elections of that year two Irish women stood as parliamentary candidates for Sinn Féin, Constance Markievicz in Dublin and Winifred Carney in Belfast, with Markievicz becoming the first female MP elected to the British House of Commons.[1] This historic election victory for a woman, albeit symbolic, added to the sense of optimism of suffrage campaigners that the parliamentary vote would bring about significant changes in women's lives and that their campaign for the vote was now over. Writing in the *Irish Citizen* in 1920, Hanna Sheehy Skeffington noted that: 'There can be no women's paper without a women's movement . . . and because since a measure, however limited, of suffrage has been granted women are forging their own destiny in practical fields of endeavour.'[2]

With the winning of the parliamentary franchise for women many suffrage campaigners in Ireland, like their counterparts in the UK, moved on to pursue other campaigns and interests requiring their commitment and expertise, for example the international peace movement and the labour movement.[3] In the Irish Free State the national question dominated the political and social landscape in the immediate post-suffrage years with the outbreak of the War of Independence in 1919 and the Civil War in 1921. A significant number of women played an active part in these conflicts, including well-known suffrage campaigners such as Jennie Wyse Power, Constance Markievicz, Mary MacSwiney and Hanna Sheehy Skeffington.[4] The acceptance of the Anglo-Irish Treaty in 1921, which sparked the outbreak of civil war, marked a further victory for women's equality with a commitment in the proposed Irish Free State Constitution to extend the parliamentary franchise to women on equal terms with men. It is worth noting however that this significant development was over-shadowed by the bitter Dáil debates on the treaty and that all six women deputies, including former suffrage campaigners, voted against the treaty, once again highlighting the difficult relationship which existed between feminism and nationalism at this time.[5]

Under the terms of the 1920 Government of Ireland Act which resulted in the partition of Ireland, the six-county Northern Ireland State was established with a devolved government dominated by a Unionist majority. In the first election to the Northern Ireland parliament, the Ulster Women's Unionist Council promoted male rather than female candidates in order to 'preserve the safety of the Unionist cause'.[6] Two women were elected, both widows of Unionist MPs.[7] There were never more than four women at any one time in the Northern Ireland parliament and none of the women elected represented the nationalist community.

In the south, the 1922 Free State Constitution, enacted following the victory of the pro-treaty side in the Civil War, further guaranteed the rights of Irish women citizens in the Irish Free State. The constitution confirmed the right of women to vote at twenty-one, on equal terms with men and Article 3 of the new constitution stated that 'every person, without distinction of sex, shall . . . enjoy the privileges and be subject to the obligations of such citizenship'. Women in the Irish Free State now had full rights to political citizenship, six years before women in Britain and Northern Ireland and five female TDs were elected to the Dáil in 1923, the greatest number of successful female candidates until the 1977 general election.[8] Optimism on the part of suffrage campaigners was understandable and voiced by Esther Roper in a letter to Hanna Sheehy Skeffington when she wrote that: 'Never had there been such a firm foundation of justice and freedom guaranteed by any country of its women citizens'.[9]

'AN EMPTY FORMULA'?

Yet in spite of the success of the suffrage campaign, the recognition of the contribution of women to the nationalist struggle and the early victories of female candidates in national elections, gender equality 'without distinction of sex' was not forthcoming in the Irish Free State. Indeed, by 1943 Hanna Sheehy Skeffington felt compelled to state that the contribution made by women to the nationalist cause and to the formation of the new state was 'long forgotten' and the guarantee of equal citizenship for Irish men and women reduced to a mere 'empty formula'.[10] Sheehy Skeffington, along with fellow activists and women's organisations, believed that legislation enacted during the 1920s and 1930s had deliberately and systematically undermined the rights of Irish women to equal citizenship. In Northern Ireland the demand for the right of women to equal citizenship was stifled by the pre-occupation of the Unionist government with maintaining the Union and the under-representation of nationalist women in the political process. As Myrtle Hill argues: 'The determination of women themselves to strengthen both the local unionist power base and the all-important link with Britain and Empire should not be underestimated.'[11]

There is little doubt that consecutive Irish governments, the Catholic Church and the majority of Irish citizens understood the primary role of women in the newly independent Ireland to be that of wife and mother. This had been the norm long before independence and, in spite of the extension of the franchise, continued to be the norm in the new Irish Free State.[12] What alarmed former suffrage campaigners and women's groups was not this assumption that most women wished to work within the home but the fact that a woman's domestic role appeared to undermine her rights as an equal citizen. These fears were justified when legislation passed throughout the 1920s and 1930s placed restrictions on women's citizenship rights on the grounds that men and women had different functions in society and different duties as citizens. In addition, women continued to be under-represented in both national and local government with only six women elected to the Dáil throughout the 1920s and 1930s. Women's employment opportunities and wage rates were also less favourable than male workers and as a result large numbers of young women were leaving the state throughout the 1920s and 1930s in search of better economic opportunities abroad.[13]

In light of such realities it would appear that the parliamentary franchise for women had not significantly improved or enhanced the position of women in Irish society. This experience was not unique to

Ireland. Women in the new German Weimar Republic were granted the parliamentary vote in 1919 but went on to endure a political system that sought the 'restoration of traditional gender roles in the home and workplace'.[14] In Britain and Northern Ireland, following a brief surge of progressive legislation in the immediate post suffrage period,[15] women's organisations continued to campaign with varying degrees of success for social and economic equality for women. Their efforts led veteran British suffrage campaigner Eleanor Rathbone to remark in 1936 that 'no doubt some of us exaggerated [the power of the vote]'.[16]

This chapter will explore the possibility that Irish feminists and suffrage campaigners may also have exaggerated the power of the vote for women to significantly enhance women's lives in the Irish Free State. The motives for the implementation of discriminatory legislation throughout the 1920s and 1930s will be uncovered and the reaction of female activists and women's organisations to these restrictions on their citizenship rights will be highlighted. The question of whether or not the majority of women in the Irish Free State were either aware or concerned about their rights to equal citizenship must be addressed and their alleged 'damnable patience'[17] in allowing themselves to be under-represented in national politics examined. By providing an account of the 1943 general election, in which four independent female candidates stood on 'women's issues', the limited progress of women's political, economic and social status in the first twenty-one years of the Free State's existence becomes apparent. This assessment in turn allows for conclusions to be drawn about the impact that the parliamentary franchise had on the lives of Irish women throughout the formative years of the Irish Free State.

THE JURIES ACTS

The implementation of discriminatory legislation by both the Cumann na nGaedheal and Fianna Fáil governments of the 1920s and 1930s has received considerable attention from historians in recent years.[18] What becomes clear from the legislation enacted and the response of women's groups to these new laws is that a discourse was taking place between the state and women's societies about the precise meaning and definition of women's citizenship in the Irish Free State long after the enfranchisement of women. It is in the implementation of the 1924 and 1927 Juries Acts that this debate can most vividly be illustrated. In 1924 Kevin O'Higgins, Minister for Justice in the Cumann na nGaedheal government, announced his plan to introduce new legislation which would allow women but not men to exempt themselves from jury service. This legislation was in direct contravention of the 1919 Sex Disqualification (Removal) Act and Article 3 of the Free State Constitution as it differentiated between the citizenship rights of men and women solely on the grounds of sex. Rosemary Cullen Owens points out that O'Higgins justified his actions by stating that his intention was to remove unwilling women jurors from the jury rolls, thereby allowing women, presumed to be busy with the responsibilities of home and family, to avoid participating in time-consuming jury service. By implication, the legislation was therefore a matter of efficiency and convenience rather than one of gender discrimination.[19]

In spite of such assurances, a number of women's organisations were not convinced and condemned the proposed legislation. One of the groups to lead this protest was the Irish Women's Citizens' and Local Government Association (later renamed the Irish Women's Citizens' Association). This organisation was set up in 1923 when the suffrage society, the Irish Women's Suffrage and Local Government Association, merged with the Irish Women's Association of Citizenship. The aim of the new society was 'to bring together all Irishwomen of all politics and all creeds for the study and practise of good citizenship'.[20] The emphasis here on the practise of good citizenship is significant as it represented a logical progression from the fight for the vote to an attempt to inform and educate women on how to use their vote wisely. Membership of the new association included well-known suffrage campaigners, for example Lucy Kingson, Rosamund Jacob and Jennie Wyse Power. The re-formation of this former suffrage society and the continued involvement of stalwart members makes clear that as early as 1923 some feminist campaigners were willing to continue with their campaign for women's rights and were aware of the need for such work despite the winning of the vote for women.

If any of those involved in the suffrage movement did believe that the fight for women's equality was over, the 1924 Juries Bill quickly disabused them of that notion. In response to the proposed legislation, the Irish Women's Citizens' Association argued that 'women had no right to evade any duties and responsibilities involved in citizenship' and went on to condemn the bill as 'derogatory to women if women could escape sitting on juries due to sex alone'.[21] Although supported by two leading women's societies, the National Council of Women and the National University Women Graduates Association,[22] the campaign against the bill did not receive the support of politicians or senators within the Oireachtas and the bill passed successfully through the Dáil and Senate.[23] The situation had changed however by 1927 when Minister O'Higgins announced plans to remove women altogether from jury rolls. This time women's groups were better prepared and won wider support in opposing his plans, with the support of a number of female senators proving crucial to the campaign.

Defending the new legislation in the Dáil, O'Higgins argued that he was justified in removing women's names from jury lists as a matter of course in light of the large numbers of women who had requested exemptions under the 1924 Act.[24] A significant number of women had requested exemption from jury service but it could be argued that given such a right men would also be as keen to absent themselves from what for many could be considered a chore and an inconvenience. Firmly basing their argument on the principle of equality for men and women, those protesting against the bill once again highlighted the discrepancy between this proposed legislation and Article 3 of the constitution. In addition, it was argued that women facing trial by jury had the right to be judged by peers of the same gender who may have greater empathy with their plight. Some of the leading voices in this well organised protest included Hanna Sheehy Skeffington, a member of the National Council of Women and Women Graduates' Association, Mary Hayden, who was president of both the National Council of Women and the Women Graduates' Association and a member of the Women's Citizens' Association and Jennie Wyse Power, former president of Cumann na mBan and also a member of the Irish Women's Citizens' Association.

This small but influential network of women succeeded in mounting a concerted campaign against the bill and all members of the Dáil were sent letters outlining the implications of the bill for women. The campaign benefited in particular from the support it received from Jennie Wyse Power and Eileen Costello in the Senate where the two senators condemned the government for attempting to deprive women of their basic duties and rights of citizenship. Wyse Power made it clear that her protest was 'entirely influenced by the fact that if this Bill becomes law the civic spirit that is developing in women will be arrested'.[25] Echoing such views, Senator Costello also focussed on the role of women as citizens and argued that women had a duty of citizenship to sit on juries and that 'any attempt to exempt women from this duty was an injustice'.[26] It is worth noting that the only female representative in the Dáil during this debate, Margaret Collins-O'Driscoll, did not raise any objections and voted in line with her party, Cumann na nGaedheal. Although Minister O'Higgins dismissed the protests of women in the Senate and outside the Oireachtas as unrepresentative of the vast majority of Irishwomen, he was forced to make an amendment to the bill in the wake of such objections. When the 1927 Juries Act was passed, women were excluded from jury service but individual women did have the right to apply to sit on a jury if they so desired.

The debates surrounding the 1924 and 1927 Juries Acts illustrated the conflicting definitions of citizenship for women emerging in the Irish Free State. On the one hand, feminists argued that women were entitled to the same rights of citizenship as men, whilst the state appeared to favour a more gender-based definition with women's role clearly defined by her domestic duties. In the Dáil debates on the 1927 Juries Bill, Kevin O'Higgins expressed his firm belief that a woman's 'normal and natural function was to have children'.[27] When using such an explanation to defend the removal of women from jury rolls it is no wonder that women's groups were alarmed that the association of women solely with their work as wives and mothers would impinge upon their citizenship rights. Even more alarming was O'Higgins' dismissal of the guarantee of equality contained in the 1922 Constitution when he announced in the Dáil that 'a few words in a Constitution do not wipe out the difference between the sexes, either physical or mental or temperamental or emotional'.[28] It was difficult however for women campaigners in the 1920s and 1930s to convince legislators and the general public of the danger that such pronouncements held for women's right to equality. O'Higgins reflected a widely held belief that women seeking a role in public life were an exception and that the majority of women had few interests beyond their domestic concerns. This view was endorsed by the Catholic Church, which clearly identified the position of women in society as that of wives and mothers. The papal encyclical, Rerum Novarum (1891), had stated categorically that: 'Woman is by her nature fitted for home work and it is this which is best adapted to preserve her modesty and promote the good upbringing of children and the well being of the family.'[29] In a country where 93 per cent of the population were practising Catholics, these views were extremely influential.

WOMEN'S EMPLOYMENT RIGHTS

Women's societies were not just concerned with the right of women to sit on juries. Their involvement in the protest against the 1925 Civil Service (Amendment) Bill, the marriage bar and Section 16 of the 1935

Conditions of Employment Act displayed the willingness of these groups to object to any attempts by the state to limit the employment opportunities of women. Equal access to employment, like the right to participate in public life, was considered to be a basic entitlement of all citizens in a democratic society. This principle was seen to be undermined when the Cumann na nGaedheal government announced plans to restrict entry to higher grades of the civil service on the grounds of gender alone. This would mean that women would not be eligible to sit entry examinations for certain grades and would therefore be deprived of opportunities for promotion and salary increases. The motive for such a move appeared to be a desire on the part of the Minister for Finance, Mr Blythe, to have the power to limit certain civil service roles to one particular sex, although the reason why this should be so was not explained.[30]

Aware of the threat that this plan presented to the employment rights of women, the Irish Women's Citizens' Association, the National Council of Women and the Women Graduates' Association came together to highlight the discrimination inherent in the bill. Leading the campaign, the Irish Women's Citizens' Association declared that: 'In the view of the women's organisations the question is one of principle. To them the test for appointment to any office should be the fitness of the candidate to discharge the duties of that office – the question asked should be, not are these candidates men or women, but are they competent to do the work.'[31] In sharp contrast to these views, Margeret Collins-O'Driscoll supported the proposed amendment in the Dáil, arguing that she 'failed to see how it infringed upon women's rights under the Constitution'.[32] As Mary Clancy argues, it is likely that Collins-O'Driscoll's loyalty to Cumann na nGaedheal influenced her response.[33]

Party loyalty was not a matter of concern for Senators Jennie Wyse Power and Eileen Costello, who spoke energetically against the bill in the Senate. Wyse Power argued that women who had played such an important role in the nationalist struggle should not be deprived of their right to serve the new state in the higher ranks of the civil service. Eileen Costello denounced the bill as 'morally wrong' and 'monstrously unfair' and highlighted the fact that such a restriction on employment rights was also a restriction on citizenship rights.[34] Although the bill was passed in the Dáil, it was defeated in the Senate, mainly due to the efforts of Wyse Power and Costello, and plans to limit women's opportunities in the civil service were abandoned. This victory for the women's societies should not be underestimated. It can be argued that only a very small minority of women would be qualified for these higher grades and so the matter was of little relevance to the majority of women. It was true that only an elite of well-educated women would be excluded from promotion but it was the fact that such exclusion would be based purely on the grounds of gender that led women's groups to protest so vigorously against the bill. That their efforts resulted in the withdrawing of the proposed amendment was a significant victory for women's rights at that time.

Campaigns against the public service marriage bar and legislation allowing limits to be placed on the number of women working in industry, both implemented by the new Fianna Fáil government, were not so successful. Throughout the 1930s, women's groups, including the National Council of Women and the newly formed Joint Committee of Women's Societies and Social Workers, set up in 1935, argued for the removal of the marriage bar.[35] A leading member of the society, Mary Kettle, acknowledged that the majority of married women did not work or wish to work outside the home. Nevertheless, she argued that the marriage bar discriminated against single women who were denied promotional opportunities by employers who made the assumption that they would marry and so be forced to resign. Despite such concerns, the marriage bar remained in place throughout the 1930s and 1940s, reflecting the desire of the Irish government, in common with other European governments during the economic depression of the inter-war period, to protect male employment regardless of the right of female citizens to similar opportunities. It is worth noting that the Irish Women's Workers Union,[36] led by the former suffrage campaigner, Louie Bennett, did not campaign against the public service marriage bar, illustrating the support for the concept of the family wage amongst the Irish trade union movement during this period.

It was this desire to shore up male employment rates that explains the inclusion of Section 16 in the 1935 Conditions of Employment Act. This allowed the Minister for Industry and Commerce to limit the number of women working in any given industry. The numbers of women employed in the industrial sector had risen steadily since the 1920s, causing alarm amongst politicians and male trade union leaders that women workers would lower wage levels and take men's jobs.[37] Once again, a number of women's organisations showed their willingness to speak out against the proposed legislation. The Irish Women's Workers Union led the campaign as the clause directly affected its membership but was joined by middle class feminist women's organisations including the National Council of Women and the Women Graduates' Association.

The IWWU argued that equal pay for equal work would ensure that women workers would not undercut their male counterparts but were not supported in this demand by the wider trade union movement. In campaigning against the bill, women's groups used a range of tactics originating from the suffrage campaign and developed during subsequent battles. Letters were written to national newspapers outlining the unfairness of the bill in relation to working class women, deputations sent to members of the Dáil, including the Minister for Industry and Commerce, Seán Lemass, public meetings held and leaflets distributed to the public. International endorsement of the campaign came from the Women's Consultative Committee at the League of Nations. Support was also forthcoming from female members of the Senate. Jennie Wyse Power, together with Kathleen Clarke and Kathleen Brown, tabled an amendment, later defeated, to remove Section 16.[38] In contrast the three female members of the Dáil, Bridget Redmond (FG), Mary Reynolds (FG) and Margaret Pearse (FF), made no comment on the controversial elements of the bill. Their silence caused frustration amongst Irish feminists but confirmed the prediction made by Lucy Kingston in 1918 'that "the woman-element in politics" will be inextricably bound up with party feeling'.[39]

The 1936 Conditions of Employment Act was passed with Section 16 intact, although, as Mary Daly points out, women were never excluded from industrial employment on the basis of the act and were to benefit the most from expanding employment opportunities in the new light industries.[40] The campaign against Section 16 did, however, have some positive outcomes for women activists at this time. As suggested earlier, a wide range of women's groups were galvanised into action by the campaign and co-operation was achieved between middle-class pressure groups and the working class IWWU. The strength of feeling generated by the campaign led, as Rosemary Cullen Owens writes, to the establishment by the National Council of Women of a Standing Committee to monitor future legislation affecting women.[41]

The experience gained by women's organisations during this campaign in terms of planning and organisation, the use of the media, lobbying techniques and the ability to address public meetings were all skills that older members of the groups had gained during the suffrage campaign. The use of such tactics during the protest campaigns of the 1920s and 1930s allowed new and younger members the opportunity to acquire the confidence and experience needed to challenge discriminatory legislation using accepted constitutional means. Just as in the UK there was no attempt to return to civil disobedience or violent methods to further women's equality. Women's organisations campaigning for equality at this time accepted that women were now part of the political process and so should work within the confines of a legal democratic system to achieve their demands for reform.

Despite the ability of women's groups to attract media attention during the 1920s and successfully bring about amendments to the 1927 Juries Act and the suspension of the 1925 Civil Service (Amendment) Bill, organisations such as the Women's Citizens' Association and the Women Graduates' Association remained small, mainly Dublin based pressure groups. These societies were content to exploit the high public profile of a number of their older members, for example Hanna Sheehy Skeffington and Mary Hayden, rather than attempt to recruit large numbers of women from all around the country.[42]

CUMANN NA MBAN

In contrast to the women's groups mentioned above, Cumann na mBan, the Irish republican women's organisation set up in 1914, appeared to be much more successful in recruiting younger women from all over the twenty-six counties.[43] Cumann na mBan had voted against the 1921 Treaty and in line with Sinn Féin refused to recognise the legitimacy of the new Irish State. The organisation, however, remained an important recruiting ground for women whose republicanism and desire for a united Ireland took precedence over the demands of feminist and mainstream women's organisations for gender equality and women's rights within the twenty-six county Irish Free State.

Cumann na mBan were active throughout the 1920s and 1930s in drawing attention to the plight of republican prisoners and were engaged in a range of IRA activities including the procurement of arms, street protests and civil disobedience.[44] The fact that the organisation did not recognise the Irish Free State meant that it was not in a position to campaign against discriminatory legislation even if individual members of the organisations had wished to do so. There is little doubt that the failure of Cumann na mBan and the wider women's movement to join together to support demands for women's equality was a major setback for the cause of women's rights in the decades following enfranchisement. Working together, these groups would have presented a more inclusive and accurate representation of Irish women and thereby strengthened their demand for reform. This missed opportunity again reflects the deep divisions within Irish society and the dilemmas faced by those who believed in both republican and feminist ideology.

THE 1937 CONSTITUTION

The ability of women's groups to mount effective campaigns to challenge any further attempts to undermine women's citizenship rights was put to the test with the publication of the draft 1937 Constitution. The controversy surrounding the drafting of the new constitution and the campaign against the implementation of certain articles by a number of women's organisations has been written about in detail elsewhere.[45] The intention here is to focus on the success of the women campaigners to force amendments to a number of crucial articles and to explore the way in which this campaign led to the establishment of a women's political party. During the Dáil debate in May 1937 on the new constitution, objections were raised outside the Dáil by the now established network of women's organisations including the Women Graduates' Association, the IWWU, the National Council of Women and the Joint Committee of Women's Societies and Social Workers. Using tried and trusted techniques, the groups lobbied TDs, sent deputations to the Taoiseach, held public meetings and wrote numerous letters to the press highlighting the dangers in the new constitution for the citizenship rights of women. It is worth noting that Cumann na mBan also protested against the new constitution but based their objections on the grounds of political sovereignty and independence rather than on any threat to the rights of women citizens.[46]

Raising their objections to Articles 9 and 16, which dealt with citizenship qualification and voting rights, a deputation representing feminist women's organisations met with de Valera to argue that the omission of the phrase 'without distinction of sex' in these articles could undermine the right of Irish women to vote or hold citizenship. De Valera's response was that the guarantee of equality was 'otiose, redundant and indeed meaningless',[47] but in light of pressure brought to bear by women's groups did agree to re-insert the term into Article 16. An amendment was also made to Article 45 that in its original wording referred to the 'inadequate strength of women' in a clause relating to the right of citizens to engage in paid work. Fearing that women may be excluded from their choice of occupation on the grounds of gender, women's groups objected and the offending words were removed. The success of the women's campaign in achieving these changes should not be undermined and were achieved with little if no help from the three sitting female TDs.[48]

Following its successful passage through the Dáil, the date for a national referendum on the new constitution was set for 1 July 1937, the same date as the general election. This opportunity allowed women's organisations to appeal for the first time directly to voters and a well-run and highly publicised campaign was organised. Public meetings, handbills and letters to the papers urged voters to reject the constitution on the grounds that it undermined the citizenship rights of women. It was argued that Article 40.1, which allowed the state to take into account 'differences of capacity, physical and moral, and of social function', left women vulnerable to discrimination on the grounds of either their presumed physical weakness or their traditional role as wives and mothers. Article 41.1.1 appeared to alter the definition of women's citizenship when it stated that 'by her life within the home, woman gives to the State a support without which the common good cannot be achieved'. Article 41.2.2 went on to state that women should not be forced into paid work 'to the neglect of their duties in the home'. The IWWU objected to these articles, which appeared to recognise only the work of wives and mothers and ignored the contribution that women made to the labour force at this time. There was also concern that women may be restricted to unpaid domestic work which the state appeared to consider the ideal and normal occupation for Irish women.

The fact that women's groups identified the threat inherent in these articles is extremely significant. It demonstrates a keen understanding on their part of the concept of equal citizenship and the dangers arising from any attempt to designate separate public duties to men and women. Different duties for citizens could result in different rights. Mary E. Daly has argued that the recognition of women's domestic work in the constitution was a good thing as it reflected the reality of the lives of the majority of Irish women.[49] There is no doubt that to have women's unpaid work acknowledged in a national constitution in the 1930s was a progressive and welcome development. However, the benefits of such praise are quickly undermined when the record of discriminatory legislation passed during the 1920s and 1930s is considered. It is in this context that the very genuine and justified concerns of feminist campaigners can be best understood. The attempt in Articles 40 and 41 to define women's primary role as a wife and mother could, it was argued by women's groups, lead directly to further restrictive legislation in the areas of employment and civil rights. It should also be noted that, despite the recognition given to women's unpaid work in the constitution, no proposals were forthcoming at that time for the provision of family allowances or other measures which would assist women in performing their traditional role.

When put to the country, the constitution was passed by a small majority and so a gender-based definition of women's citizenship had become enshrined in the state's constitution.[50] It was clear that a number of factors had led to the failure of women voters to come out en masse and vote 'no' to the new constitution. Party political loyalties were strong in this post civil war era and the representation of women in the constitution clearly did reflect the norm for the majority of women and the accepted role for women as ordained by the Catholic Church. Moreover, the debate in Dublin about the status of women in the constitution had little appeal or relevance to women who struggled to feed and clothe their families on a daily basis. It was this recognition by women's groups that their campaign was not reaching the mass of Irish women that led in November 1937 to the setting up of the Women's Social and Political League, the first independent women's party in Ireland. With backing from the Joint Committee of Women's Societies and Social Workers, the National Council of Women and the Women Graduates' Association, the aim of the party was to inform and organise women voters and to educate them about their rights and duties as equal citizens. It was also hoped that the party would work towards increasing the representation of independent women in the Dáil. Amongst the leading supporters of the new party were Hanna Sheehy Skeffington, Mary Kettle, Mary Hayden and Dorothy McArdle, names repeatedly associated with the campaign for women's equality in Ireland. The plan for an independent women's party was, however too ambitious for a group lacking adequate financial backing and popular support. Within a year the party had changed its name from Political to Progressive and had decided to focus instead on lobbying and campaign work, joining the network of women's organisations already active at this time.

WOMEN CANDIDATES AND THE 1943 GENERAL ELECTION

The women's party may have failed but the desire to win effective representation for women in the Dáil had not diminished. Twenty-five years after women had won the parliamentary franchise, four independent women candidates stood in the 1943 general election in an attempt to ensure that political representation for women would result in the enhancement of the status of women in Ireland. Hanna Sheehy Skeffington, now chairperson of the Women's Social and Progressive League, stood in Dublin South on a platform of equal rights and welfare reform. In her manifesto, Sheehy Skeffington proclaimed that: 'There can be no true democracy where there is not complete economic and political freedom for the entire nation both men and women.'[51] Included in her election manifesto was the demand for equal pay for equal work, equal opportunities for women, the restoration of full jury rights, equal pension rights and the removal of 'the many disabilities, economic, social and domestic from which Irish women at present suffer'.[52] Acknowledging the hardships experienced by many housewives and mothers in Ireland during the Emergency years, the campaign called for the introduction of family allowances, free school meals, clean milk and a health programme to halt the spread of TB. Sheehy Skeffington also focussed on the failure of women deputies in the Dáil to fight for women's rights and welfare. The three sitting female TDs, Redmond, Rice and Reynolds, were accused of being silent on all matters affecting women's lives and acting always as obedient party followers.[53]

The Women's Social and Progressive League co-ordinated Sheehy Skeffington's campaign in Dublin and were supported by like-minded feminist groups including the Women Graduates' Association and the Irish Women's Citizens' Association. Also endorsing the campaign was the Irish Countrywomen's Association[54] and the newly formed Irish Housewives Association, set up in 1942 by a number of Dublin women including Hilda Tweedy and Andree Sheehy Skeffington, daughter-in-law to Hanna Sheehy Skeffington. Both the ICA and the Housewives Association were concerned with welfare issues relating to women and children and were effective in highlighting the miserable conditions many women endured whilst fulfilling their traditional and expected roles as housewives and mothers.

Outside of Dublin, the three other independent women candidates were Margaret Ashe, who stood in Galway West, Mary Anne Philips and Mary Corbett, both of whom stood in Tipperary. Like Sheehy Skeffington, all three women had experience of local government and stood on platforms highlighting the needs of women within their constituencies. Mary Anne Philips called for the introduction of equal pay, family allowances and improved childcare and housing. Mary Corbett included family allowances, free school meals and greater employment opportunities for boys and girls in her local area to stem the flow of emigration. Margaret Ashe focussed on housing and other welfare issues. Had they won, Rosemary Cullen Owens writes, the four independent women candidates would have formed 'the nucleus of a Women's Party in the Dáil'.[55] All four were, however, badly defeated, with only Margaret Ashe retaining her deposit.[56]

CONCLUSION

Writing five months after her defeat in the 1943 General Election, Hanna Sheehy Skeffington asked the pertinent question: 'Is the Dáil a fit place for a woman? The answer of the electorate would appear to be NO.'[57] Twenty-five years after winning the vote, it did appear that women were not willing to use that vote to increase their representation in the Dáil or to prevent the implementation of discriminatory legislation. It could be argued, therefore, that the vote had made little difference to Irish women's lives and had done little to enhance their position within Irish society. There is no doubt that, had Irish women voted for female candidates supporting an equality agenda and voiced their opposition to gender biased legislation, the possibility of greater strides towards equality could have been achieved by 1943. The fact that some success was forthcoming in preventing or amending unjust legislation proves that point.

Sheehy Skeffington and her supporters had to accept, however, that many women voted along traditional family lines and that, for a majority of women, engagement with politics was limited and perhaps not relevant to their lives or circumstances. The continuing activities of Cumann na mBan also demonstrated that, for some women, republicanism was more important than equal rights. The influence of Catholic social teaching was another important factor and devout women may have felt uncomfortable supporting the call for equal rights when the Church continually endorsed the domestic role of women within the family and did little to encourage women to engage in public life. It would be wrong, however, to suggest, as the journalist Anna Kelly did in February 1943, that following the extension of the parliamentary franchise 'what, after all the dreadful prognostications, came to pass? Nothing. Women voted and returned home to normality'.[58]

The continued campaigning of former suffrage activists and a small but effective network of women's organisations ensured that the debate surrounding the nature of women's citizenship and the role of women in Irish society remained at the centre of Irish politics throughout the 1920s, 1930s and early 1940s. This discourse may not have radically improved the lives of Irish women in the short term but it did draw attention to the fact that once granted, citizenship rights within a democratic society had to be protected, and that women were entitled to the same citizenship rights as men. The activities of Dublin based pressure groups ensured that a link was maintained between the suffrage movement and subsequent campaigns for women's equality. The indefatigable efforts of women such as Hanna Sheehy Skeffington, Mary Hayden, Mary Kettle and Jennie Wyse Power to fight against any attempt to compromise women's rights demonstrated that they and the groups they represented had not 'overestimated the power of the vote'. This was their victory and their success.

NOTES

1. As a member of Sinn Féin, Constance Markievicz did not recognise the Westminster parliament and refused to take up her seat.
2. *Irish Citizen*, September 1920, cited in M. Luddy, *Hanna Sheehy Skeffington* (Dundalk: Historical Association of Ireland, 1995), p. 34.
3. For a full discussion of the role of women in these campaigns, see R. Cullen Owens, *A Social History of Women in Ireland 1870–1970* (Dublin: Gill and Macmillan, 2005), pp. 127–54 & 190–214.
4. See M. Ward, *Unmanageable Revolutionaries: Women and Irish nationalism* (Dingle: Pluto Press, 1983) and S. McCoole, *No Ordinary Women: Irish Female Activists in the Revolutionary Years 1900–1923* (Dublin: The O'Brien Press, 2004).
5. The six female Dáil deputies were: Mary MacSwiney, Ada English, Margaret Pearse, Constance Markievicz, Kathleen Clarke and Kate O'Callaghan. Luddy, *Hanna Sheehy Skeffington*, p. 35.
6. M. Hill, *Women in Ireland* (Belfast: Blackstaff Press, 2003), p. 90.
7. Dehra Chichester served for thirty five years and Julia McMordie served for only four years. Chichester was silent on women's issues whilst McMordie supported the appointment of female police officers and argued for equal allowances and pensions for female officers. For more information, see M. McNamara and P. Mooney (eds), *Women in Parliament, Ireland: 1918–2000* (Dublin: Wolfhound Press, 2000), pp. 222–3.
8. Of the five female TDs elected in 1923 only one, Margaret Collins-O'Driscoll (Cumann na nGaedheal), took her seat. As Sinn Féin members, the other four women did not recognise the Irish Free State. See M. Manning, 'Women in Irish National and Local Politics 1922–77', in M. MacCurtain & D. O'Corrain (eds), *Women in Irish Society: The historical dimension* (Dublin: Arlen House, 1978).
9. Esther Roper to Hanna Sheehy Skeffington, 19 June 1935.
10. H. Sheehy Skeffington, *General Election Manifesto* 1943.
11. M. Hill, *Women in Ireland*, p. 93.
12. As Mary E. Daly argues, the overwhelming majority of Irish women, married, widowed and single, were based within the home during the 1920s and 1930s. See M.E. Daly, 'Women in the Irish Free State, 1922–39: The Interaction Between Economics and Ideology', *Journal of Women's History*, Vol. 6 & 7, (Winter/Spring) 1995, p. 111.

13. For the period 1926–36 female emigration stood at 9,420 in comparison to 7,255 male emigrants from the Irish Free State. Ireland had one of the highest levels of female emigration in Europe at this time. R.E. Kennedy, *The Irish, Emigration, Marriage and Fertility* (Berkeley: University of California Press, 1973), p. 78.

14. L. Abrams and E. Harvey, 'Introduction: Gender and Gender Relations in German History', in Abrams and Harvey (eds), *Gender Relations in German History: power, agency and experience from the sixteenth to the twentieth century* (London: UCL Press, 1996), p. 6.

15. Legislation passed during this period included the 1919 Sex Disqualification (Removal) Act, the 1923 Matrimonial Causes Act and the 1925 Guardianship of Infants Act.

16. E. Rathbone, 'Changes in Public Life', in R. Strachey (ed.), *Our Freedom and its Results* (London: Hogarth Press, 1936), p. 16.

17. A phrase first used by James Connolly in 1915 and again by Hanna Sheehy Skeffington in 1943 in relation to women's rights. H. Sheehy Skeffington, *General Election Manifesto*, 1943.

18. See, for example, C. Beaumont, 'Gender, citizenship and the state in Ireland, 1922–1990' in S. Brewster, V. Crossman, F. Becket and D. Alderson (eds), *Ireland in Proximity: History, Gender, Space* (London: Routledge, 1999); Cullen Owens, *A social history of women in Ireland;* and M. Valiulis, 'Power, Gender and Identity in the Irish Free State', *Journal of Women's History* Vol 6 & 7, (Winter/Spring, 1995).

19. Cullen Owens, *A social history of women in Ireland*, p. 252.

20. *United Irishwomen*, Vol. 1, No. 4, November 1925

21. *United Irishwomen*, Vol. 1, No. 4, November 1925.

22. The National University Women Graduates' Association was set up in 1902 to promote the educational rights of women. A significant number of members were also involved in the suffrage campaign, including Hanna Sheehy Skeffington, Mary Hayden, Mary Macken and Agnes O'Farrelly. The National Council of Women was established in 1924 as an umbrella organisation for women's groups. Membership of the Council included a diverse range of women's societies, including the Mothers' Union, the United Irishwomen (ICA) and the Irish Women's Citizens' and Local Government Association. The aim of the Council was to 'promote co-operation among women all over Ireland interested in social welfare'.

23. Mary Clancy writes that neither Collins-O'Driscoll nor any of the women senators challenged the 1924 Juries Bill, suggesting that they did not perceive any threat to equal rights. See M. Clancy, 'Aspects of Women's Contribution to the Oireachtas Debate in the Irish Free State, 1922–1937', in M. Luddy and C. Murphy (eds), *Women Surviving* (Dublin: Poolbeg, 1989), p. 222.

24. In County Dublin, 3,276 women were exempted from jury service in 1924. Valiulis, 'Power, gender and identity', p. 123.

25. Cited in M. Clancy, 'Aspects of Women's Contribution to the Oireachtas Debate', p. 222.

26. Clancy, 'Aspects of Women's Contribution to the Oireachtas Debate', p. 223.

27. Clancy, 'Aspects of Women's Contribution to the Oireachtas Debate', p. 223.

28. Cited in Cullen Owens, *A social history of women in Ireland*, p. 255.

29. For a full discussion on the influence of Catholic Social Teaching on definitions of citizenship for women in the Irish Free State, see C. Beaumont, 'Women, Citizenship and Catholicism in the Irish Free State, 1922–1948', *Women's History Review*, Vol. 6, No. 4, 1997.

30. Cullen Owens, *A social history of women in Ireland*, p. 253.

31. *United Irishwomen* Vol. 1, No. 7, 1926.

32. Clancy, 'Aspects of Women's Contribution to the Oireachtas Debate', p. 217.
33. Clancy, 'Aspects of Women's Contribution to the Oireachtas Debate', p. 217.
34. Clancy, 'Aspects of Women's Contribution to the Oireachtas Debate', p. 218.
35. The Joint Committee of Women's Societies and Social Workers was set up to safeguard the welfare of women and children. Membership of the Committee included the National Council of Women, the Mothers' Union and the Irish Women's Citizens' Association.
36. The Irish Women's Workers Union was set up in 1917 to protect the interests of working class women employed in industry.
37. See M.E. Daly, 'Women in the Irish Free State', p. 110.
38. Cullen Owens, *A social history of women in Ireland*, pp. 265–70.
39. L.O. Kingston, 'The Irishwoman's outlook', *The Englishwoman*, 37 (January–March 1918) cited in M. Luddy, *Women in Ireland 1800–1918: a documentary history* (Cork: Cork University Press, 1995), p. 288.
40. Daly, 'Women in the Irish Free State', p. 110.
41. Cullen Owens, *A social history of women in Ireland*, p. 270.
42. In evidence to the Committee of Vocational Education in 1940, membership for the Women's Citizens Association was given as 187 and the Women Graduates' Association recorded 300 members, (evidence to the Committee on Vocational Education (National Library of Ireland, Ms941, no. 200, vol. 20, 1940).
43. For an account of the history of Cumann na mBan see Ward, *Unmanageable Revolutionaries.*_
44. L. Ryan, *Gender, Identity and The Irish Press, 1922–1937: Embodying the Nation* (New York: The Edwin Mellen Press, 2002) pp. 223–52.
45. See, for example, C. Beaumont, 'Women and the Politics of Equality: The Irish Women's Movement 1930–1943', in M. Valiulis and M. O'Dowd (eds), *Women and Irish History* (Dublin: Wolfhound Press, 1997) and Cullen Owens, *A social history of women in Ireland*, pp. 271–9.
46. L. Ryan, *Gender, Identity and the Irish Press*, p. 145.
47. *The Irish Press*, 11 May 1937.
48. Mary Clancy writes that Margaret Pearse did not speak, Bridget Redmond only under pressure and Helena Concannon spoke in favour of the Constitution in line with her party, Fianna Fáil. Clancy, 'Aspects of Women's Contribution to the Oiraeachtas Debate', p. 224.
49. Daly, 'Women in the Irish Free State', p. 112.
50. An all-party Oireachtas Committee on the Constitution is currently reviewing the wording of Article 41 in order to remove the gender bias contained within the Article. *The Irish Times* 19 January 2006.
51. Sheehy Skeffington, *General Election Manifesto*, 1943.
52. Women's Social and Progressive League, leaflet n.d.
53. Ibid.
54. The ICA, formally known as the United Irishwomen, was set up in 1910 to represent the needs and interests of rural women.
55. Cullen Owens, *A social history of women in Ireland*, p. 282.
56. It is worth noting that the first independent female candidate was elected to the Northern Ireland parliament in 1944. Irene Calvert was successful in a bye-election to a university seat and stood on a platform of putting 'the women's point of view'. She resigned in 1953.
57. H. Sheehy Skeffington, 'Women in Politics', in *The Bell* Vol. 7, No. 2 November 1943, p. 143.
58. *Irish Times Pictorial*, 6 February 1943.

Index

Page numbers in *italics* refer to illustrations